AF593270

CAST YOUR OWN Horoscope

TALILA STAN

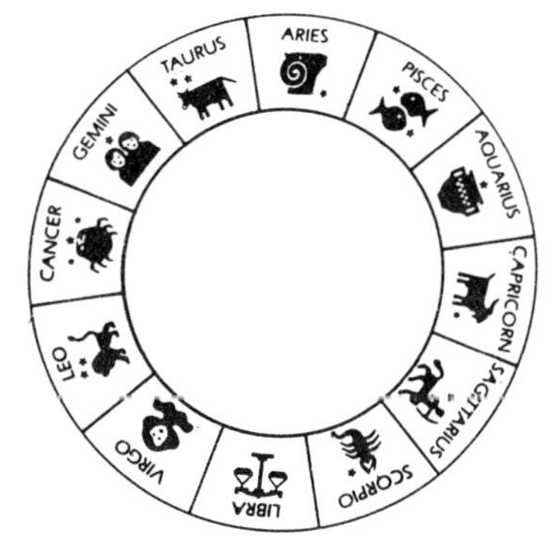

W.H. ALLEN · LONDON
1986

Set in Baskerville and Univers by
Phoenix Photosetting, Chatham, Kent
Printed and bound in Great Britain by
Anchor Brendon Ltd, Tiptree, Essex
for the Publishers W.H. Allen & Co. Plc
44 Hill Street, London W1X 8LB

Editorial Consultant: Jane Struthers

British Library Cataloguing in Publication Data

Stan, Talila
Cast your own horoscope.
1. Horoscopes
I. Title
133.5′42 BF1728.A2

ISBN 0-491-03923-9

Acknowledgements

I wish to thank those of my friends and acquaintances who agreed to uncover the secrets of the innermost 'chambers' of their horoscope Houses and contribute to the research that has led to the writing of this book, which gives for the first time in astrological literature a thorough and detailed description of the twelve Signs' influence in each of the twelve Houses of the horoscope.

I also wish to express my gratitude to Marianne Meisels, Nina Davies and my mother Aviva Stan who helped me in the arduous task of translation and turned it into a labour of love. I would also like to thank Jane Struthers and Mike Bailey, my editors, for their much appreciated suggestions.

Talila Stan

CONTENTS

FOREWORD

I'm sure you know your Sun sign — it couldn't be simpler, since it merely depends on the month in which you were born. If you were born between 21 March and 21 April, for instance, you know that you're an Aries, or in astrological terminology, your Sun sign is Aries. But if you're not sure, turn to page 16 to discover your Sun sign.

From what you've read about your Sun sign, you're convinced that there's some truth to astrology. However, you probably found that the description was too general — like one of those old-fashioned silhouettes which give a true profile of the subject, but with the details missing. After all, everybody who was born during the same thirty-day period shares the same Sun sign. Or, to put it more simply, each Sun sign refers to one-twelfth of all humanity.

But the Sun sign isn't the only factor in astrology. Were it based merely on the Sun signs, we would be divided into only 12 types and this, of course, isn't so. Everyone knows that human nature is much more complex than that. I've often heard people say things like, 'I know five Scorpios and, although they share some characteristics, they are also very different in many ways.' Or, 'I know someone who was born on the same day I was, and we have hardly anything in common.' Surprising? Not really, because although these people were born under the same Sun sign, each of them has a different Ascendant, or rising sign.

THE ASCENDANT

Your Sun sign depends on the month in which you were born, so its influence is very general. Your Ascendant, on the other hand, is determined by the hour and place of your birth and is therefore much more individual. One person whose Sun sign is Aries may have their Ascendant in Taurus; another Arian may have Sagittarius as their Ascendant, yet another may have Leo, or Aries, or Scorpio, or any one of the 12 signs.

The Ascendant shows us the details missing in the Sun sign's silhouette, and helps us paint a true astrological picture. Every one of us is a mixture of the characteristics of our Ascendant (calculated by the hour of birth) with the characteristics of our Sun sign (determined by the month of birth), which explains the many differences and variations existing between people born under the same Sun sign. Blending the characteristics of the Ascendant with those of the Sun sign also explains any contradictions and conflicts in an individual's character. It is this mixture of Sun sign and Ascendant in each one of us which weaves the rich and complicated fabric of human nature.

We've now seen that the 12 signs of the zodiac are not only divided into the 12 Sun signs, but also into a second grouping — the 12 Ascendants, or rising signs. So, mankind is not divided into just 12 groups, but into 144 basic types — and even this is only the tip of the iceberg. There are many other factors in the horoscope, each one adding something to the fabric of human nature, some of which I will deal with in the next chapter.

Yet, despite the fact that the Ascendant is so important, most people have never even heard of it, and very few people know which of the 12 signs is their rising sign. Why?

The answer is very simple. Your Sun sign is determined by the month in which you were born. But calculating your Ascendant working from the hour and place in which you were born, *was* a much more complicated procedure. These calculations, which are based on precise astronomical and geographical data, required the skills of an astrologer. Until now, that is! But after reading this book, you won't need to consult an astrologer to discover your Ascendant. With the aid of this book, you can be your own astrologer.

THE MAGIC FORMULA

Here, for the first time, is a new method which is revolutionary in its simplicity. Using this magic formula you'll be able to work out your Ascendant all by yourself, in a matter of minutes. I developed it with one idea in mind: to enable every reader to discover their Ascendant without complicated calculations — but with reliable results! The formula given in the next chapter is so simple that even a schoolchild can follow it. And yet, despite its simplicity, its rate of accuracy is extremely high — 97 per cent!

YOUR ASCENDANT IS THE KEY TO YOUR HOROSCOPE

The horoscope is divided into 12 sections, called Houses, which symbolize the 12 main spheres of life, such as love, health, career and finances. The 12 signs of the zodiac rotate around the Houses, completing a circle every 24 hours. Therefore, your horoscope contains all 12 signs and all 12 Houses, the only question being, which sign influences which House? In other words, which sign do you have in your House of love, which in your House of health, in your House of finances and every other area which interests you?

Your Ascendant, which is also the first sign in your horoscope, gives you the answer to these questions. How?

Since it's the sign at the beginning of your horoscope, the Ascendant is always in the First House. It thereby influences that sphere of your life symbolized by this House — your personality and the circumstances of your life. Once you've discovered your Ascendant, which is in the First House of your horoscope, it's very easy to determine which sign you have in each of the remaining 11 Houses, as I'll explain in the next chapter. The remainder of the book deals with interpreting the meaning of each sign in each of the 12 Houses.

Pleasant reading!

Talila Stan

SIGNS AND HOUSES

My instant horoscope, presented for the first time in this book, is based on the concept of signs and Houses. The Houses, as I have already explained, symbolize the various aspects of life such as love, money, family and career, whereas the signs found in the different Houses indicate your lucky sign for each particular aspect of your life. In the following chapters of this book you will find detailed descriptions of the significance of each of the 12 signs in each of the dozen Houses. Extensive attention will be given to the Ascendant — the sign situated in the First House at the time of birth.

However, before turning to the magic formula that will reveal which of the 12 signs is your Ascendant, as well as which sign influences each aspect of your life, let's see what a sign and a House are.

THE SIGNS

Picture the zodiac as a giant ferris wheel, sweeping across the heavens from east to west, carrying with it the Sun, the Moon and the eight planets. The zodiac is divided into 12 segments, each 30 degrees wide, which are the signs.

The signs and the central concepts they represent are:

Aries — pioneering spirit, assertiveness
Taurus — productivity, earthiness
Gemini — communication, versatility
Cancer — sensitivity, domesticity
Leo — power, love of honour, creativity
Virgo — censoriousness, pedantic attention to detail
Libra — need for harmony and union
Scorpio — depth, secretiveness
Sagittarius — optimism, openness
Capricorn — purposefulness, ambition
Aquarius — originality, individualism
Pisces — sensitivity, otherworldliness

EVERY SIGN HAS A RULING PLANET

The zodiac is like a vast, heavenly, circular path in which the Sun, Moon and Planets all move, each at its own pace. The Sun, Moon and planets (I will call these heavenly bodies 'the planets' from now on) traverse all the signs. Nevertheless, there is a special affinity between each of the planets and the sign considered to be under its influence, or rule.

Each sign is ruled by one or two planets:

Aries	— Mars	Libra	— Venus
Taurus	— Venus	Scorpio	— Pluto, Mars
Gemini	— Mercury	Sagittarius	— Jupiter
Cancer	— the Moon	Capricorn	— Saturn
Leo	— the Sun	Aquarius	— Uranus, Saturn
Virgo	— Mercury	Pisces	— Neptune, Jupiter

And each planet has a particular significance:
The Sun — self-expression, vitality, power
The Moon — sensitivity and feelings, response
Mercury — intelligence, mobility
Venus — love, beauty, harmony
Mars — energy, impulses and urges
Jupiter — expansion, plenty, optimism
Saturn — restrictions and limitations, pessimism
Uranus — originality, inventiveness
Neptune — spirituality, nebulousness
Pluto — renewal, elimination

A sixteenth-century wood engraving depicting the Moon as a woman – the Moon rules the sign of Cancer.

Each planet may express itself in either a positive or a negative manner. For example, Jupiter's beneficent influence results in optimism and plenty, while its negative influence gives rise to complacency and smugness, wastefulness, exaggeration and over-indulgence.

Each of the 12 signs reflects, to a great extent, the traits of its ruling planet. Aries, for example, ruled by Mars (symbolizing energy and impulses) has a pronounced tendency to assertive self-expression and to impulses not always properly controlled.

Further indications of the characteristics of the signs are supplied by the Elements and Qualities. Each of the signs belongs to one of the four Elements (Fire, Earth, Air, Water), and to one of the three Qualities (Cardinal, Fixed, Mutable). Each sign comprises, therefore, the characteristics of both its Element and Quality.

ELEMENTS AND QUALITIES

Astrology divides the 12 signs into two groupings. The first are the four Elements (Fire, Earth, Air, Water), each consisting of three signs. The second are the three Qualities (Cardinal, Fixed, Mutable), each consisting of four signs.

The Elements — Fire, Earth, Air, Water

Fire: Aries, Leo, Sagittarius — fiery, ardent, extroverted, energetic.
Earth: Taurus, Virgo, Capricorn — earthy, materialistic, purposeful and cautious.
Air: Gemini, Libra, Aquarius — rational, intelligent, communicative, intellectually and spiritually inclined.
Water: Cancer, Scorpio, Pisces — emotional, sensitive, intuitive, introverted.

The Qualities — Cardinal, Fixed, Mutable

Cardinal: Aries, Cancer, Libra, Capricorn — active, outgoing.
Fixed: Taurus, Leo, Scorpio, Aquarius — persevering, stable, resistant to change.
Mutable: Gemini, Virgo, Sagittarius, Pisces — changeable, adaptable.

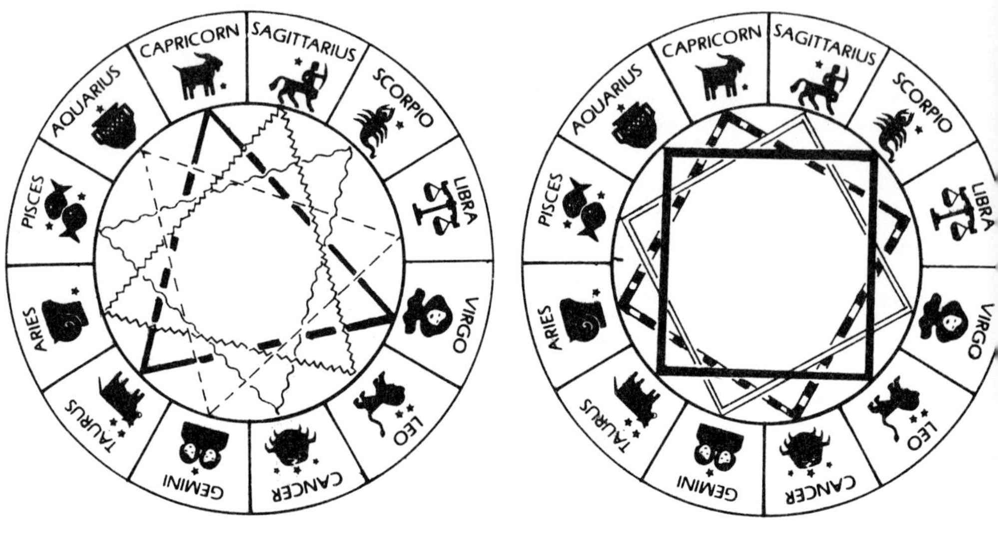

The Elements

Fire
Earth
Air
Water

The Qualities

Cardinal
Fixed
Mutable

Each sign reflects the nature of the Element and the Quality it belongs to and thus, simply by knowing the sign's Element and Quality, we gain some understanding of its nature.

Each of the three signs of a particular Element belongs to a different Quality. For example, each of the Fire signs — Aries, Leo and Sagittarius — is of a different Quality: Aries is Cardinal, Leo is Fixed, and Sagittarius is Mutable. Thus, there are three kinds of Fire: Cardinal, Fixed and Mutable Fire. This pattern holds true for the other Elements as well: each of the three Earth, three Air and three Water signs belongs to a different Quality. So, although three signs are of the same Element, and four signs are of the same Quality, the particular combination of Element with Quality is unique to each one of the signs, as is shown in the table opposite.

Index to the signs according to the Elements and Qualities

	ELEMENT OF FIRE	ELEMENT OF EARTH	ELEMENT OF AIR	ELEMENT OF WATER
CARDINAL QUALITY	**ARIES** The combination of Fire with the Cardinal Quality results in dynamism and activity.	**CAPRICORN** The combination of Earth with the Cardinal Quality results in an ability to put great efforts into attaining materialistic and earthly goals.	**LIBRA** The Cardinal Quality gives impetus and direction to the intellectual ability so characteristic of Air, which is thus given renewed energy.	**CANCER** The Watery need for emotional security provides the impetus necessary for activity symbolized by Cardinality.
FIXED QUALITY	**LEO** Fire and the enthusiasm associated with it, tempered by the Fixed Quality, are expressed in a more restrained manner than in Aries, and are channelled into creativity and management.	**TAURUS** The combination of Earth with the Fixed Quality results in earthiness, love of constancy and stubbornness.	**AQUARIUS** The combination of Air with the Fixed Quality results in loyalty to an ideal and constancy of opinions. The Air of Aquarius is usually still — but this may be the quiet before the storm . . .	**SCORPIO** The combination of the emotional Water Element with the Fixed Quality results in stable and very strong feelings.
MUTABLE QUALITY	**SAGITTARIUS** The combination of Fire and Mutability indicates constant motion and a love of travel and wide, open spaces.	**VIRGO** The combination of Earth with the Mutable Quality results in a realistic approach to many and varied aspects of life, sometimes expressed in a very practical outlook.	**GEMINI** The combination of Air with the Mutable Quality results in a great many areas of interest, in a tendency to spread oneself thin, and in a lack of perseverance.	**PISCES** The combination of the emotional Water Element with the Mutable Quality results in emotional adaptability, and in the ability to identify emotionally with others.

THE POLAR CONNECTION — COMPLEMENTARY OPPOSITES

There is a special bond between the polar signs — the signs in opposition to one another in the zodiac. This is a strong interrelationship in which a sign's characteristics complement those of its polar opposite. In Aries, for example, the 'I' or ego is strongly emphasized, while in its polar opposite, Libra, the emphasis is on the other person. The polar signs are:

Aries — Libra

Taurus — Scorpio

Gemini — Sagittarius

Cancer — Capricorn

Leo — Aquarius

Virgo — Pisces

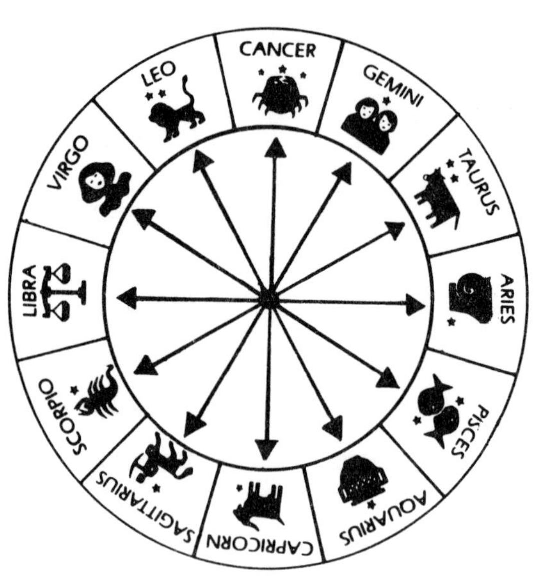

THE SIGNS AND HUMAN ANATOMY

Each of the signs has an affinity with a specific part of the body. Starting with the first of the signs, Aries, which rules the head, down to the last sign, Pisces, which rules the feet, the signs rule the human body, from top to bottom, in the following order:

Aries — head

Taurus — neck, throat

Gemini — arms, hands, respiratory system

Cancer — chest, womb, stomach

Leo — heart, back

Virgo — intestines

Libra — kidneys

Scorpio — reproductive and sexual organs

Sagittarius — pelvis

Capricorn — knees

Aquarius — calves, circulatory system

Pisces — feet

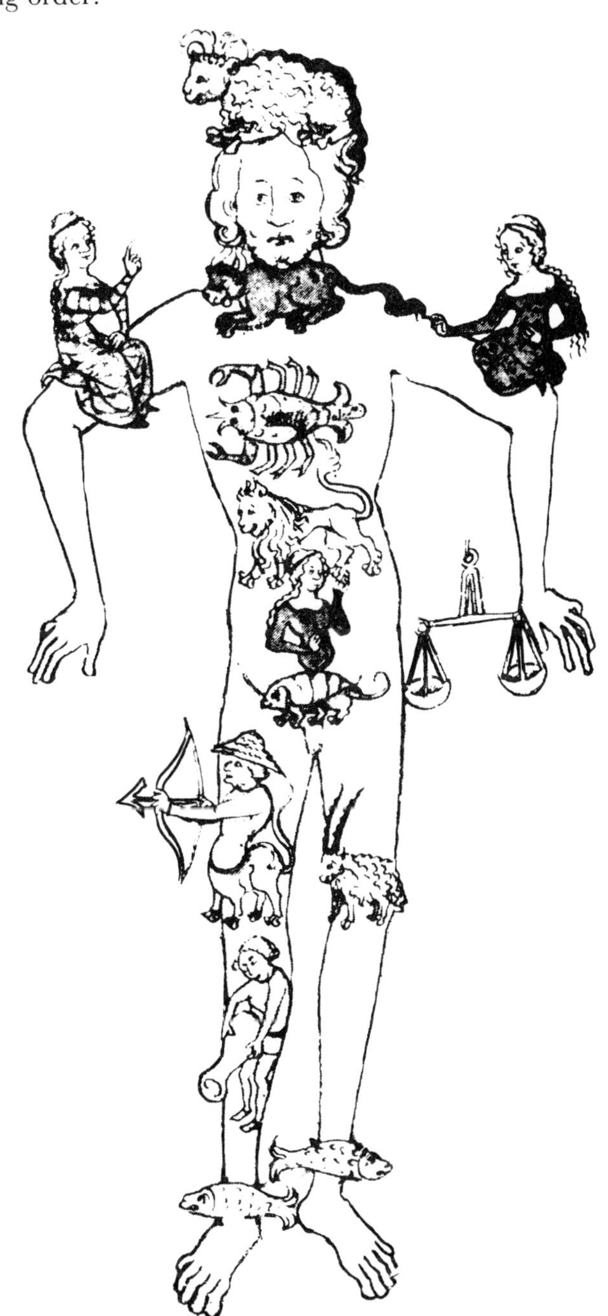

WHAT IS YOUR SUN SIGN?

This is the sign in which the Sun is found on the date of your birth. As the Earth orbits the Sun, in the course of one year, the Sun appears to be passing through the 12 signs of the zodiac, staying in each sign for approximately one month.

These are the dates during which the Sun is found in each sign:

Aries —	21 March to 21 April
Taurus —	21 April to 22 May
Gemini —	22 May to 22 June
Cancer —	22 June to 23 July
Leo —	23 July to 23 August
Virgo —	23 August to 23 September
Libra —	23 September to 23 October
Scorpio —	23 October to 23 November
Sagittarius —	23 November to 23 December
Capricorn —	23 December to 21 January
Aquarius —	21 January to 19 February
Pisces —	19 February to 21 March

The dates given here are correct to within one day, plus or minus. Only by using a detailed Ephemeris (a book that gives the precise movements of each of the planets for a given period of time) is it possible to determine the exact day and hour when the Sun moves from one sign into another.

The Sun sign

In March the Sun is seen in the sign of Pisces. A month later the Earth has moved approximately 30 degrees in its orbit, and from its new position the Sun is seen in the sign of Aries.

WHAT IS YOUR ASCENDANT?

This is the sign rising on the eastern horizon of your birthplace at the time of your birth. That is why it is known as your Ascending or rising sign. The Ascendant is situated in the First House of the horoscope — the House of personality.

As a result of the Earth's daily spin on its own axis, the zodiac seems to make a complete turn of the heavens, from east to west, every 24 hours. As there are 12 signs in the zodiac, a new sign rises on the eastern horizon approximately every two hours. The sign rising on the eastern horizon of your birthplace at the time of your birth is your Ascendant. Is there any difference between Ascendants and Sun signs, and do they influence us in different ways? I will enlarge upon this subject in the introduction to the chapter 'The First House', which deals extensively with the influence of the 12 Ascendants.

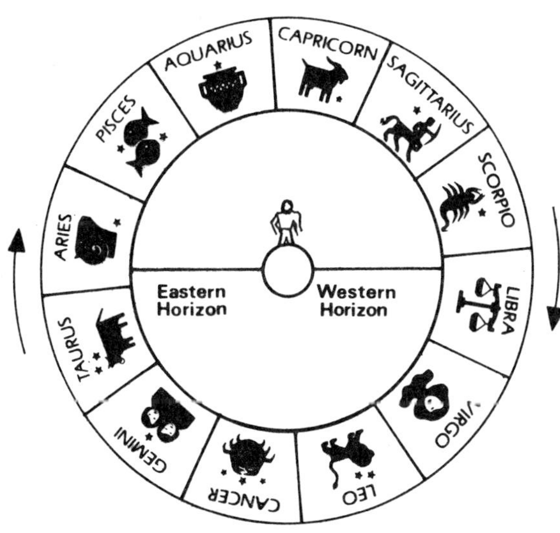

The Ascendant sign

The zodiac takes roughly 24 hours to orbit the Earth and approximately every two hours a new sign rises on the eastern horizon. The sign that was rising on the eastern horizon of your birthplace at the time you were born is your Ascendant.

THE HOUSES

As I mentioned in the Foreword, each of the 12 Houses represents a different area of life. Here are the keywords of the symbolism of each of the Houses (a further explanation of the significance of each of the Houses can be found in the introductions to the sections dealing with the Houses):

First House — the personality
Second House — property, money
Third House — mentality, short journeys
Fourth House — home and family
Fifth House — love, children, creativity
Sixth House — health, work
Seventh House — others in close connections, marriage, partnerships
Eighth House — sex, shared possessions, inheritance, death
Ninth House — abstract thought, long journeys
Tenth House — career
Eleventh House — friends, attitude to social problems
Twelfth House — the subconscious, seclusion, institutions of confinement

The first six Houses are personal, centering on the individual, while the latter six relate to the individual's extension of himself in his contacts with the external world.

As a result of the Earth's 24-hour spin on its axis, the Sun, Moon, planets and 12 signs seem to revolve in the heavens, passing through each of the 12 Houses in every 24-hour period. But, what are these 12 Houses?

The Houses may be defined as a division of the vast heavenly spaces into 12 spheres of influence, the starting point of the division being the eastern horizon of any location, where the Sun rises at dawn. The importance astrology ascribes to the eastern horizon stems from the fact that the planets and the signs, which appear to revolve around the Earth every 24 hours, emerge first on the eastern horizon, as they rise out of the invisible sky (the opposite hemisphere to yours) into the visible one (the hemisphere in which you live).

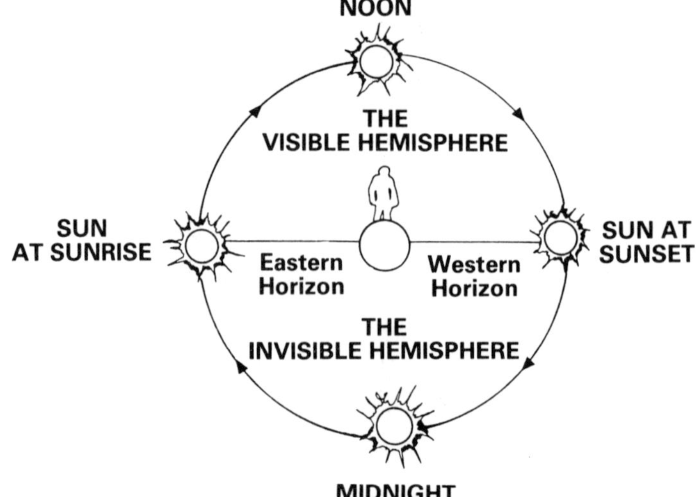

There are several systems of house division, each of which enjoys the enthusiastic support of devoted followers. The system presented here is both the most ancient and the simplest of these, and is known as the Equal House System, since it divides the heavens into 12 equal wedges of 30 degrees each. This system of division is the one followed by the prestigious British Faculty of Astrological Studies and eminent astrologers such as Margaret Hone and Jeff Mayo.

THE SIGNS IN THE HOUSES

During the course of every 24-hour period, the signs of the zodiac pass through the 12 Houses, from east to west. Each of the 12 signs stays for approximately two hours in each of the Houses. While staying in a given House the sign acts in its own characteristic way, influencing the area of life represented by that House. For example, Sagittarius (optimism and expansion) in the Second House (representing money), indicates generosity and an optimistic, open attitude towards money, while Virgo (censoriousness) in the same House indicates a critical, even nit-picking approach to anything related to finances.

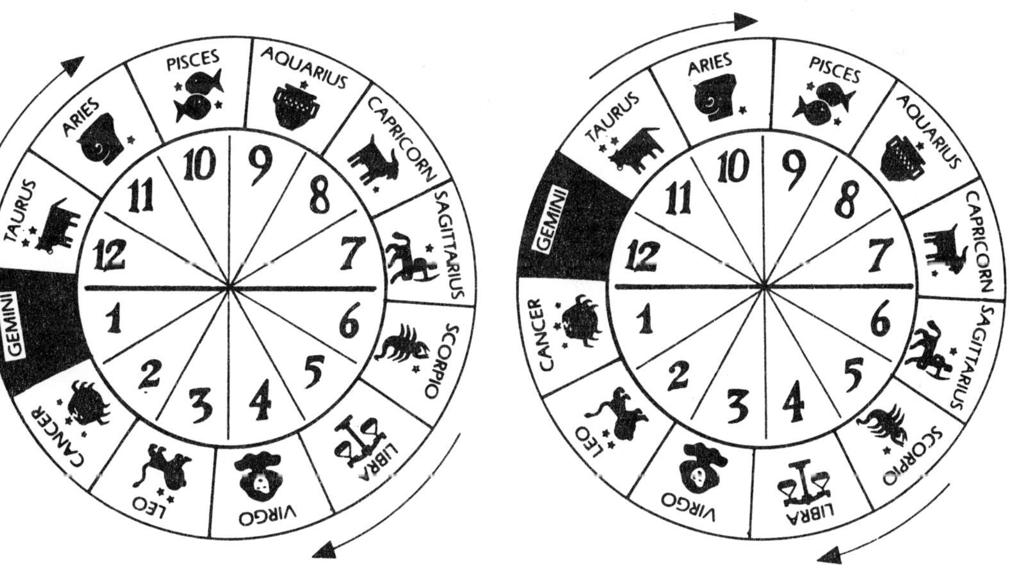

During the day each of the 12 signs passes through the 12 Houses clockwise, lodging in each House for about two hours. For example, in the drawing on the left, Gemini is in the First House; in the drawing on the right we see the situation two hours later – Gemini is now in the Twelfth House and Cancer has risen to the First House.

The magic formula in the following chapter will show you which sign influences each of the 12 Houses of your horoscope. But what does the sign, twinkling in a certain House, portend? The second part of this book is dedicated to a detailed analysis of the typical influence each of the 12 signs exerts over the dozen Houses.

THE PLANETS IN THE HOUSES

The Sun, Moon and the eight planets seem to revolve in the heavens together with the zodiac, and are swept from east to west in a circle which takes them through the 12 Houses.* While one of the signs is present in each of the 12 Houses, the planets are unevenly distributed throughout the Houses. Thus, while not every House has a planetary lodger, several planets may be crowded into a single House. When a planet is in a particular House, it influences the life area represented by that House. Let us return to the example given above, in which Sagittarius is in the Second House, a situation which, by itself, would indicate an optimistic approach to monetary matters, generosity, and financial success. If the Sun, Venus or Jupiter is also in the Second House, the generosity and financial success, symbolized by Sagittarius, are given added emphasis. If, on the other hand, Saturn, the Planet of restrictions and limitations, is in the Second House, the abundance symbolized by Sagittarius will be somewhat limited. At the same time, Saturn will serve to restrain the Sagittarian tendency to financial frivolity and speculation.

If you wish to discover which planets were in which of your Houses at the time of your birth, either buy, or borrow from a library, an Ephemeris for the year in which you were born, which will contain all the information you need to know.

*Besides their apparent motion, each of the planets moves at its own pace through the zodiac. But except for the rapidly moving Moon, which advances at the rate of about 12 degrees per day, the planets' independent motion is exceedingly slow — the fastest among them advances only about one degree a day. It is, therefore, possible to compare the planets to a group of school children sitting obediently, almost perfectly still, on a huge ferris wheel (the zodiac) which turns them inexorably from east to west.

THE MAGIC FORMULA

The formula which enables you
to calculate your own instant horoscope
and discover which of the 12 signs
is your Ascendant

Now it's time to disclose the secret of the Magic Formula which is published here for the first time. I developed this formula so that every reader could easily discover the main data of his or her horoscope, without getting involved in lengthy and wearisome calculations. Indeed, this new formula is so simple that within a few minutes you can work out your own instant horoscope! This will show you which sign is your Ascendant (the sign placed in the First House of your horoscope) and which signs influence each area of your life, represented by the other 11 Houses.

HOW TO USE THE FORMULA

The basic information you need to discover your Ascendant is knowledge of your date, time and place of birth. Now simply apply this formula:

DAILY CODE + TIME OF BIRTH + REGIONAL CODE = ASCENDANT CODE

Add together your DAILY CODE (see pages 25–28 for the Daily Code Tables), your TIME OF BIRTH (check with the Tables of Time Changes on pages 29–34 for local adjustments) and your REGIONAL CODE (see pages 35–43 for the Regional Code Maps). The resulting figure, expressed in hours and minutes, is your ASCENDANT CODE. Look it up with the aid of the Ascendant Zone Maps and Code Tables (see pages 45–59) and you will discover your Ascendant sign.

Opposite is a sample calculation and instructions for your own formula. Follow them to discover your Ascendant sign.

Before starting your calculations it is important to note that all figures are given in hours and minutes and are expressed as part of the 24-hour clock. Thus if you add 10:10 and 00:55, the correct result is 11:05 (and not 10:65!).

SAMPLE FORMULA

Birthday of subject – 16 September 1960 at 15:20 in London

	hrs : mins
DAILY CODE	+ 22 : 58
TIME OF BIRTH (adjusted after reference to the Tables of Time Changes)	+ 14 : 20
REGIONAL CODE for London	+ 00 : 40
	= 37 : 58
	– 24 : 00
If, as here, the final figure exceeds 24 hours, simply subtract 24:00 to arrive at the **ASCENDANT CODE**	= 13 : 58

Reference to the Ascendant Zone Map for Great Britain shows that London is in Zone 5; thus the subject's Ascendant, listed in Zone 5 of the Ascendant Code Table for People Born in Great Britain, is revealed as:

SAGITTARIUS

YOUR FORMULA

	hrs : mins
DAILY CODE refer to Daily Code Tables	+ :
TIME OF BIRTH refer to Tables of Time Changes and adjust if necessary	+ :
REGIONAL CODE refer to Regional Code Maps	+ :
(if the final figure exceeds 24 hours, subtract 24:00) **= ASCENDANT CODE**	= :

Now that you know your Ascendant Code, simply refer to the relevant Ascendant Code Map for the Zone of your birthplace and look up the accompanying Ascendant Code Table to discover your Ascendant sign. There are no more calculations to be done – your instant horoscope is ready.

If your Ascendant Code is on the borderline of two Ascendants, you should read the relevant personality profiles as described in the next section of the book, The First House. You must then decide which profile most accurately describes you (be honest!). Fortunately the signs that are adjacent are distinct from one another in their characteristics and so it should not be difficult to find your true Ascendant.

WHICH SIGN OCCUPIES EACH OF YOUR HOUSES?

Now that you have found out which of the 12 signs is your Ascendant, you have the key to discovering which sign is in each of the 12 houses of your horoscope. The Ascendant resides in the First House of the horoscope and the rest of the signs follow, in their astrological order, in each of the remaining 11 Houses. For example, if your Ascendant is Leo, then the sign that follows it in the zodiac – Virgo – is in your Second House, and so on.

THE WHEEL OF FORTUNE

You must now consult the Wheel of Fortune on the cover of this book. Turn the Wheel until the words '1st House' appear in the window of your Ascendant sign. The remaining Houses will automatically appear in their correct signs.

THE 12 HOUSES AND THE SIGNS AFFECTING THEM

Having used the magic formula, by now you will have discovered which of the 12 signs is your Ascendant (the sign in the First House of your horoscope), and which sign inhabits and thus influences each of the other Houses.

Each of the next 12 chapters is devoted to one of the 12 Houses. Each chapter describes the influence exerted by every single sign over the area of life symbolized by that particular House. The signs in the First House (the Ascendants) will be enlarged upon in the next chapter, which is devoted to the First House.

DAILY CODE TABLES

With these tables you can find your DAILY CODE, according to the day and month you were born (the year doesn't matter). For example, if you were born on 10 November in Great Britain the table shows that your DAILY CODE is 2:35.

Daily Code Table for People Born in

GREAT BRITAIN AND IRELAND

DAY	JAN	FEB	MAR	APRIL	MAY	JUNE	JULY	AUG	SEPT	OCT	NOV	DEC
1	6:00	8:02	9:53	11:56	13:54	15:56	17:54	19:57	21:59	23:57	1:59	3:58
2	6:04	8:06	9:57	11:59	13:58	16:00	17:58	20:00	22:03	00:01	2:03	4:01
3	6:08	8:10	10:01	12:03	14:02	16:04	18:02	20:04	22:07	00:05	2:07	4:05
4	6:12	8:14	10:05	12:07	14:06	16:08	18:06	20:08	22:11	00:09	2:11	4:09
5	6:16	8:18	10:09	12:11	14:10	16:12	18:10	20:12	22:15	00:13	2:15	4:13
6	6:19	8:22	10:13	12:15	14:14	16:16	18:14	20:16	22:18	00:17	2:19	4:17
7	6:23	8:26	10:17	12:19	14:17	16:20	18:18	20:20	22:22	00:21	2:23	4:21
8	6:27	8:30	10:21	12:23	14:21	16:24	18:22	20:24	22:26	00:25	2:27	4:25
9	6:31	8:33	10:25	12:27	14:25	16:28	18:26	20:28	22:30	00:29	2:31	4:29
10	6:35	8:37	10:29	12:31	14:29	16:32	18:30	20:32	22:34	00:33	2:35	4:33
11	6:39	8:41	10:33	12:35	14:33	16:35	18:34	20:36	22:38	00:36	2:39	4:37
12	6:43	8:45	10:37	12:39	14:37	16:39	18:38	20:40	22:42	00:40	2:43	4:41
13	6:47	8:49	10:41	12:43	14:41	16:43	18:42	20:44	22:46	00:44	2:47	4:45
14	6:51	8:53	10:45	12:47	14:45	16:47	18:46	20:48	22:50	00:48	2:51	4:49
15	6:55	8:57	10:49	12:51	14:49	16:51	18:50	20:52	22:54	00:52	2:54	4:53
16	6:59	9:01	10:52	12:55	14:53	16:55	18:53	20:56	22:58	00:56	2:58	4:57
17	7:03	9:05	10:56	12:59	14:57	16:59	18:57	21:00	23:02	1:00	3:02	5:01
18	7:07	9:09	11:00	13:03	15:01	17:03	19:01	21:04	23:06	1:04	3:06	5:05
19	7:11	9:13	11:04	13:07	15:05	17:07	19:05	21:08	23:10	1:08	3:10	5:09
20	7:15	9:17	11:08	13:11	15:09	17:11	19:09	21:11	23:14	1:12	3:14	5:12
21	7:19	9:21	11:12	13:14	15:13	17:15	19:13	21:15	23:18	1:16	3:18	5:16
22	7:22	9:25	11:16	13:18	15:17	17:19	19:17	21:19	23:22	1:20	3:22	5:20
23	7:26	9:29	11:20	13:22	15:21	17:23	19:21	21:23	23:26	1:24	3:26	5:24
24	7:30	9:33	11:24	13:26	15:25	17:27	19:25	21:27	23:29	1:28	3:30	5:28
25	7:34	9:37	11:28	13:30	15:28	17:31	19:29	21:31	23:33	1:32	3:34	5:32
26	7:38	9:41	11:32	13:34	15:32	17:35	19:33	21:35	23:37	1:36	3:38	5:36
27	7:42	9:44	11:36	13:38	15:36	17:39	19:37	21:39	23:41	1:40	3:42	5:40
28	7:46	9:48	11:40	13:42	15:40	17:43	19:41	21:43	23:45	1:43	3:46	5:44
29	7:50	9:51	11:44	13:46	15:44	17:46	19:45	21:47	23:49	1:47	3:50	5:48
30	7:54		11:48	13:50	15:48	17:50	19:49	21:51	23:53	1:51	3:54	5:52
31	7:58		11:52		15:52		19:53	21:55		1:55		5:56

Daily Code Table for People Born in

CANADA

DAY	JAN	FEB	MAR	APRIL	MAY	JUNE	JULY	AUG	SEPT	OCT	NOV	DEC
1	4:40	6:42	8:33	10:36	12:34	14:36	16:34	18:37	20:39	22:37	0:39	2:38
2	4:44	6:46	8:37	10:39	12:38	14:40	16:38	18:40	20:43	22:41	0:43	2:41
3	4:48	6:50	8:41	10:43	12:42	14:44	16:42	18:44	20:47	22:45	0:47	2:45
4	4:52	6:54	8:45	10:47	12:46	14:48	16:46	18:48	20:51	22:49	0:51	2:49
5	4:56	6:58	8:49	10:51	12:50	14:52	16:50	18:52	20:55	22:53	0:55	2:53
6	4:59	7:02	8:53	10:55	12:54	14:56	16:54	18:56	20:58	22:57	0:59	2:57
7	5:03	7:06	8:57	10:59	12:57	15:00	16:58	19:00	21:02	23:01	1:03	3:01
8	5:07	7:10	9:01	11:03	13:01	15:04	17:02	19:04	21:06	23:05	1:07	3:05
9	5:11	7:13	9:05	11:07	13:05	15:08	17:06	19:08	21:10	23:09	1:11	3:09
10	5:15	7:17	9:09	11:11	13:09	15:12	17:10	19:12	21:14	23:13	1:15	3:13
11	5:19	7:21	9:13	11:15	13:13	15:15	17:14	19:16	21:18	23:16	1:19	3:17
12	5:23	7:25	9:17	11:19	13:17	15:19	17:18	19:20	21:22	23:20	1:23	3:21
13	5:27	7:29	9:21	11:23	13:21	15:23	17:22	19:24	21:26	23:24	1:27	3:25
14	5:31	7:33	9:25	11:27	13:25	15:27	17:26	19:28	21:30	23:28	1:31	3:29
15	5:35	7:37	9:29	11:31	13:29	15:31	17:30	19:32	21:34	23:32	1:34	3:33
16	5:39	7:41	9:32	11:35	13:33	15:35	17:33	19:36	21:38	23:36	1:38	3:37
17	5:43	7:45	9:36	11:39	13:37	15:39	17:37	19:40	21:42	23:40	1:42	3:41
18	5:47	7:49	9:40	11:43	13:41	15:43	17:41	19:44	21:46	23:44	1:46	3:45
19	5:51	7:53	9:44	11:47	13:45	15:47	17:45	19:48	21:50	23:48	1:50	3:49
20	5:55	7:57	9:48	11:51	13:49	15:51	17:49	19:51	21:54	23:52	1:54	3:52
21	5:59	8:01	9:52	11:54	13:53	15:55	17:53	19:55	21:58	23:56	1:58	3:56
22	6:02	8:05	9:56	11:58	13:57	15:59	17:57	19:59	22:02	0:00	2:02	4:00
23	6:06	8:09	10:00	12:02	14:01	16:03	18:01	20:03	22:06	0:04	2:06	4:04
24	6:10	8:13	10:04	12:06	14:05	16:07	18:05	20:07	22:09	0:08	2:10	4:08
25	6:14	8:17	10:08	12:10	14:08	16:11	18:09	20:11	22:13	0:12	2:14	4:12
26	6:18	8:21	10:12	12:14	14:12	16:15	18:13	20:15	22:17	0:16	2:18	4:16
27	6:22	8:24	10:16	12:18	14:16	16:19	18:17	20:19	22:21	0:20	2:22	4:20
28	6:26	8:28	10:20	12:22	14:20	16:23	18:21	20:23	22:25	0:23	2:26	4:24
29	6:30	8:31	10:24	12:26	14:24	16:26	18:25	20:27	22:29	0:27	2:30	4:28
30	6:34		10:28	12:30	14:28	16:30	18:29	20:31	22:33	0:31	2:34	4:32
31	6:38		10:32		14:32		18:33	20:35		0:35		4:36

Daily Code Table for People Born in

AUSTRALIA, NEW ZEALAND AND SOUTH AFRICA

DAY	JAN	FEB	MAR	APRIL	MAY	JUNE	JULY	AUG	SEPT	OCT	NOV	DEC
1	5:40	7:42	9:33	11:36	13:34	15:36	17:34	19:37	21:39	23:37	1:39	3:38
2	5:44	7:46	9:37	11:39	13:38	15:40	17:38	19:40	21:43	23:41	1:43	3:41
3	5:48	7:50	9:41	11:43	13:42	15:44	17:42	19:44	21:47	23:45	1:47	3:45
4	5:52	7:54	9:45	11:47	13:46	15:48	17:46	19:48	21:51	23:49	1:51	3:49
5	5:56	7:58	9:49	11:51	13:50	15:52	17:50	19:52	21:55	23:53	1:55	3:53
6	5:59	8:02	9:53	11:55	13:54	15:56	17:54	19:56	21:58	23:57	1:59	3:57
7	6:03	8:06	9:57	11:59	13:57	16:00	17:58	20:00	22:02	00:01	2:03	4:01
8	6:07	8:10	10:01	12:03	14:01	16:04	18:02	20:04	22:06	00:05	2:07	4:05
9	6:11	8:13	10:05	12:07	14:05	16:08	18:06	20:08	22:10	00:09	2:11	4:09
10	6:15	8:17	10:09	12:11	14:09	16:12	18:10	20:12	22:14	00:13	2:15	4:13
11	6:19	8:21	10:13	12:15	14:13	16:15	18:14	20:16	22:18	00:16	2:19	4:17
12	6:23	8:25	10:17	12:19	14:17	16:19	18:18	20:20	22:22	00:20	2:23	4:21
13	6:27	8:29	10:21	12:23	14:21	16:23	18:22	20:24	22:26	00:24	2:27	4:25
14	6:31	8:33	10:25	12:27	14:25	16:27	18:26	20:28	22:30	00:28	2:31	4:29
15	6:35	8:37	10:29	12:31	14:29	16:31	18:30	20:32	22:34	00:32	2:34	4:33
16	6:39	8:41	10:32	12:35	14:33	16:35	18:33	20:36	22:38	00:36	2:38	4:37
17	6:43	8:45	10:36	12:39	14:37	16:39	18:37	20:40	22:42	00:40	2:42	4:41
18	6:47	8:49	10:40	12:43	14:41	16:43	18:41	20:44	22:46	00:44	2:46	4:45
19	6:51	8:53	10:44	12:47	14:45	16:47	18:45	20:48	22:50	00:48	2:50	4:49
20	6:55	8:57	10:48	12:51	14:49	16:51	18:49	20:51	22:54	00:52	2:54	4:52
21	6:59	9:01	10:52	12:54	14:53	16:55	18:53	20:55	22:58	00:56	2:58	4:56
22	7:02	9:05	10:56	12:58	14:57	16:59	18:57	20:59	23:02	1:00	3:02	5:00
23	7:06	9:09	11:00	13:02	15:01	17:03	19:01	21:03	23:06	1:04	3:06	5:04
24	7:10	9:13	11:04	13:06	15:05	17:07	19:05	21:07	23:09	1:08	3:10	5:08
25	7:14	9:17	11:08	13:10	15:08	17:11	19:09	21:11	23:13	1:12	3:14	5:12
26	7:18	9:21	11:12	13:14	15:12	17:15	19:13	21:15	23:17	1:16	3:18	5:16
27	7:22	9:24	11:16	13:18	15:16	17:19	19:17	21:19	23:21	1:20	3:22	5:20
28	7:26	9:28	11:20	13:22	15:20	17:23	19:21	21:23	23:25	1:23	3:26	5:24
29	7:30	9:31	11:24	13:26	15:24	17:26	19:25	21:27	23:29	1:27	3:30	5:28
30	7:34		11:28	13:30	15:28	17:30	19:29	21:31	23:33	1:31	3:34	5:32
31	7:38		11:32		15:32		19:33	21:35		1:35		5:36

TABLES OF TIME CHANGES

Table of Time changes for People born in

GREAT BRITAIN AND IRELAND

Including Summer Time, Double Summer Time and British Standard Time

If your birthday falls on or between any of the dates given in this table, subtract the number of hours shown in order to obtain your TIME OF BIRTH.

Year	Dates	Hours
1916	21 May – 1 Oct	1 hr
1917	8 April – 17 Sept	1 hr
1918	24 March – 30 Sept	1 hr
1919	30 March – 29 Sept	1 hr
1920	28 March – 25 Oct	1 hr
1921	3 April – 3 Oct	1 hr
1922	26 March – 8 Oct	1 hr
1923	22 April – 16 Sept	1 hr
1924	13 April – 21 Sept	1 hr
1925	19 April – 4 Oct	1 hr
1926	18 April – 3 Oct	1 hr
1927	10 April – 2 Oct	1 hr
1928	22 April – 7 Oct	1 hr
1929	21 April – 6 Oct	1 hr
1930	13 April – 5 Oct	1 hr
1931	19 April – 4 Oct	1 hr
1932	17 April – 2 Oct	1 hr
1933	9 April – 8 Oct	1 hr
1934	22 April – 7 Oct	1 hr
1935	14 April – 6 Oct	1 hr
1936	19 April – 4 Oct	1 hr
1937	18 April – 3 Oct	1 hr
1938	10 April – 2 Oct	1 hr
1939	16 April – 19 Nov	1 hr
1940	25 Feb – 31 Dec	1 hr
1941	1 Jan – 3 May	1 hr
	4 May – 10 Aug	2 hrs
	11 Aug – 31 Dec	1 hr
1942	1 Jan – 4 April	1 hr
	5 April – 9 Aug	2 hrs
	10 Aug – 31 Dec	1 hr
1943	1 Jan – 3 April	1 hr
	4 April – 15 Aug	2 hrs
	16 Aug – 31 Dec	1 hr
1944	1 Jan – 1 April	1 hr
	2 April – 17 Sept	2 hrs
	18 Sept – 31 Dec	1 hr
1945	1 Jan – 1 April	1 hr
	2 April – 15 July	2 hrs
	16 July – 31 Dec	1 hr
1946	14 April – 6 Oct	1 hr
1947	16 March – 12 April	1 hr
	13 April – 10 Aug	2 hrs
	11 Aug – 2 Nov	1 hr
1948	14 March – 31 Oct	1 hr
1949	3 April – 30 Oct	1 hr
1950	16 April – 22 Oct	1 hr
1951	15 April – 21 Oct	1 hr
1952	20 April – 26 Oct	1 hr
1953	19 April – 4 Oct	1 hr
1954	11 April – 3 Oct	1 hr
1955	17 April – 2 Oct	1 hr
1956	22 April – 7 Oct	1 hr
1957	14 April – 6 Oct	1 hr
1958	20 April – 5 Oct	1 hr
1959	19 April – 4 Oct	1 hr
1960	10 April – 2 Oct	1 hr
1961	26 March – 29 Oct	1 hr
1962	25 March – 28 Oct	1 hr
1963	31 March – 27 Oct	1 hr
1964	22 March – 25 Oct	1 hr
1965	21 March – 24 Oct	1 hr
1966	20 March – 23 Oct	1 hr
1967	19 March – 29 Oct	1 hr
1968	18 Feb – 31 Dec	1 hr
1969	1 Jan – 31 Dec	1 hr
1970	1 Jan – 31 Dec	1 hr
1971	1 Jan – 31 Oct	1 hr
1972	19 March – 29 Oct	1 hr
1973	18 March – 28 Oct	1 hr
1974	17 March – 27 Oct	1 hr
1975	16 March – 26 Oct	1 hr
1976	21 March – 24 Oct	1 hr
1977	20 March – 23 Oct	1 hr
1978	19 March – 29 Oct	1 hr
1979	18 March – 28 Oct	1 hr
1980	16 March – 26 Oct	1 hr
1981	29 March – 25 Oct	1 hr
1982	28 March – 24 Oct	1 hr
1983	27 March – 23 Oct	1 hr
1984	25 March – 28 Oct	1 hr
1985	31 March – 27 Oct	1 hr
1986	30 March – 26 Oct	1 hr

Table of Time Changes for People Born in

CANADA

Including Daylight Saving Time (DST) and War Time

Unfortunately, for the purposes of calculating your TIME OF BIRTH, the irregular observance of **DST** in Canada, particularly between the two world wars, makes it difficult to be absolutely precise. Further information may be obtained from The Dominion Bureau of Statistics Secretary, Library Division, Tunney's Pasture, Ottawa 3, Ontario, Canada. However, I am sure that the following will satisfy just about everybody!

WAR TIME

During the war years the whole of Canada observed War Time between these dates:

World War I	14 April 1918 – 31 Oct 1918
World War II	9 Feb 1942 – 30 Sept 1945
In Ontario and Quebec	19 Sept 1940 – 30 Sept 1945

If your birthday falls on or between these dates, subtract 1 hour to obtain your TIME OF BIRTH.

DST

DST was introduced at different times in different territories. The NORTH WEST TERRITORIES and the YUKON have never kept it. Here is a list of the territories that have observed it and the year in which they officially began to do so.

ALBERTA – 1972

ARCTIC ISLANDS –1972

BRITISH COLUMBIA – 1947

LABRADOR – 1951

MANITOBA – 1967

NEW BRUNSWICK – 1966

NEWFOUNDLAND – 1951

NOVA SCOTIA – 1972

ONTARIO – 1974

PRINCE EDWARD ISLANDS – 1962

QUEBEC (see note) – 1972

SASKATCHEWAN – 1972

If DST applies in your case and your birthday falls on or between the dates in this table, subtract 1 hour to arrive at your TIME OF BIRTH. The official DST dates are as follows:

1946	28 April – 29 Sept	1967	30 April – 29 Oct
1947	27 April – 28 Sept	1968	28 April – 27 Oct
1948	25 April – 26 Sept	1969	27 April – 26 Oct
1949	24 April – 25 Sept	1970	26 April – 25 Oct
1950	30 April – 24 Sept	1971	25 April – 31 Oct
1951	29 April – 30 Sept	1972	30 April – 29 Oct
1952	27 April – 28 Sept	1973	29 April – 28 Oct
1953	26 April – 27 Sept	1974	28 April – 27 Oct
1954	25 April – 26 Sept	1975	27 April – 26 Oct
1955	24 April – 25 Sept	1976	25 April – 31 Oct
1956	29 April – 30 Sept	1977	24 April – 30 Oct
1957	28 April – 29 Sept	1978	30 April – 29 Oct
1958	27 April – 28 Sept	1979	29 April – 28 Oct
1959	26 April – 27 Sept	1980	27 April – 26 Oct
1960	24 April – 25 Sept	1981	26 April – 25 Oct
1961	30 April – 24 Sept	1982	25 April – 31 Oct
1962	29 April – 28 Oct	1983	24 April – 30 Oct
1963	28 April – 27 Oct	1984	29 April – 28 Oct
1964	26 April – 25 Oct	1985	28 April – 27 Oct
1965	25 April – 31 Oct	1986	27 April – 26 Oct
1966	24 April – 30 Oct		

Note on Quebec

If you were born in QUEBEC between 1942 and 1969 please note the following adjustments to your TIME OF BIRTH, which must be made in addition to the calculation for DST:

28 Sept 1942 – 9 June 1952: add 1 hour if born east of longtitude 68°

1 Nov 1953 – 29 Oct 1961: subtract 1 hour if born west of longtitude 68° in the counties of RIMOUSKI, RIVIERE-DU-LOUP, TEMISCOUATA, SAGUENAY, MATANE

1 Nov 1962 – 23 Oct 1969: subtract 1 hour if born in TEMISCOUATA

Table of Time Changes for People Born in

AUSTRALIA

Including Daylight Saving Time (DST)

DST has been observed as follows in Australia. If your birthday falls on or between the dates given, subtract 1 hour in order to obtain your TIME OF BIRTH. Please note the territorial exceptions that follow the main table.

1917	1 Jan – 25 March
1918–1941	not kept but see TASMANIA
1942	1 Jan – 29 March
1942/3	27 Sept – 28 March
1943/4	3 Oct – 26 March
1945–1970	not kept but see TASMANIA
1971/2	24 Oct – 27 Feb
1972/3	29 Oct – 4 March
1973/4	28 Oct – 3 March
1974/5	27 Oct – 2 March
1975/6	26 Oct –7 March
1976/7	31 Oct – 6 March
1977/8	30 Oct – 5 March
1978/9	29 Oct – 4 March
1979/80	28 Oct – 2 March
1980/1	26 Oct – 1 March
1981/2	25 Oct – 5 March
1982/3	31 Oct – 6 March
1983/4	30 Oct – 4 March
1984/5	28 Oct – 3 March
1985/6	27 Oct – 16 March

NORTHERN TERRITORY discontinued DST in 1945

QUEENSLAND last observed DST in 1971/2.

SOUTH AUSTRALIA did not observe DST in 1971/72.

TASMANIA also kept DST as follows:

1917/8	28 Oct – 3 March
1918/9	27 Oct – 2 March
1967/8	1 Oct – 31 March
1968/9	27 Oct – 9 March
1969/70	26 Oct – 8 March
1970/1	25 Oct – 14 March

WESTERN AUSTRALIA last observed DST in 1942/3 and has not kept it since with the exception of 1974/5.

Table of Time Changes for People Born in

NEW ZEALAND

Including Daylight Saving Time and New Zealand Standard Time

Those people born before or during 1945 should subtract 30 minutes from their TIME OF BIRTH before consulting the table below.

If your birthday falls on or between any of the dates in the following table, subtract the amount of time indicated in order to arrive at your TIME OF BIRTH.

1927/8	6 Nov – 4 March	1 hr
1928/9	14 Oct – 17 March	½ hr
1929/30	13 Oct – 16 March	½ hr
1930/1	12 Oct – 15 March	½ hr
1931/2	11 Oct – 20 March	½ hr
1932/3	9 Oct – 19 March	½ hr
1933/4	8 Oct – 29 April	½ hr
1934/5	30 Sept – 28 April	½ hr
1935/6	29 Sept – 26 April	½ hr
1936/7	27 Sept – 25 April	½ hr
1937/8	26 Sept – 24 April	½ hr
1938/9	25 Sept – 30 April	½ hr
1939/40	24 Sept – 28 April	½ hr
29 Sept 1940 – 31 Dec 1945		½ hr
1974/5	27 Oct – 2 March	1 hr
1975/6	26 Oct – 7 March	1 hr
1976/7	31 Oct – 6 March	1 hr
1977/8	30 Oct – 5 March	1 hr
1978/9	29 Oct – 4 March	1 hr
1979/80	28 Oct – 2 March	1 hr
1980/1	26 Oct – 1 March	1 hr
1981/2	25 Oct – 5 March	1 hr
1983/4	30 Oct – 4 March	1 hr
1984/5	28 Oct – 3 March	1 hr
1985/6	27 Oct – 2 March	1 hr

Table of Time Changes for People Born in

SOUTH AFRICA

If born on or between 19 September 1943 and 19 March 1944, unless you were born in SOUTH WEST AFRICA, subtract 1 hour to obtain your TIME OF BIRTH.

If born in NATAL on or between 27 July 1942 and 21 March 1943 subtract 1 hour to obtain your TIME OF BIRTH.

If born in TRANSVAAL, CAPE PROVINCE, ORANGE FREE STATE, SOUTH WEST AFRICA on or between 20 September 1942 and 21 March 1943, subtract 1 hour to obtain your TIME OF BIRTH.

REGIONAL CODE MAPS

GREAT BRITAIN AND IRELAND
Regional Code Map

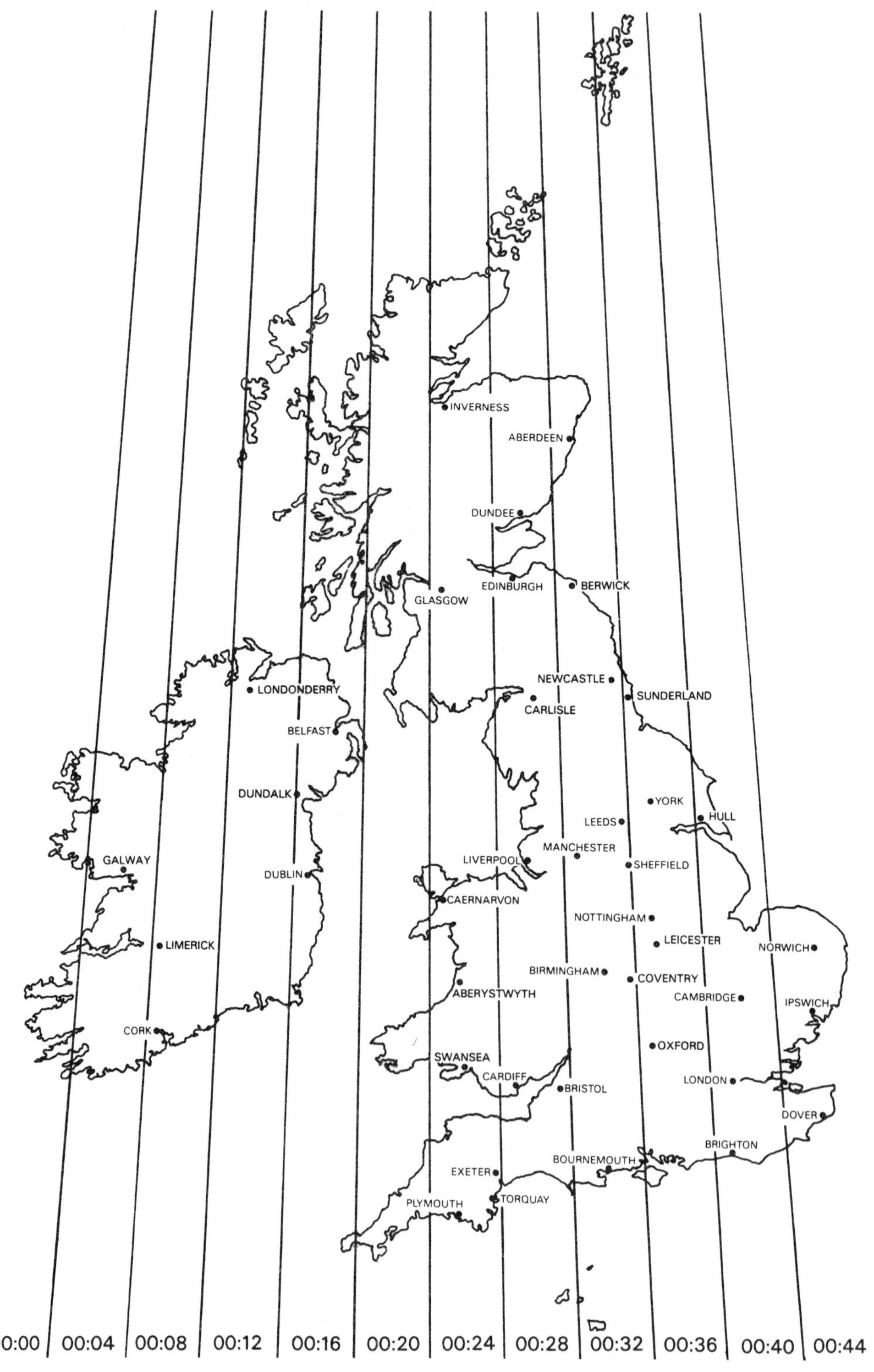

To discover your REGIONAL CODE, find your place of birth on the map and note the time band in which it is located. If you were born on or very close to a line separating two time zones, take an average of the two times.

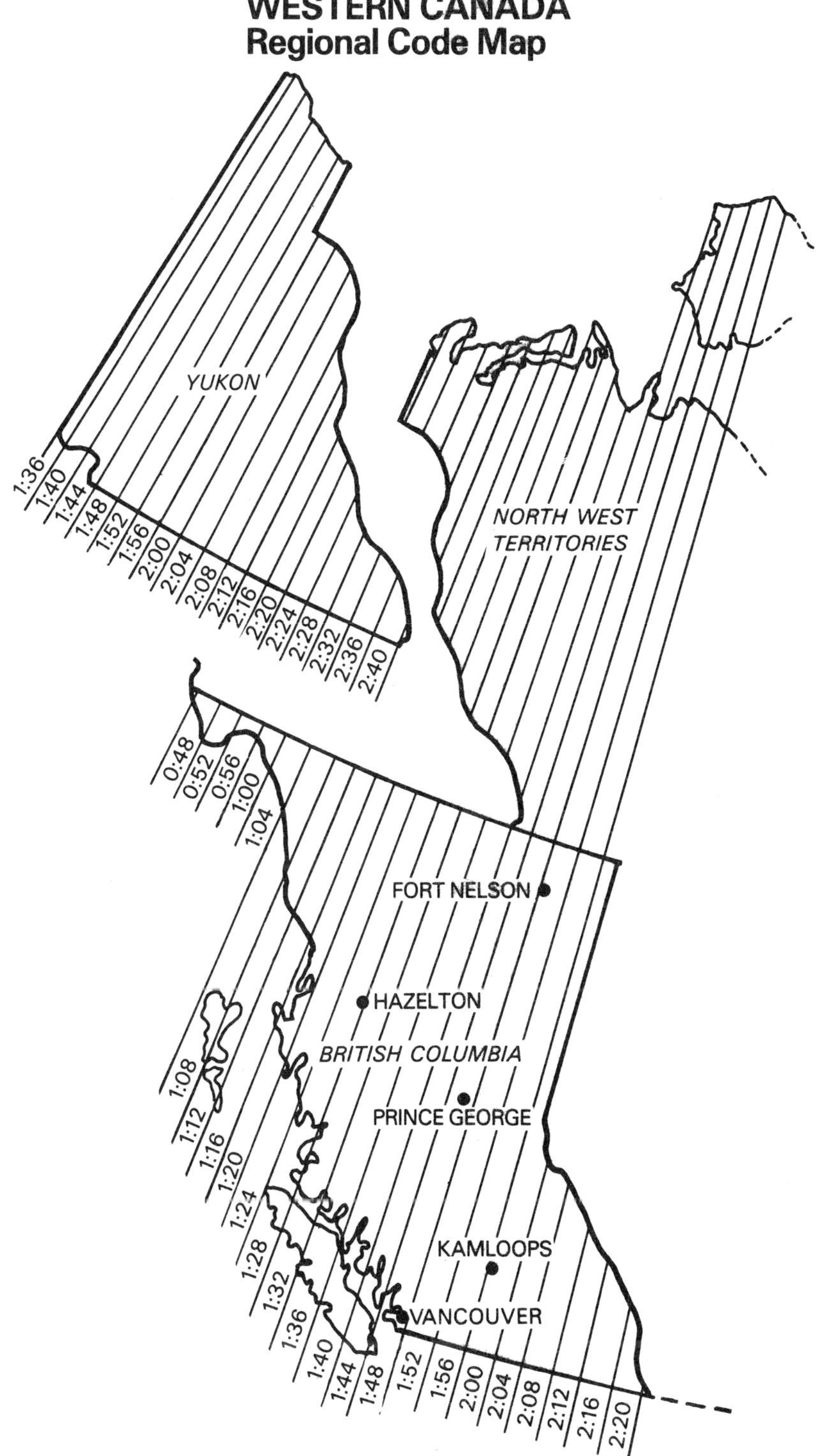

To discover your REGIONAL CODE, find your place of birth on the map and note the time band in which it is located. If you were born on or very close to a line separating two time zones, take an average of the two times.

CENTRAL CANADA
Regional Code Map

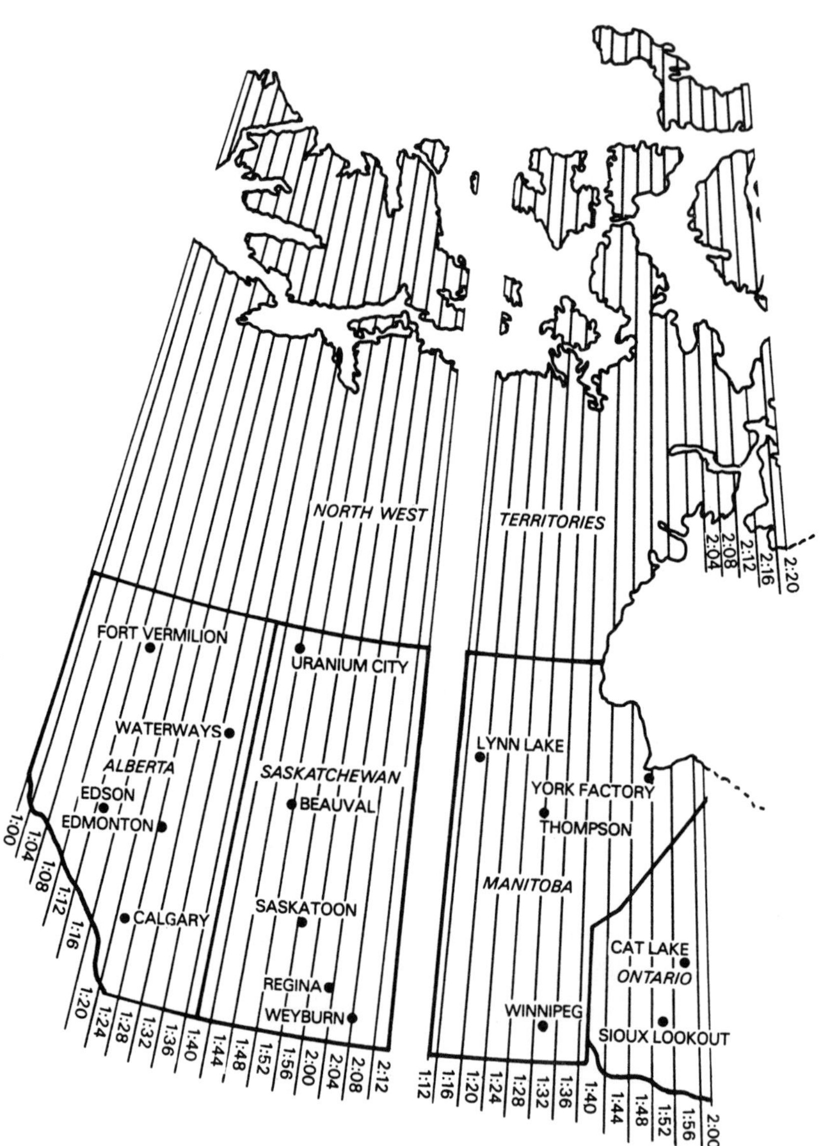

To discover your REGIONAL CODE, find your place of birth on the map and note the time band in which it is located. If you were born on or very close to a line separating two time zones, take an average of the two times.

EASTERN CANADA
Regional Code Map

AUSTRALIA
Regional Code Map

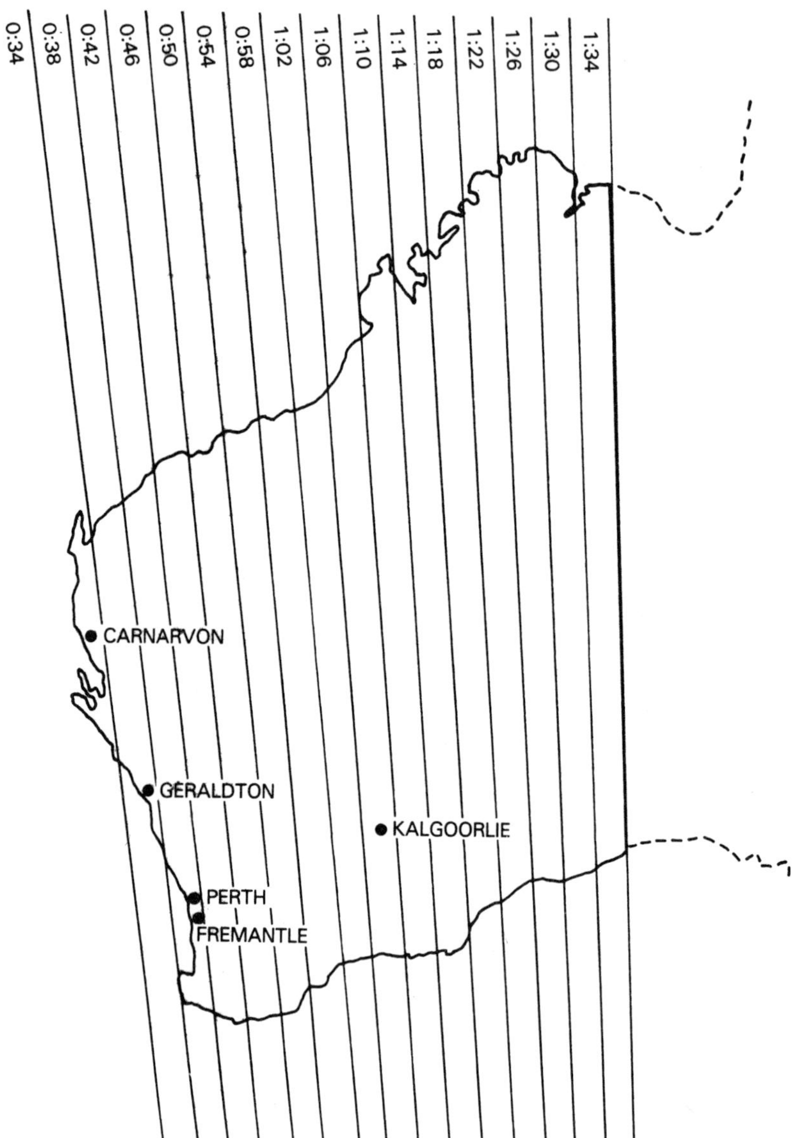

To discover your REGIONAL CODE, find your place of birth on the map and note the time band in which it is located. If you were born on or very close to a line separating two time zones, take an average of the two times.

0:14
0:18
0:22
0:26
0:30
0:34
0:38
0:42
0:46
0:50
0:54
0:58
1:02
1:06
1:10
1:14
DARWIN
CAIRNS
TOWNSVILLE
WINTON
ALICE SPRINGS
CHARLEVILLE
CUNNAMULLA
BRISBANE
BROKEN HILL
ARMIDALE
ADELAIDE
SYDNEY
CANBERRA
HORSHAM
MELBOURNE
LAUNCESTON
HOBART
0:08
0:12
0:16
0:20
0:24
0:28
0:32
0:36
0:40
0:44
0:48
0:52

NEW ZEALAND
Regional Code Map

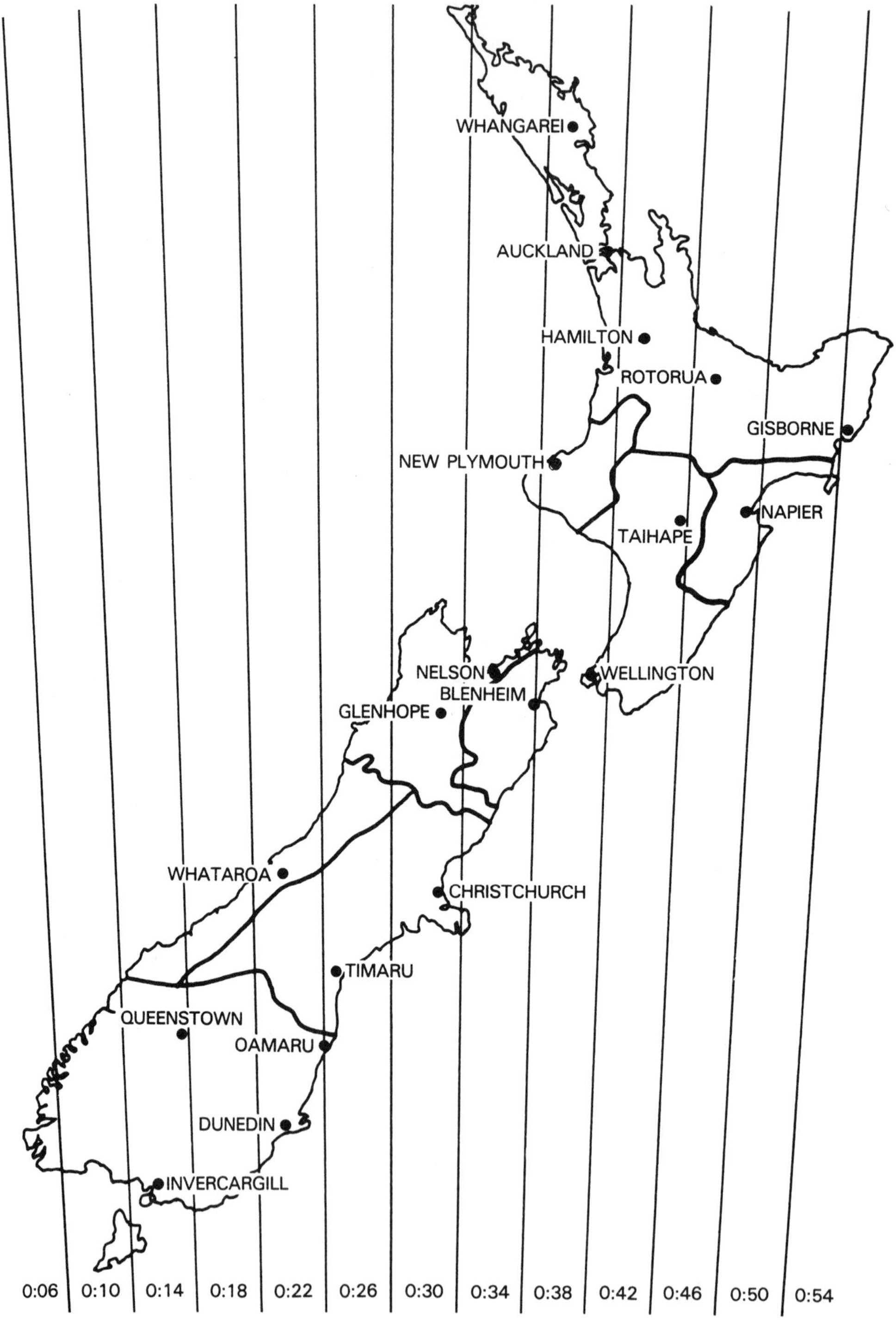

WHANGAREI
AUCKLAND
HAMILTON
ROTORUA
GISBORNE
NEW PLYMOUTH
NAPIER
TAIHAPE
WELLINGTON
NELSON
BLENHEIM
GLENHOPE
WHATAROA
CHRISTCHURCH
TIMARU
QUEENSTOWN
OAMARU
DUNEDIN
INVERCARGILL

0:06 | 0:10 | 0:14 | 0:18 | 0:22 | 0:26 | 0:30 | 0:34 | 0:38 | 0:42 | 0:46 | 0:50 | 0:54

To discover your REGIONAL CODE, find your place of birth on the map and note the time band in which it is located. If you were born on or very close to a line separating two time zones, take an average of the two times.

SOUTH AFRICA
Regional Code Map

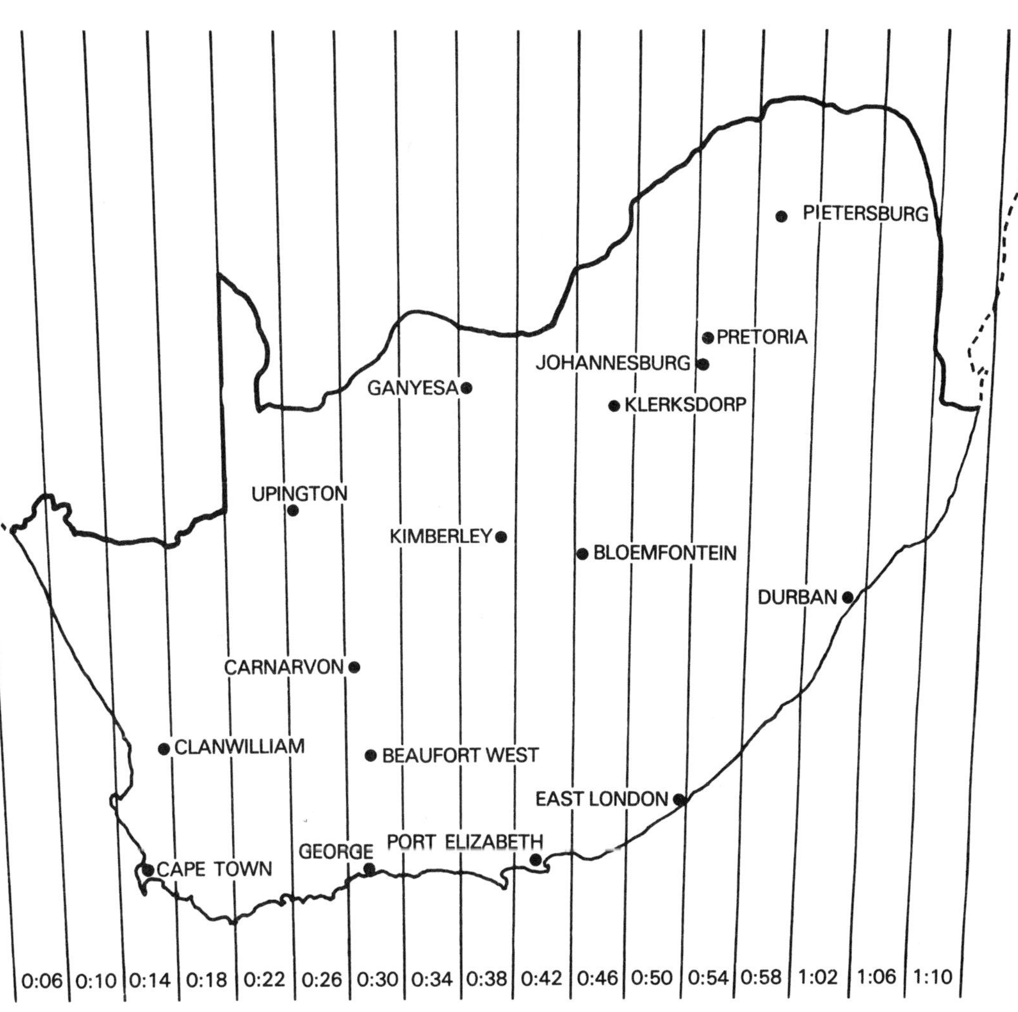

To discover your REGIONAL CODE, find your place of birth on the map and note the time band in which it is located. If you were born on or very close to a line separating two time zones, take an average of the two times.

ASCENDANT ZONE MAPS AND CODE TABLES

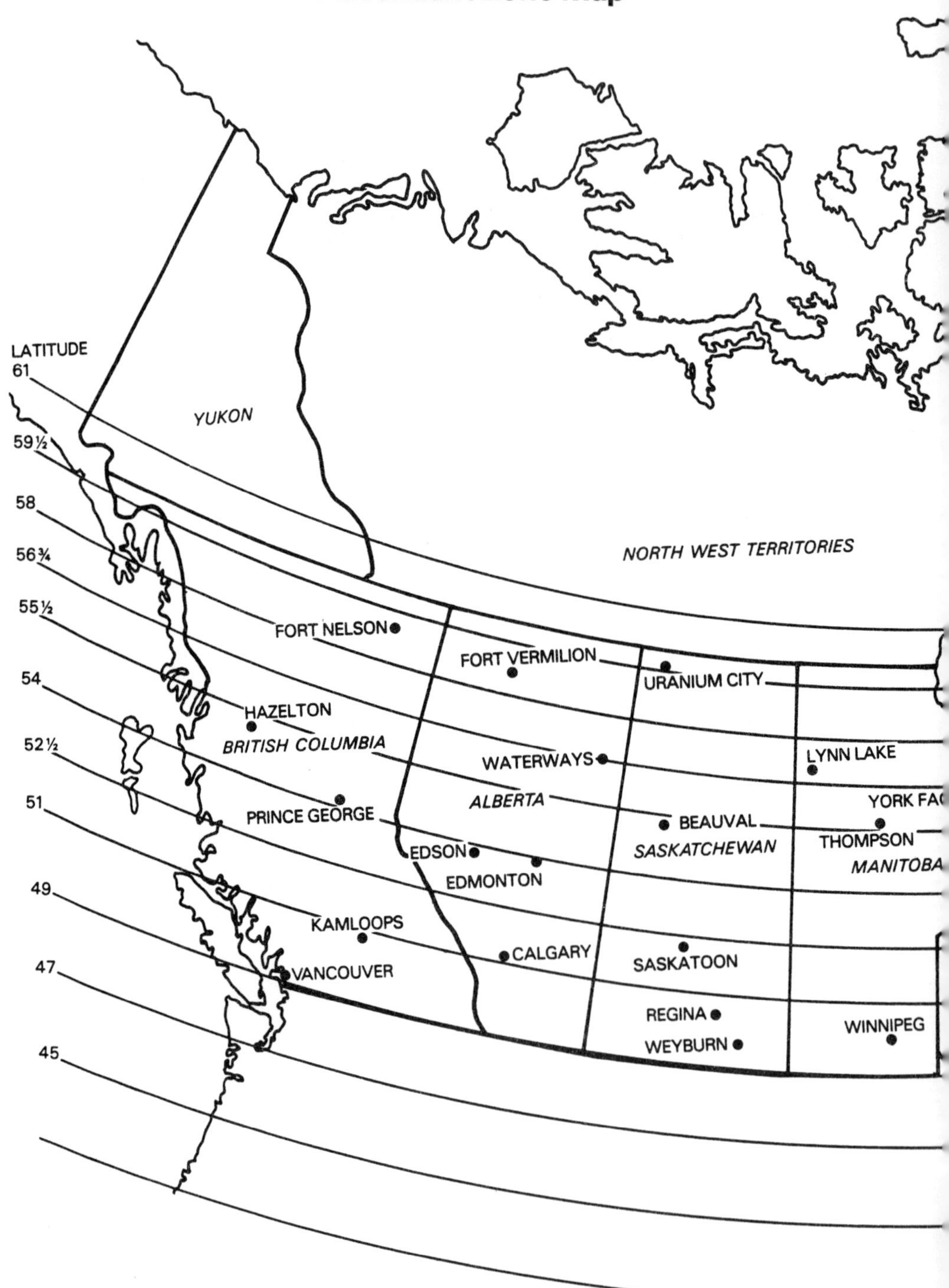
CANADA
Ascendant Zone Map
LATITUDE
61
59½
58
56¾
55½
54
52½
51
49
47
45
YUKON
NORTH WEST TERRITORIES
FORT NELSON
FORT VERMILION
URANIUM CITY
HAZELTON
BRITISH COLUMBIA
WATERWAYS
LYNN LAKE
ALBERTA
PRINCE GEORGE
BEAUVAL
THOMPSON
SASKATCHEWAN
MANITOBA
EDSON
EDMONTON
KAMLOOPS
CALGARY
SASKATOON
VANCOUVER
REGINA
WEYBURN
WINNIPEG

Locate the Zone of your birthplace on this map before referring to your Ascendant Code Table to discover your Ascendant sign.

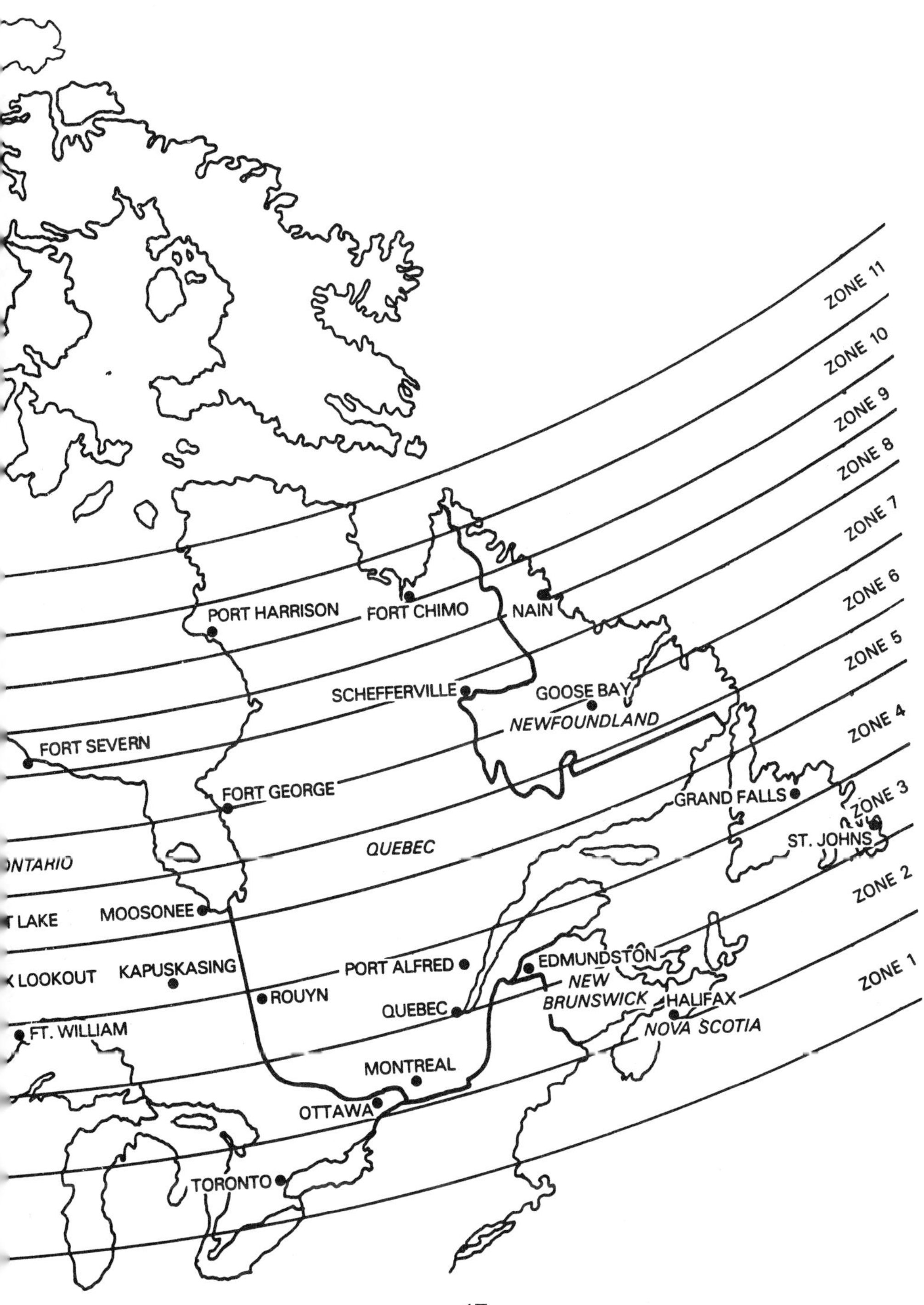

GREAT BRITAIN AND IRELAND
Ascendant Zone Map

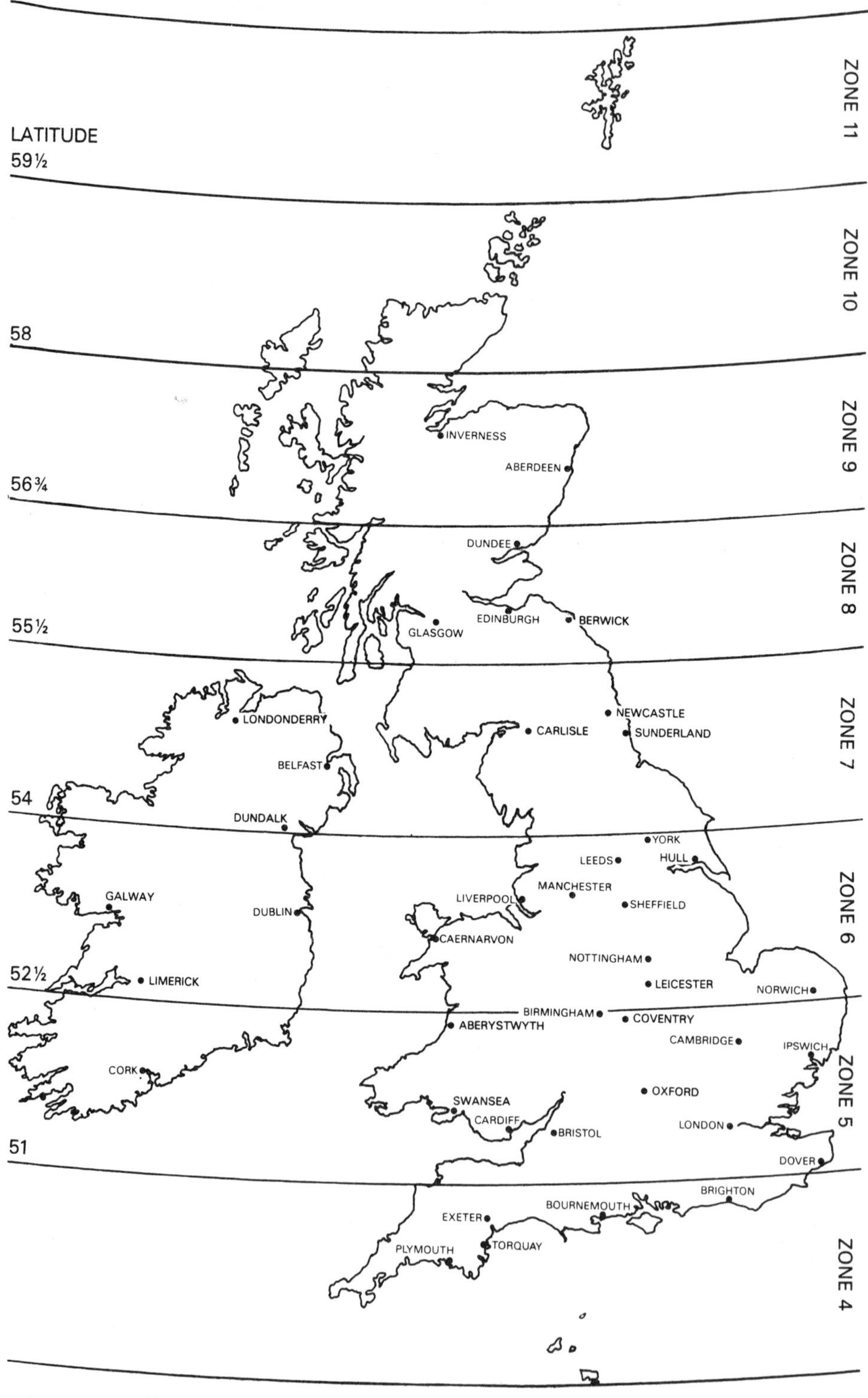

Locate the Zone of your birthplace on this map before referring to your Ascendant Code Table to discover your Ascendant sign.

ASCENDANT CODE TABLE FOR PEOPLE BORN IN GREAT BRITAIN, IRELAND AND CANADA

Zone 1

ASCENDANT CODE	ASCENDANT
0:00 – 0:47	CANCER
0:47 – 3:24	LEO
3:24 – 6:00	VIRGO
6:00 – 8:37	LIBRA
8:37 – 11:13	SCORPIO
11:13 – 13:38	SAGITTARIUS
13:38 – 15:30	CAPRICORN
15:30 – 16:52	AQUARIUS
16:52 – 18:00	PISCES
18:00 – 19:07	ARIES
19:07 – 20:29	TAURUS
20:29 – 22:21	GEMINI
22:21 – 24:00	CANCER

Zone 2

ASCENDANT CODE	ASCENDANT
0:00 – 0:38	CANCER
0:38 – 3:19	LEO
3:19 – 6:00	VIRGO
6:00 – 8:41	LIBRA
8:41 – 11:21	SCORPIO
11:21 – 13:48	SAGITTARIUS
13:48 – 15:39	CAPRICORN
15:39 – 16:57	AQUARIUS
16:57 – 18:00	PISCES
18:00 – 19:03	ARIES
19:03 – 20:21	TAURUS
20:21 – 22:12	GEMINI
22:12 – 24:00	CANCER

Zone 3

ASCENDANT CODE	ASCENDANT
0:00 – 0:32	CANCER
0:32 – 3:16	LEO
3:16 – 6:00	VIRGO
6:00 – 8:45	LIBRA
8:45 – 11:28	SCORPIO
11:28 – 13:56	SAGITTARIUS
13:56 – 15:46	CAPRICORN
15:46 – 17:01	AQUARIUS
17:01 – 18:00	PISCES
18:00 – 18:59	ARIES
18:59 – 20:14	TAURUS
20:14 – 22:04	GEMINI
22:04 – 24:00	CANCER

Zone 4

ASCENDANT CODE	ASCENDANT
0:00 – 0:24	CANCER
0:24 – 3:12	LEO
3:12 – 6:00	VIRGO
6:00 – 8:49	LIBRA
8:49 – 11:36	SCORPIO
11:36 – 14:06	SAGITTARIUS
14:06 – 15:51	CAPRICORN
15:54 – 17:05	AQUARIUS
17:05 – 18:00	PISCES
18:00 – 18:56	ARIES
18:56 – 20:05	TAURUS
20:05 – 21:54	GEMINI
21:54 – 24:00	CANCER

Zone 5

ASCENDANT CODE	ASCENDANT
0:00 – 0:18	CANCER
0:18 – 3:10	LEO
3:10 – 6:00	VIRGO
6:00 – 8:50	LIBRA
8:50 – 11:41	SCORPIO
11:41 – 14:13	SAGITTARIUS
14:13 – 15:59	CAPRICORN
15:59 – 17:08	AQUARIUS
17:08 – 18:00	PISCES
18:00 – 18:54	ARIES
18:54 – 20:00	TAURUS
20:00 – 21:47	GEMINI
21:47 – 24:00	CANCER

Zone 6

ASCENDANT CODE	ASCENDANT
0:00 – 0:13	CANCER
0:13 – 3:06	LEO
3:06 – 6:00	VIRGO
6:00 – 8:54	LIBRA
8:54 – 11:48	SCORPIO
11:48 – 14:20	SAGITTARIUS
14:20 – 16:05	CAPRICORN
16:05 – 17:11	AQUARIUS
17:11 – 18:00	PISCES
18:00 – 18:49	ARIES
18:49 – 19:55	TAURUS
19:55 – 21:39	GEMINI
21:39 – 24:00	CANCER

Zone 7

ASCENDANT CODE	ASCENDANT
0:00 – 0:04	CANCER
0:04 – 3:02	LEO
3:02 – 6:00	VIRGO
6:00 – 8:58	LIBRA
8:58 – 11:56	SCORPIO
11:56 – 14:30	SAGITTARIUS
14:30 – 16:13	CAPRICORN
16:13 – 17:15	AQUARIUS
17:15 – 18:00	PISCES
18:00 – 18:45	ARIES
18:45 – 19:47	TAURUS
19:47 – 21:30	GEMINI
21:30 – 24:00	CANCER

Zone 8

ASCENDANT CODE	ASCENDANT
0:00 – 2:57	LEO
2:57 – 6:00	VIRGO
6:00 – 9:03	LIBRA
9:03 – 12:06	SCORPIO
12:06 – 14:44	SAGITTARIUS
14:44 – 16:23	CAPRICORN
16:23 – 17:19	AQUARIUS
17:19 – 18:00	PISCES
18:00 – 18:41	ARIES
18:41 – 19:37	TAURUS
19:37 – 21:16	GEMINI
21:16 – 23:54	CANCER
23:54 – 24:00	LEO

Zone 9

ASCENDANT CODE	ASCENDANT
0:00 – 2:54	LEO
2:54 – 6:00	VIRGO
6:00 – 9:06	LIBRA
9:06 – 12:12	SCORPIO
12:12 – 14:52	SAGITTARIUS
14:52 – 16:29	CAPRICORN
16:29 – 17:23	AQUARIUS
17:23 – 18:00	PISCES
18:00 – 18:37	ARIES
18:37 – 19:31	TAURUS
19:31 – 21:08	GEMINI
21:08 – 23:48	CANCER
23:48 – 24:00	LEO

Zone 10

ASCENDANT CODE	ASCENDANT
0:00 – 2:50	LEO
2:50 – 6:00	VIRGO
6:00 – 9:10	LIBRA
9:10 – 12:22	SCORPIO
12:22 – 15:04	SAGITTARIUS
15:04 – 16:40	CAPRICORN
16:40 – 17:27	AQUARIUS
17:27 – 18:00	PISCES
18:00 – 18:33	ARIES
18:33 – 19:20	TAURUS
19:20 – 20:56	GEMINI
20:56 – 23:38	CANCER
23:38 – 24:00	LEO

Zone 11

ASCENDANT CODE	ASCENDANT
0:00 – 2:46	LEO
2:46 – 6:00	VIRGO
6:00 – 9:14	LIBRA
9:14 – 12:29	SCORPIO
12:29 – 15:14	SAGITTARIUS
15:14 – 16:46	CAPRICORN
16:46 – 17:30	AQUARIUS
17:30 – 18:00	PISCES
18:00 – 18:29	ARIES
18:29 – 19:14	TAURUS
19:14 – 20:46	GEMINI
20:46 – 23:31	CANCER
23:31 – 24:00	LEO

AUSTRALIA
Ascendant Zone Map

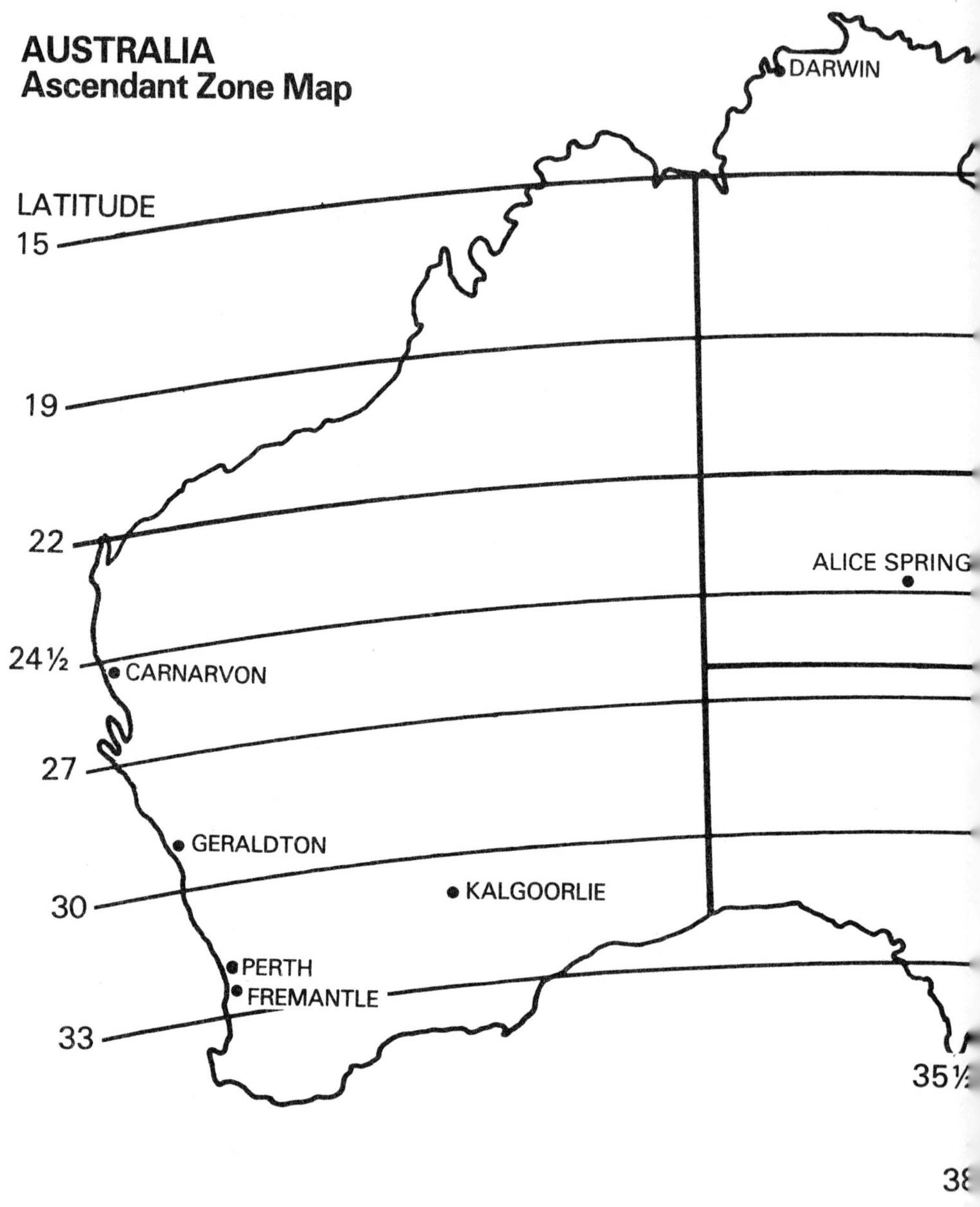

Locate the Zone of your birthplace on this map before referring to your Ascendant Code Table to discover your Ascendant sign.

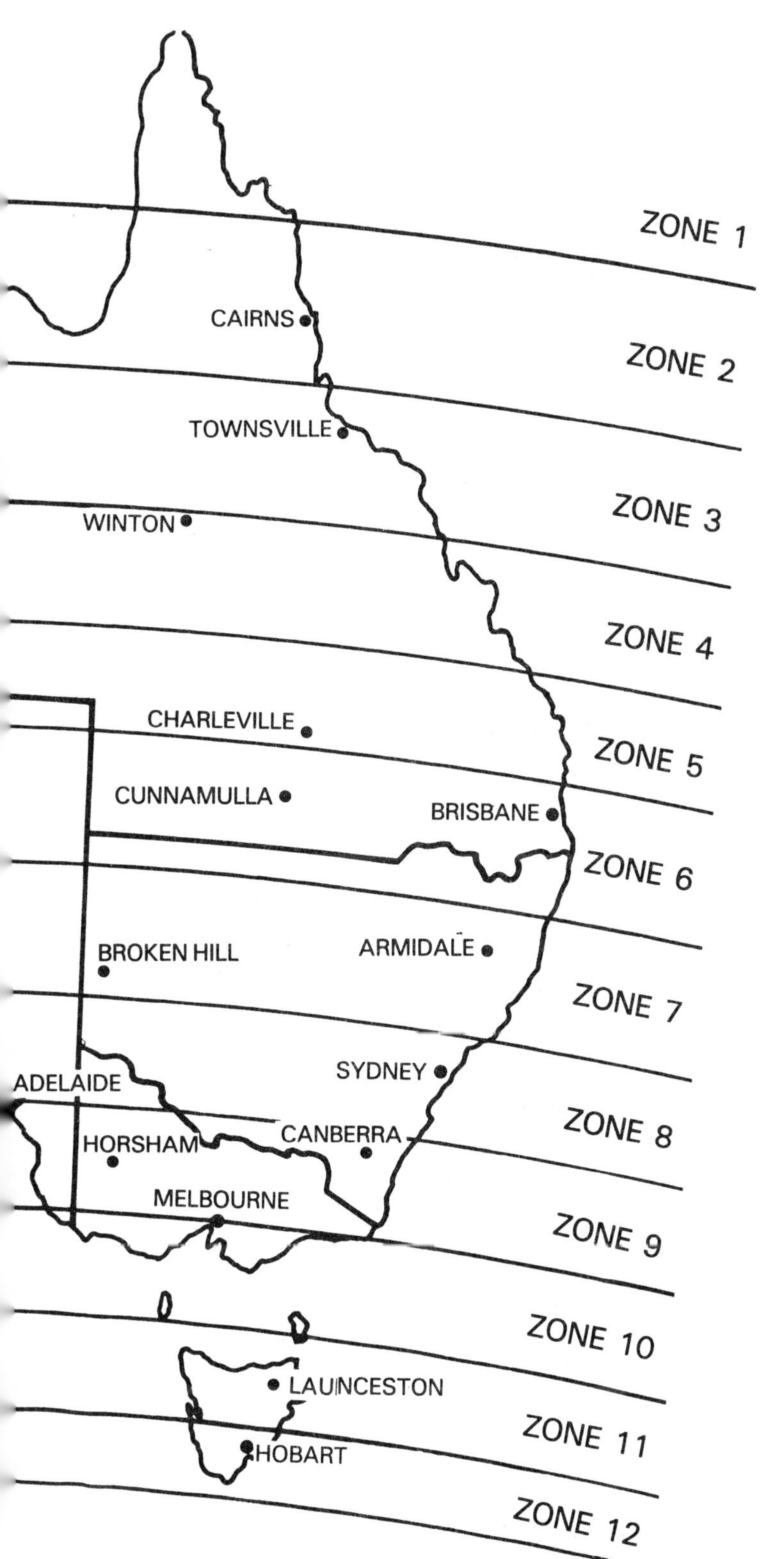
ZONE 1
CAIRNS
ZONE 2
TOWNSVILLE
ZONE 3
WINTON
ZONE 4
CHARLEVILLE
ZONE 5
CUNNAMULLA
BRISBANE
ZONE 6
BROKEN HILL
ARMIDALE
ZONE 7
SYDNEY
ADELAIDE
ZONE 8
HORSHAM
CANBERRA
MELBOURNE
ZONE 9
ZONE 10
LAUNCESTON
ZONE 11
HOBART
ZONE 12

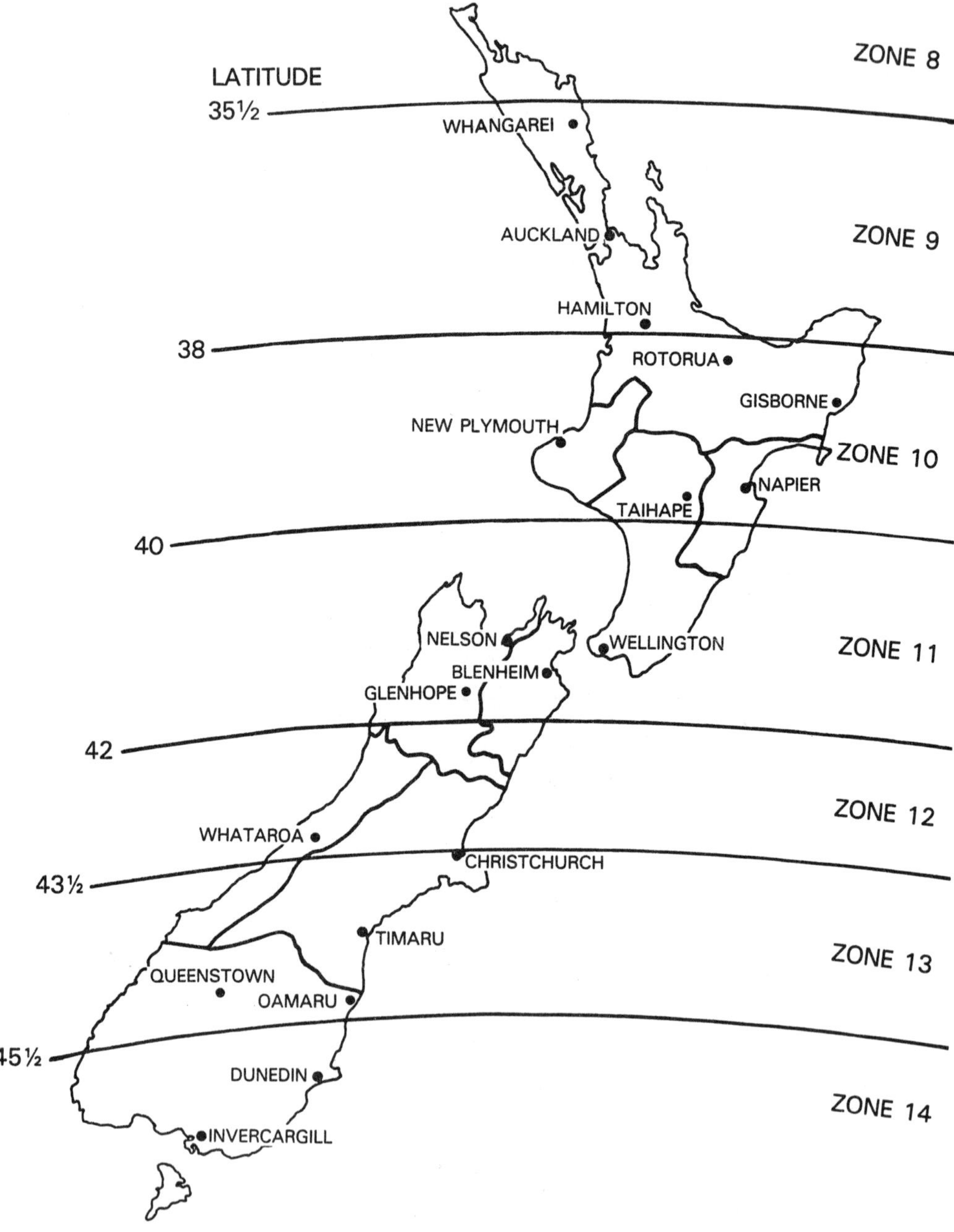

Locate the Zone of your birthplace on this map before referring to your Ascendant Code Table to discover your Ascendant sign.

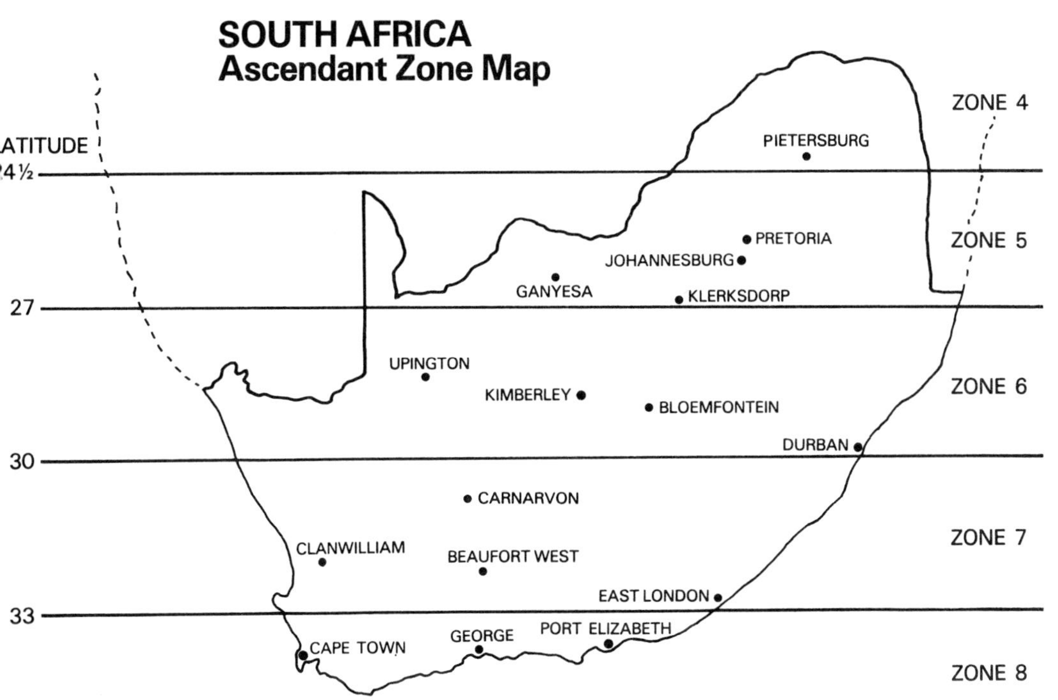

Locate the Zone of your birthplace on this map before referring to your Ascendant Code Table to discover your Ascendant sign.

ASCENDANT CODE TABLE FOR PEOPLE BORN IN AUSTRALIA, NEW ZEALAND AND SOUTH AFRICA

Zone 1

ASCENDANT CODE	ASCENDANT
0:00 – 0:23	GEMINI
0:23 – 2:28	CANCER
2:28 – 4:19	LEO
4:19 – 6:00	VIRGO
6:00 – 7:40	LIBRA
7:40 – 9:32	SCORPIO
9:32 – 11:38	SAGITTARIUS
11:38 – 13:49	CAPRICORN
13:49 – 15:57	AQUARIUS
15:57 – 18:00	PISCES
18:00 – 20:02	ARIES
20:02 – 22:10	TAURUS
22:10 – 24:00	GEMINI

Zone 2

ASCENDANT CODE	ASCENDANT
0:00 – 0:31	GEMINI
0:31 – 2:34	CANCER
2:34 – 4:23	LEO
4:23 – 6:00	VIRGO
6:00 – 7:37	LIBRA
7:37 – 9:26	SCORPIO
9:26 – 11:30	SAGITTARIUS
11:30 – 13:43	CAPRICORN
13:43 – 15:54	AQUARIUS
15:54 – 18:00	PISCES
18:00 – 20:06	ARIES
20:06 – 22:17	TAURUS
22:17 – 24:00	GEMINI

Zone 3

ASCENDANT CODE	ASCENDANT
0:00 – 0:37	GEMINI
0:37 – 2:40	CANCER
2:40 – 4:26	LEO
4:26 – 6:00	VIRGO
6:00 – 7:34	LIBRA
7:34 – 9:19	SCORPIO
9:19 – 11:23	SAGITTARIUS
11:23 – 13:37	CAPRICORN
13:37 – 15:51	AQUARIUS
15:51 – 18:00	PISCES
18:00 – 20:09	ARIES
20:09 – 22:23	TAURUS
22:23 – 24:00	GEMINI

Zone 4

ASCENDANT CODE	ASCENDANT
0:00 – 0:42	GEMINI
0:42 – 2:45	CANCER
2:45 – 4:29	LEO
4:29 – 6:00	VIRGO
6:00 – 7:31	LIBRA
7:31 – 9:15	SCORPIO
9:15 – 11:17	SAGITTARIUS
11:17 – 13:32	CAPRICORN
13:32 – 15:47	AQUARIUS
15:47 – 18:00	PISCES
18:00 – 20:12	ARIES
20:12 – 22:27	TAURUS
22:27 – 24:00	GEMINI

Zone 5

ASCENDANT CODE	ASCENDANT
0:00 – 0:50	GEMINI
0:50 – 2:50	CANCER
2:50 – 4:31	LEO
4:31 – 6:00	VIRGO
6:00 – 7:30	LIBRA
7:30 – 9:10	SCORPIO
9:10 – 11:10	SAGITTARIUS
11:10 – 13:27	CAPRICORN
13:27 – 15:46	AQUARIUS
15:46 – 18:00	PISCES
18:00 – 20:15	ARIES
20:15 – 22:33	TAURUS
22:33 – 24:00	GEMINI

Zone 6

ASCENDANT CODE	ASCENDANT
0:00 – 0:55	GEMINI
0:55 – 2:54	CANCER
2:54 – 4:34	LEO
4:34 – 6:00	VIRGO
6:00 – 7:26	LIBRA
7:26 – 9:05	SCORPIO
9:05 – 11:05	SAGITTARIUS
11:05 – 13:23	CAPRICORN
13:23 – 15:43	AQUARIUS
15:43 – 18:00	PISCES
18:00 – 20:17	ARIES
20:17 – 22:38	TAURUS
22:38 – 24:00	GEMINI

Zone 7

ASCENDANT CODE	ASCENDANT
0:00 – 1:02	GEMINI
1:02 – 3:01	CANCER
3:01 – 4:37	LEO
4:37 – 6:00	VIRGO
6:00 – 7:23	LIBRA
7:23 – 8:59	SCORPIO
8:59 – 10:58	SAGITTARIUS
10:58 – 13:17	CAPRICORN
13:17 – 15:39	AQUARIUS
15:39 – 18:00	PISCES
18:00 – 20:21	ARIES
20:21 – 22:43	TAURUS
22:43 – 24:00	GEMINI

Zone 8

ASCENDANT CODE	ASCENDANT
0:00 – 1:09	GEMINI
1:09 – 3:07	CANCER
3:07 – 4:40	LEO
4:40 – 6:00	VIRGO
6:00 – 7:19	LIBRA
7:19 – 8:53	SCORPIO
8:53 – 10:51	SAGITTARIUS
10:51 – 13:10	CAPRICORN
13:10 – 15:36	AQUARIUS
15:36 – 18:00	PISCES
18:00 – 20:23	ARIES
20:23 – 22:49	TAURUS
22:49 – 24:00	GEMINI

Zone 9

ASCENDANT CODE	ASCENDANT
0:00 – 1:15	GEMINI
1:15 – 3:13	CANCER
3:13 – 4:43	LEO
4:43 – 6:00	VIRGO
6:00 – 7:17	LIBRA
7:17 – 8:48	SCORPIO
8:48 – 10:44	SAGITTARIUS
10:44 – 13:05	CAPRICORN
13:05 – 15:33	AQUARIUS
15:33 – 18:00	PISCES
18:00 – 20:26	ARIES
20:26 – 22:55	TAURUS
22:55 – 24:00	GEMINI

Zone 10

ASCENDANT CODE	ASCENDANT
0:00 – 1:21	GEMINI
1:21 – 3:17	CANCER
3:17 – 4:46	LEO
4:46 – 6:00	VIRGO
6:00 – 7:14	LIBRA
7:14 – 8:43	SCORPIO
8:43 – 10:39	SAGITTARIUS
10:39 – 13:00	CAPRICORN
13:00 – 15:31	AQUARIUS
15:31 – 18:00	PISCES
18:00 – 20:29	ARIES
20:29 – 23:00	TAURUS
23:00 – 24:00	GEMINI

Zone 11

ASCENDANT CODE	ASCENDANT
0:00 – 1:28	GEMINI
1:28 – 3:23	CANCER
3:23 – 4:48	LEO
4:48 – 6:00	VIRGO
6:00 – 7:12	LIBRA
7:12 – 8:37	SCORPIO
8:37 – 10:33	SAGITTARIUS
10:33 – 12:55	CAPRICORN
12:55 – 15:28	AQUARIUS
15:28 – 18:00	PISCES
18:00 – 20:32	ARIES
20:32 – 23:05	TAURUS
23:05 – 24:00	GEMINI

Zone 12

ASCENDANT CODE	ASCENDANT
0:00 – 1:35	GEMINI
1:35 – 3:28	CANCER
3:28 – 4:52	LEO
4:52 – 6:00	VIRGO
6:00 – 7:08	LIBRA
7:08 – 8:31	SCORPIO
8:31 – 10:25	SAGITTARIUS
10:25 – 12:49	CAPRICORN
12:49 – 15:25	AQUARIUS
15:25 – 18:00	PISCES
18:00 – 20:35	ARIES
20:35 – 23:11	TAURUS
23:11 – 24:00	GEMINI

Zone 13

ASCENDANT CODE	ASCENDANT
0:00 – 1:42	GEMINI
1:42 – 3:34	CANCER
3:34 – 4:55	LEO
4:55 – 6:00	VIRGO
6:00 – 7:05	LIBRA
7:05 – 8:25	SCORPIO
8:25 – 10:18	SAGITTARIUS
10:18 – 12:44	CAPRICORN
12:44 – 15:22	AQUARIUS
15:22 – 18:00	PISCES
18:00 – 20:38	ARIES
20:38 – 23:16	TAURUS
23:16 – 24:00	GEMINI

Zone 14

ASCENDANT CODE	ASCENDANT
0:00 – 1:48	GEMINI
1:48 – 3:39	CANCER
3:39 – 4:57	LEO
4:57 – 6:00	VIRGO
6:00 – 7:03	LIBRA
7:03 – 8:21	SCORPIO
8:21 – 10:12	SAGITTARIUS
10:12 – 12:39	CAPRICORN
12:39 – 15:20	AQUARIUS
15:20 – 18:00	PISCES
18:00 – 20:41	ARIES
20:41 – 23:21	TAURUS
23:21 – 24:00	GEMINI

THE FIRST HOUSE

The personality, physical characteristics, life circumstances (especially during childhood).

The Ascendant versus the Sun sign

Is the influence exerted by the Ascendant (determined by the hour of birth) identical to the influence exerted by the Sun sign, which is determined by the date of birth? In other words, does the character of the person whose Ascendant, or rising sign, is Sagittarius resemble that of the person whose Sun sign is Sagittarius?

Basically, the influence wielded by a sign is similar whether it functions as the Ascendant or the Sun sign, since its fundamental characteristics remain the same. However, there is a subtle difference between the sign's respective modes of expression. So, even though the same sign is involved, its influence as the Sun sign is not identical to its influence as the Ascendant. Why?

The Sun, in astrological symbolism, represents the spiritual and eternal, while the Earth represents the material and worldly aspects of life, so the influence of the Sun sign is expressed in our spiritual lives and character traits. In contrast, the power of the Ascendant (determined by the earth's horizon) is seen primarily in earthly circumstances. So, the Sun sign symbolizes our inner being, and the Ascendant, our external circumstances. A certain overlapping is inevitable, however, and the distinction is not always quite as clear-cut as that. Indeed, the Ascendant influences not only one's circumstances but also those character traits developed as a result of them. Conversely, the Sun sign may express itself in external circumstances – for character is also fate.

This example illustrates how the same sign expresses itself as a Sun sign and as an Ascendant.

When Sagittarius, the sign of expansion, acts as Sun sign, its power expresses itself mainly in the person's wide mental horizons and journeys of the spirit. On the other hand, when Sagittarius is the Ascendant, the urge to expand one's horizons will occur on a more physical level, in a broadening of earthly horizons through distant journeys. Nevertheless, those whose Sun sign is Sagittarius may travel far and wide across the globe while those with a Sagittarian Ascendant may be given to flights of the spirit. As you can see, the difference in the effect of a sign as the Sun sign or Ascendant isn't always so cut and dried. This is true of most signs, with the exception of Taurus and Scorpio. Here, the difference is more substantial, perhaps because these signs are the most powerful in the zodiac.

The Earth sign of Taurus symbolizes the good earth *par excellence* – the Garden of Eden. The essential difference between Taurus as Sun sign or as Ascendant lies in a different conception of the idea of the Garden of Eden. Those who have Taurus as their Ascendant, conceive this idea in an earthly, sensuous manner, longing to experience these pleasures now, while for many of those whose Sun sign is Taurus, the Garden of Eden is a spiritual idea, a vague memory of a different, better existence which they long for and attempt to recreate here, for the benefit of mankind. These ideas may, at times, seem Utopian, but even while a person whose Sun sign is Taurus may try to reach for the Moon, his or her feet are firmly planted on the ground. Thanks to this realistic approach to life, Sun Taureans find practical ways of making their vision come true. Creative thinkers, philosophers and men of vision such as Buddha, Socrates, Shakespeare, Kant, Freud, Karl Marx and Theodor Herzl all have Taurus as their Sun sign, which is the one most richly populated by the spiritual giants of the human race, with the possible exceptions of Aquarius and Pisces. Taurus as the Ascendant, on the other hand, is perhaps the most poorly represented when it comes to outstanding people. I made this interesting discovery quite recently, and attribute the fact that so few famous people have Taurus as their rising sign to their too-complacent nature which shies away from challenge, risk or anything that may interfere with their state of contentment.

In Taurus' polar sign, Scorpio, there is also a marked difference between Scorpio's expression as the Sun sign, and as the Ascendant. But while Taurus is blessed with a measure of sweetness, Scorpio has been given a drop of venom. Thus, when Scorpio is the Sun sign, this venomous side might express itself in rather poisonous character traits; but when Scorpio is the Ascendant, its venom may be seen in external circumstances. This difference will be enlarged upon in the section describing Scorpio as the Ascendant. Although the description of the signs in the First House relates mainly to the Ascendants, most of it refers to Sun signs as well. I have pointed out any qualities which I feel are specific to the Ascendant, and not relevant to the Sun sign.

ARIES — THE RAM

Symbol — The Ram leading the flock

Ruling planet — Mars, the planet of war

Element — Fire

Quality — Cardinal

Anatomical area under Aries' influence — The head

Polar sign — Libra

No matter how old they are, people with Aries as their Sun sign or as their Ascendant (also known as the rising sign) have a fresh, youthful quality and a zest for life. This is the first sign of the zodiac, and represents the hope and promise of spring after the dark days of winter. Aries is also the first of the Fire signs, and denotes an active and dynamic personality, full of sparks — sometimes, they become a real display of fireworks!

People with Aries as their Sun or rising sign are independent, daring, impulsive and active, and radiate an attractive and infectious fervour, like the ram leading the flock. The Arian pioneering spirit, vision, energy and dash make them burn with originality and make them leaders in every sphere. Many people can get carried away by the Arian enthusiasm, obeying their call of 'Follow me!'. Nevertheless, that doesn't always happen immediately, because sometimes Arians blaze new and apparently dangerous trails, which people at first fear to follow, biding their time until the Rams have paved the way. However, Arian enthusiasm soon begins to wane, for those born under this fiery sign have no patience for old flames, and are forever seeking new challenges, leaving others to tie up the loose ends of all their old ventures.

Arians are courageous and adventurous, and yearn for new, challenging and varied experiences. At times they can be too daring, because they love playing with fire and flirting with danger. They are hasty and impulsive, leaping before they look and always diving in head-first, so it is small wonder that their heads are the most vulnerable parts of their bodies!

They never stop to think before swinging into action, never learn from experience, and will repeat the same mistakes over and over again. Learn from experience? The fervent, stormy pace at which they lead their lives leaves no time for them to stop and reflect. Although usually very intelligent, and sometimes quite brilliant, even their greatest admirers (of which there will be many) can't call them wise. But why should they stop to think? After all, Arians have no doubts — everything is crystal clear to them, and shooting from the hip, they will fire off quick answers to any questions that come their way. Even in the fields of philosophy and religion they don't show any intellectual humility, and will stride confidently along paths of the spiritual world that even respected philosophers fear to tread. To hesitate, waver, consider — all these are traits of Aries' polar sign Libra, which is autumnal in season and nature, and is of a much more mature disposition. The essential difference between the two signs is seen in the contrast between autumn's mellow hues and the vivid colours of spring, the season when, following the hibernation of winter, the forces of life burst forth, setting the earth ablaze in a riot of green flame that erupts in the brilliant, vibrant colours of Nature set abloom.

Arians burn with confidence and trust — especially when they are investing it in themselves. They are the children of the zodiac, self-centred and convinced that the world revolves around them. Everything is seen in terms of their own egos, and is taken very personally. These offsprings of spring are forever jumping to conclusions, and are always convinced that they are in the right. The problem is that their opinions, which are usually formed through personal motives, tend to be childish and over-simplified. It is difficult for them to accept any creed or viewpoint that is different from their own and, being hot-headed and quick-tempered, they are easily dragged into quarrels and arguments. They argue heatedly and with passion, and you don't have to add fuel to the flames to make them enraged, and finally set them blazing. Luckily, although they lose their tempers swiftly and dramatically, they recover their equanimity just as easily, and never bear grudges. (Think of a child having a tantrum, and you've got a good picture of an angry Arian!) A burst of temper can lead to violence, however, and even if they are not aggressive physically, they can attack verbally.

Not only intolerant, Arians are impatient too, like the children they really are. Once they know what they want, they must have it immediately — 'I want it *now*!' is a favourite Arian phrase! The metal associated with this sign is iron, and Arians certainly believe in striking while the iron is hot. As well as being assertive, they don't stand on ceremony or bother with niceties. They are not people to beat about the bush or to take 'no' for an answer. (You try saying 'no' to an Arian, and see what happens!) Instead, they express their considerable wills in a very straightforward, open and direct manner, ramming headlong anyone or anything that gets in the way. In fact, they can cause a lot of headaches, not only to themselves but to those around them as well.

This is perhaps the least materialistic of the 12 signs, with the possible exceptions of Sagittarius and Pisces. Arians like to travel light, moving freely down the highway of life. 'Why be burdened with possessions?' they ask. All of their worldly goods can fit into a knapsack, and if even that is too heavy, they are always willing to jettison the excess baggage by giving it away to their friends. They have a liberal attitude towards money and their cheque-books are always open, their credit cards at the ready. The idea that they may ever lack for something never crosses their minds. But even if it does, they will brush the thought aside — why worry? After all, they have themselves, which is more than enough! That's why Arians are burdened neither with worries, nor with possessions. This is particularly true of those who have Aries as their Sun sign. People with Aries

Ascendants, on the other hand, may develop a somewhat more serious approach to money, particularly as they grow older.

Some Arians certainly don't suffer from lack of self-confidence or self-appreciation. Sometimes it seems to be quite the reverse! (You could say that when self-esteem was being handed out, Arians elbowed their way to the head of the queue!) These people are convinced that everything they do is highly important and full of meaning. Both the Ram and the Ewe have very large egos, but they display their swollen heads in different ways.

Arian women are very liberated, but still feel that society prevents them from enjoying the freedom of self-expression that it grants men, so many of them find an artistic outlet when they want to express themselves. This is one of the most creative signs of the zodiac, and many talented artists have Aries as their Sun sign or Ascendant. However, some Arians (usually women) treat the arts as a means of boosting their own egos, and furthering their ambitions for recognition. A woman with an Aries Ascendant may write poetry that she publishes at her own expense, and then inflicts on all her friends. Or, she may decide that she is a painter, and proclaim it to the world. Popping into an acquaintance's house (some Arians are bold battering Rams who usually arrive unannounced, as they're always confident of a warm welcome), she will present her hosts with some of her sketches, all of which have one artistic feature in common — her big, bold signature! Unfortunately, she'll soon make another impromptu visit to ensure that her pictures have been given pride of place. The walls of her own home will be crowded with paintings and photographs focusing on a central theme — her own portrait, painted from every possible angle!

In fact, narcissism is a strong element in the Arian make-up, so it's no wonder that the sign is prominent in the horoscopes of most movie actresses. But even when the Arian woman's desire for stardom remains just a dream, she'll always see herself as a prima donna, putting on airs and graces. It's curious how Arians tend to extremes of behaviour, from the very natural and direct in most cases, to the utter artificiality and phoniness of those few black sheep who enjoy pulling the wool over everyone's eyes. The charts of women who behave like this often show a considerable emphasis on Pisces — the sign of imagination, delusions and dreams.

It's not just the women who like showing off — some Arian men also blow their own trumpets with gusto, announcing their virtues and successes in ringing tones. Even if they don't have anything to shout about, they'll compensate for that with some fabulous fables and tall tales. This type of Ram is the eternal proof that sometimes there *can* be smoke without fire! Pathological lying and a tendency to deck themselves out in a borrowed golden fleece is more characteristic of the men of this sign than the women. (After all, modern art has given legitimacy to anyone posing as a poetess or artist.) So, the next time a man assures you that he is a test pilot or a rich oil tycoon, you'd better check his birthdate quickly!

I've already said that Arians tend to go to extremes. Most of them are very honest, natural and direct, but quite a few act in a very artificial manner, bluffing their way through life. The straightforwardness of the open, candid Arian is reflected in the strong, clear facial features of the typical Ram or Ewe. The palms of their hands may have few lines, but these will be strongly and clearly defined. While some Arians have equally uncomplicated characters, others are almost primeval in their absolute simplicity. They pride themselves on being devoid of any complexes or hang-ups, and are immune to self-doubt. Should they face any knotty problems, they will solve them in a characteristically simple and straightforward way, cutting the Gordian knot like Alexander the Great.

Arians need to admire someone, and if it isn't themselves, they may become enthusiastic fans of a football team or a person who embodies their ideals of power and virility. As most Arians are extremely athletic and competitive, they are often very successful in sports. Men born under this sign are particularly drawn to football, and if they play the game themselves, they often specialize in headers. Being the first sign of the zodiac, Arians need to be first in everything else, too, especially when they are driving. They can turn a motorway into a race-track, and some of them drive so fast that they should really own pilots' licences, in case their cars ever leave the ground!

There's nothing wishy-washy about an Arian's appearance. The men

The dynamic and youthful personality of Ezar Weizman, combined with his military achievements as an outstanding Israeli Defence Minister and Commander of the Israeli Air Force, is characteristic of Martial Aries as the Ascendant sign.

Fiery Aries, which bestows energy, boldness and vigour, is Barbra Streisand's Ascendant sign – contributing substantially to her artistic achievements.

are very masculine, muscular, athletic, wiry and clean-cut, with ruddy complexions and often a reddish gleam to their hair. And as if that weren't enough, red is their favourite colour. Usually, they don't have an ounce of spare fat, as their bodies burn up surplus calories to produce energy and warmth. Anyone sharing an Arian man's bed won't need an electric blanket or a hot water bottle, even on the coldest of winter nights!

When Arian women are beautiful, they are strikingly so. They can be divided into two main types. The first have round faces, doll-like features, large bright eyes and, as a rule, curly hair. The other type is a thoroughbred beauty with high cheek-bones, a panther-like figure and straight dark hair with a reddish shimmer, to serve as a reminder that Arian women are the daughters of the red planet, Mars. They are the very embodiment of a Red Indian chief's daughter. But don't forget that Mars is the planet of war, and Arian women are quick to anger, especially if they suspect that someone is trying to home in on their territory. When they put on their war-paint, Arian women can ram anyone — with or without horns. But luckily their wrath dies down quickly and they are soon ready to smoke the peace pipe.

Women born under this sign are convinced that anything men can do, they can do better. Not that they despise men because, on the contrary, they admire them and are ardent fans of the male sex. It's just that these

Martial Aries was the Ascendant sign of Dwight D. Eisenhower, commander of the Allied Forces in Europe in World War II and 34th president of the United States.

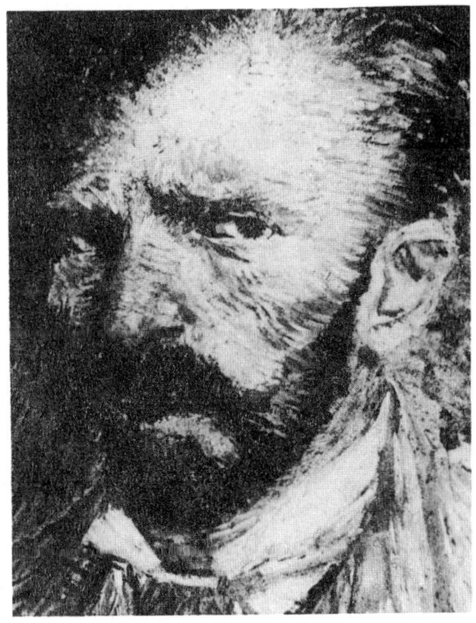

The fiery passion of Aries is reflected in the paintings of Vincent Van Gogh (Sun sign Aries). Aries' vigour and pioneering spirit also find expression in the great artist's fresh and innovative style of painting.

women are acutely aware of their inner strength and wills, and will act and think accordingly. When they find a man attractive, they don't hide it. This is not the sort of woman to drop her handkerchief and wait coyly for her hero to retrieve it. She's not even willing to wait for him to drop *his* hanky. Instead, when she likes a man, she simply makes for him like an arrow from a bow, and he won't know what's hit him, as she carries him off to her wigwam by his hair! Every conquest is another feather in her cap, which she wears like a Red Indian headdress.

Not all Arian women are aggressive. After all, Aries isn't only the sign of the Ram, but of the Lamb as well and sometimes, just for a change, these women live up to the latter image. This type of Arian woman is as gentle as a lamb and as soft as baby wool. But even she can surprise the man who has invited her to a romantic movie by saying that she's tired of hearts and flowers, and would rather see an adventure film, full of blood and guts. All of which only goes to prove that even the softest lambskin may conceal a wolf!

FAMOUS PEOPLE BORN UNDER ARIES

ARIES AS THE ASCENDANT

Willy Brandt (Sun sign Sagittarius)
Princess Caroline of Monaco (Sun sign Aquarius)
Dwight D Eisenhower (Sun sign Libra)
Thomas Hobbes (Sun sign Aries)
André Malraux (Sun sign Scorpio)
Henry Miller (Sun sign Capricorn)
John D Rockefeller (Sun sign Cancer)
Frank Sinatra (Sun sign Sagittarius)
Barbra Streisand (Sun sign Taurus)

ARIES AS THE SUN SIGN

Hans Christian Andersen (Ascendant Sagittarius)
Johann Sebastian Bach (Ascendant Cancer)
Otto von Bismarck (Ascendant Leo)
Marlon Brando (Ascendant Sagittarius)
Giacomo Casanova (Ascendant Scorpio)
Charlie Chaplin (Ascendant Scorpio)
Bette Davis (Ascendant Sagittarius)
René Descartes (Ascendant Capricorn)
Thomas Hobbes (Ascendant Aries)
Raphael (Ascendant Scorpio)
Vincent Van Gogh (Ascendant Cancer)
Emile Zola (Ascendant Sagittarius)

and the following people whose Ascendants are unknown: Bela Bartok, Anatole France, Robert Frost, Nikolai Gogol, Vladimir Nabokov, Spencer Tracy, Tennessee Williams

TAURUS — THE BULL

Symbol — The Bull

Ruling planet — Venus, the planet of love, beauty and the arts

Element — Earth

Quality — Fixed

Anatomical area under Taurus' influence — The neck and throat

Polar sign — Scorpio

Have you ever met someone who greatly values their creature comforts, yet wasn't born with the Sun in Taurus? If so, then you can be sure that their Ascendant, or rising sign, is Taurus, making them a true hedonist who yearns to indulge in all the pleasures that life has to offer.

As you might expect, most people with Taurus Ascendants are quite earthbound. Their spirits, as a rule, don't soar into the higher realms, nor are they troubled by philosophical questions which set them wondering. However, they will faithfully follow to the letter the teachings of the Greek philosopher, Epicurus, who believed in getting the most out of all sensual pleasures! As far as Taureans are concerned, the world is a sensual paradise, where we all help ourselves to the banquet of life, without having yet tasted the fruit of the tree of knowledge. In fact, knowledge doesn't concern Taurus that much. They will gladly accept the simplest explanations of spiritual matters, leaving the search for deeper meanings to their polar sign, Scorpio. Theirs are not tortured Dostoyevskian souls, thirsting for the mystical meaning of life. Quite the reverse, in fact — their needs are easily satisfied, and they're perfectly happy as long as their pastures are green.

'Eat, drink and be merry, for tomorrow we — will eat and drink again' is the Taurean motto. These people are more than happy to leave the original ending, 'For tomorrow we die', to pessimistic and complex-ridden Scorpios to contemplate. Enthusiastic believers in this world and in life-before-death, Taureans don't allow even the slightest shadow of such a gloomy thought to cloud their brows and trouble their spirits.

Don't think that all Taureans are selfishly only concerned with their own needs, because they are very sensitive to those of others, too. People with Taurus rising are especially aware of the wants of their nearest and dearest, but those born with the Sun in Taurus long to bestow the good things of the earth on the whole of humanity. It's no coincidence that many of the world's greatest philosophers and humanitarians were born with the Sun in this sign, as you will discover by reading the list at the end of this chapter.

Unlike impulsive Aries, the first sign of the zodiac, placid Taurus, the second sign, does not rush to the fore. These people are perfectly satisfied with being second-best. They are calm and serene, wanting peaceful lives in which they can cultivate their own gardens of Eden. Taureans love nature, want to be close to the earth (which is their element, after all!), and are satisfied as long as their earth is the 'good earth'.

In fact, 'salt of the earth' is one way to describe Taureans: they are genuine, truthful and reliable, with positive, frank and direct natures and easy, simple manners. These are the Good Samaritans of the zodiac, always ready to lend a helping hand, and knowing instinctively how to give the right sort of help at the right time and place. Generosity comes easily to them, and they have the happy knack of always giving the right present, managing to buy their loved ones just what they need. (And that doesn't have to be a diamond bracelet or a gold watch — it could be something as mundane, and as essential, as an electric kettle!) Taureans devote a great deal of time and thought to the presents they give, which is much more important than spending a lot of money on a gift which often is not only unnecessary, but useless as well. Thoughtfulness is certainly one of the greatest virtues of this sign.

Those born under the sign of the Bull are well-known for their love of flowers and nature, yet a male Taurean may surprise his acquaintances by saying 'I've been married for twenty years, and I've never bought my wife flowers'. Noticing his friends' puzzled expressions, he'll add 'Potted plants, yes!', without elaborating any further, since the typical Taurean is a man of few words. But there's no need to pump him for an explanation, because it takes only a little understanding of a Taurean to realize what he means — cut flowers don't last, whereas potted plants do. Flowers are here today, gone tomorrow, while a plant is for keeps. You can rely on it to last, because it has roots — and Taureans believe in roots. A plant can even become the symbol of permanence, if it's a perennial.

And permanence is something else that Taureans believe in. So, if you meet someone who barely seems to be out of the cradle, yet when looking for a job cares more about the company's pension plan than about the weekly pay-cheque, it's not hard to guess that they're a Taurean. These people are definitely not the type who live for the moment. Unstable, ephemeral things may appeal to Geminis, their next-door-neighbours in astrology, but they alarm Taureans. Geminis may be here today, gone tomorrow, but Taureans put down roots — they're not moving! They don't trust anything that's even slightly doubtful, preferring to invest in something sound, such as real estate or a solid pension fund.

Taureans have a deep aversion to change, and instead will stick to their opinions and put their considerable weight behind their views. And make no mistake, when these people take a stand, they do it properly. Their two feet will be planted firmly on the ground, and nothing will move them. Some people say that they're stubborn, while others claim they're obstinate . . . But everyone agrees that you can rely on their trustworthy, peaceful, easy-going and patient natures. Of course, there are always people who are tempted to exploit this Taurean tranquillity, but even

Taurean patience has its limits, and when a straw finally breaks the Bull's back, it's dangerous to be around! Take care, because when this Earth sign rages, the earth trembles, and when the Bull sees red, he or she runs wild, attacking and goring everything in sight. Don't push these people too far!

Comfort and luxury occupy large places in the Taurean heart, but don't confuse their great love for *la dolce vita* with laziness. The Bull is always willing to be harnessed to any task he considers positive, constructive and purposeful, and Taureans, luckily, are as strong as bulls. Commendably thorough in their work, when they plough, they plough deeply, shouldering their responsibilities and burdens without a murmur. Nor do they shrink from difficulties and obstacles in their paths — they prefer to wrestle with them, taking the bull by the horns.

Many of those born with the Sun in Taurus, or Taurus as their Ascendant, have been blessed with an excellent sense of spatial perception. Show them a sketch that doesn't mean a thing to anyone else, and they will immediately translate it into a three-dimensional figure. They're always coming up with ideas on how to make the best use of everything, and when others get confused and tied up in knots, you can trust Taureans to find the simplest and most practical solution to the problem.

Musical talent and a melodious voice are characteristic of Taurus, Elvis Presley's Ascendant sign. The famous singer was also typically Taurean in appearance: he had classic good looks, but began to put on weight in early middle age, becoming positively fat.

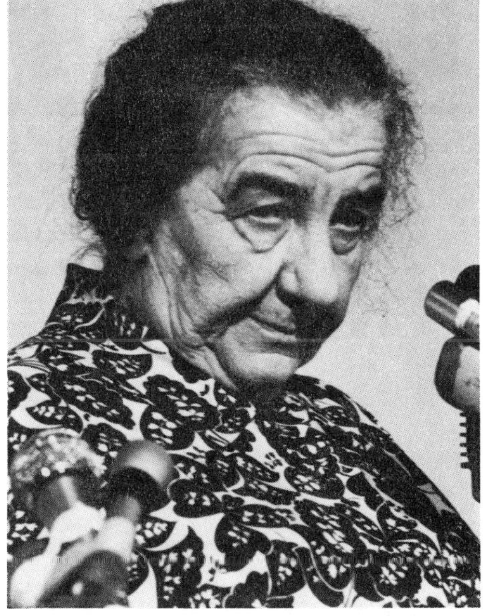

Fixity of purpose, strength of character and the basic practicality of the Earth sign – Taurus – are typical of the personality of Golda Meir (Sun sign Taurus), the first woman to serve as Israel's Prime Minister.

Being ruled by Venus, the planet of art and beauty, it's not surprising that many Taureans are artistic, particularly when it comes to singing and sculpture. However, Taurus is a very purposeful and practical sign, so these people may think that the arts are too unpredictable and flighty to provide them with good grazing grounds. The mere thought of being a penniless artist in a garret is enough to bring most of these Bulls swiftly back to the ground floor of reality. They need to feel the solid earth under their feet, and therefore are deeply opposed to building castles in the air. One thing you can be sure of — any castles they do build will have firm foundations and solid bases! Indeed, Taureans are drawn to anything connected with building and construction in general, and to architecture in particular — a sphere offering them scope for both their mathematical-spatial abilities and their artistic talents.

A strong need of security is the main characteristic of these people. They are also possessive, and everything they own — whether property, objects or people — provide them with a feeling of security. But if something rocks the boat, they'll buy themselves a treat or two by way of comfort and consolation. One Taurean bachelor in his twenties, what with one frustration and another, managed to amass not only a car, some computers, a stereo and various electrical gadgets, but also a stove, a toaster and a washing machine! Definitely a young man with a dowry . . .

Although knowing that something (or someone) belongs to them fills most Taureans with a sense of security, they feel even safer when they know that they belong to a family, clan, group, club, party, or even to a nation. Some Taureans have a highly-developed herd sense, and derive security in belonging to the largest and strongest group they can possibly find. These people are true 'squares', who will adhere to the views of the majority, toe the line and follow the flock in order to fit in.

The majority of Taureans are good-natured and easy-going, but a very few are quite different. These Bulls are ardent believers in the flesh-pots of life and the golden calf, dividing humanity into two camps: the haves and the have-nots (with a deep-rooted fear that they belong to the latter group). As a result, they have to prove to themselves again and again that they belong to the haves, and that not only the grass, but also the money, is greener on their side of the fence. They then have to convince everyone else of it, to make them turn green with envy. These Taureans relish the idea that other people's fields aren't nearly as verdant as their own, and so may try to seek out those who seem like losers, in order to help them forget their own self-doubts.

Despite the fact that most Taureans are so good-natured and considerate, they may suffer vicissitudes and pressures in their married lives, as well as many arguments about money. This is especially so with those who have Taurus rising, rather than the Sun in this sign. As a husband or wife, a Taurean is as faithful and stable as one could wish for. Their love won't diminish with the years, either — on the contrary, force of habit will strengthen their ties to their partners. These people may not be particularly brilliant or sparkling, but anyone who has learned the hard way that all that glitters is not gold, will certainly appreciate the positive qualities of their Taurean spouse.

The women of this sign can handle everything around the house, and they were definitely born with two right hands. They're particularly proud of their culinary abilities, even though they're often the only ones who enjoy their cooking! Thanks to their practical natures, they are also real handywomen, being able to do most household repair jobs, and they love pottering around their gardens.

Taurean men not only have green thumbs, but a golden touch as well, and can mend anything in the home. They are good providers, taking care of their partners' basic needs. Any woman who can be satisified with that, and doesn't want a thrilling intellectual-spiritual-romantic relationship, will be more than contented with a Taurean man. And as long as she learns to cook just like his mother (who does everything best), he'll be happy, too.

Parenthood comes easily to Taureans, who are devoted to their children. The Taurean mother isn't just a human mother — she's also Mother Earth. And not just any old earth, either, but a fertile and abundant one — a land flowing with milk and honey, from which her children will sprout forth, growing and blossoming. She does her utmost to provide her offspring with all the good things in life, raising them not only on milk, but on cream too. Sometimes, her children may feel themselves becoming over-stuffed, like the fatted calf. After all, it's well-known that even more than the calf likes to suckle, the cow loves to feed . . .

Whether male or female, Taureans are short to medium in height, and are generally rather stocky. Their features are somewhat heavy, but can be very beautiful. The most attractive Taureans of both sexes are noted for having fair and creamy complexions, serene blue eyes and a classical beauty reminiscent, particularly in profile, of a Greek statue. One typical Taurean facial characteristic is when the outer corners of the eyes tilt downwards, giving a rather sleepy expression. The Taurean nose, when it isn't straight and Greek, tends to be bulbous. Women of this sign have Rubenesque figures, and exude an aura of full-blown sensuality, like a heavy perfume, particularly if they were born with the Moon in Leo. Most Taureans are noted either for their beautiful voices (many famous singers have been born under this sign), or for the exact opposite — a rough, hoarse voice which sounds as though the speaker has a chronically sore throat. Which is hardly surprising when you consider that the throat and neck are the parts of the body ruled by this gentle giant of a sign.

FAMOUS PEOPLE BORN UNDER TAURUS

TAURUS AS THE ASCENDANT

Ludwig van Beethoven (Sun sign Sagittarius)
Jean Cocteau (Sun sign Cancer)
Vivien Leigh (Sun sign Scorpio)
Elvis Presley (Sun sign Capricorn)
George Washington (Sun sign Pisces)
Walt Whitman (Sun sign Gemini)

TAURUS AS THE SUN SIGN

Honoré de Balzac (Ascendant Leo)
Charlotte Brontë (Ascendant Virgo)
Pierre Curie (Ascendant Pisces)
Salvador Dali (Ascendant Cancer)
Leonardo da Vinci (Ascendant Sagittarius)
Queen Elizabeth II (Ascendant Capricorn)
Henry Fonda (Ascendant Pisces)
Margot Fonteyn (Ascendant Aquarius)
Sigmund Freud (Ascendant Scorpio)
Immanuel Kant (Ascendant Aquarius)
Vladimir Lenin (Ascendant Scorpio)
Niccolo Machiavelli (Ascendant Capricorn)
Karl Marx (Ascendant Aquarius)
Zubin Mehta (Ascendant Pisces)
Yehudi Menuhin (Ascendant Capricorn)
Florence Nightingale (Ascendant Virgo)
Maximilien Robespierre (Ascendant Aquarius)
Dante Gabriel Rossetti (Ascendant Gemini)
Bertrand Russell (Ascendant Capricorn)
Dr Benjamin Spock (Ascendant Aquarius)
Barbra Streisand (Ascendant Aries)
Harry S Truman (Ascendant Libra)
Joseph Turner (Ascendant Capricorn)
Orson Welles (Ascendant Gemini)

and the following people whose Ascendants are unknown: Buddha, Moshe Dayan, Knut Hamsun, Audrey Hepburn, Theodor Herzl, David Hume, Nikita Khrushchev, Sören Kierkegaard, Golda Meir, Abie Nathan, Eva Peron, William Shakespeare, Socrates

GEMINI — THE TWINS

Symbol — The Twins

Ruling planet — Mercury, the planet of intelligence and communication

Element — Air

Quality — Mutable

Anatomical area under Gemini's influence — The lungs, arms and hands

Polar sign — Sagittarius

There are always two sides to the Geminian coin, and a young pair of Twins, a boy and a girl, symbolize the duality so typical of this ever-changing sign. But even the dual human symbol of this most mercurial of the 12 signs doesn't convey the multifaceted quality of Gemini, and one is tempted to turn to the animal kingdom to borrow its colourful metaphors. With good reason, too, since Geminis are as chirpy as light-winged songbirds, and as multicoloured as butterflies. In fact, just like butterflies constantly fluttering from one flower to another, Geminis are always moving from one experience to the next. They are as variable as chameleons, as quick and imitative as little monkeys, as graceful and lithe as cats and, like cats, possess at least nine lives, if not many more.

In the zodiac, where the signs are mostly represented by animals, Gemini is the first sign symbolized by human beings and, like the first two humans, Adam and Eve, Geminis are inquisitive, ready to learn, and eager to eat the fruit of the tree of knowledge. Geminis do indeed taste the forbidden fruit, and from then on, like Adam and Eve, their souls know no peace. Their Paradise Lost seems forever to be just beyond the horizon, yet always out of reach . . . And, like the horizon, the nearer Geminians believe they are getting to it, the further their Garden of Eden recedes. For a while, it may seem to be within their grasp, only to slip away again, and lure them forever from afar. Just like the butterflies they resemble, Geminis will flit about ceaselessly in their never-ending search for the fairy-tale flower that will grant all their wishes and desires. True Geminis enjoying themselves at a party just can't help wondering what they may be missing at all those other parties being held elsewhere! They can't sit at ease in a café without their thoughts turning to the café across the street. While talking to someone, their eyes will stray to the window to watch the passers-by, and they'll glance at the door every time it opens. Their attention span being very short, these people find it difficult to focus on one specific person or topic at a time. Instead, they often do a variety of things. Their feet are in two camps at least, and they hop from person to person, activity to activity, subject to subject and place to place, but to their everlasting distress, they will never be able to be in two places at the same time. To compensate, they try to do at least two things simultaneously. For example, while chatting on the phone (a favourite Geminian activity, by the way), a typical Twin will be listening to the radio with their other ear and dashing off a letter or shopping list with their free hand. Only while dancing to this frenzied beat of life will Geminis feel truly alive.

As well as being the first of the human signs, Gemini is also the first of the Air signs, which symbolize the intellect. What's more, it is the first of the two signs ruled by Mercury, the planet of intelligence and knowledge. In mythology, Mercury is described as a youth with winged feet, who carries the caduceus, a staff overlaid with two intertwined snakes, reminiscent of the serpent that slithered down the tree of knowledge to tempt Adam and Eve. Geminis, for their part, aren't content with one tree of knowledge, but will sample a whole orchard of them, gathering tasters of information from a wide range of blossoms. But they aren't the only ones to benefit: in their ceaseless search for knowledge, they enrich everything and everyone they come into contact with. They open the minds of others, giving them an airing, dusting and shaking up their old prejudices and superstitions, thoroughly spring-cleaning them of the cobwebs and moths hiding in their crevices. The Twins give other minds new food for thought, and cause the spiritual wasteland around them to bloom. Geminis are ardent believers in education, knowledge, and the power of the written word. They are teachers, lecturers, writers, journalists or anyone who wants to further the cause of the intellect and education. Like their ruling planet Mercury, whose orbit is closest to the Sun, Geminis strive to be close to the light of knowledge at all times, and to be its torch-bearer.

Newton is said to have discovered the law of gravity when an apple fell on his head while he sat in the shade of his tree. Perhaps once upon a time, a Gemini reclining in the shadow of his tree of knowledge noticed the round fruit falling off and rolling away, thereby evoking the idea of the wheel. And indeed, the wheel — one of the greatest inventions of mankind — is quintessentially Geminian. Whether or not the wheel inventor was, in fact, a Twin, every Gemini acts as though they themselves had come up with the idea. These people are always on wheels, whether roller-skates, bicycles, motorbikes, cars or anything else that propels them along. Sometimes it seems that wheels are an integral, organic part of Geminis, from which they aren't parted even in old age. It's not unusual to see a Gemini granny dashing about on her bike, or driving her car with one hand resting nonchalantly on the steering wheel, as though the years hadn't left a mark on her. But Gemini wheels don't only turn on the road — the cogs and wheels of their brains are constantly in motion too, never rusting or seizing up, even in old age.

You'd be forgiven for thinking that all Geminis have bathed in the fountain of eternal youth. Thanks to their mental alertness, many activities and constant motion, Geminis simply have no time to grow old. Creeping old age can't hope to catch up with the fleet-footed Twin who never stays still for two seconds at a time. Even in the winter of their lives, typical Geminis remain clear-headed and mentally agile, their minds as clear as the sparkling waters of that youth-giving fountain. So it's no surprise that the Twins symbolizing this sign are always depicted as being so very young.

Without doubt, Gemini is the sign of youth, and the golden age of all Twins occurs in their early years. Thanks to their shining intelligence and quick grasp, Geminis manage, in their youth and early adulthood, to leap far ahead of their contemporaries — like the swift hare running a race against the proverbial tortoise. Yet some Geminis, who show such early promise, don't always fulfil it in adulthood. This is often due to their tendency to spread themselves too thin. They flit hither and thither on the surface, touching on many subjects but never giving any one area the serious consideration it deserves. One day, these people may discover, to their great dismay, that their heavier-footed and more serious running mates have not only caught up with them, but have overtaken them as well. Lightweight Geminis live for the moment, as long as they are in the spring and summer of their lives. But there will come a time when they find that youth and laughter are turning their backs on them, and that autumn is at their doorsteps. A miserable time indeed for those who have whiled away the summer with song, dance, and a hop, skip and a jump, and who, in their complacency, didn't bother to prepare for the rainy days ahead.

As well as being one of the most intelligent signs in the zodiac, Gemini is also the one with the quickest understanding. The Gemini mind fizzes, bubbles and sparkles like champagne, refreshing and joyous, charming the listener with its flights of fancy, wit and an airy, flippant and nonchalant sense of humour. Geminis are verbal acrobats-cum-magicians, threading words as though they were diamonds on a chain. Sometimes, though, those flashing, sparkling gems are nothing more than polished glass, and the charm is easily broken. These people can discuss any subject under the sun as though they were experts, despite the fact that their knowledge is usually minimal and very superficial! Like a peacock proudly diplaying his magnificent feathers, Geminis gladly demonstrate the wide range of their knowledge. But these are often borrowed feathers, with their brilliant ideas taken from elsewhere. Mythology tells how Mercury stole apples from the garden of Apollo, the sun god, and Geminis, ruled by Mercury, have the same tendency to take ideas from others and present them as their own, conveniently forgetting to give credit where credit is due. They're the original plagiarists! But it is quite impossible to catch these tricksters out — they're as slippery as quicksilver (mercury!), and just as difficult to get hold of. For every embarrassing question, Geminis have a ready-made answer up their sleeves. Like a tennis pro (a typical Gemini sport), they have a crushing return for every lob. Their reflexes and responses are equally quick in speech as in motion, and on their own ground — the spoken word — they are invincible, with complete and utter control of language. While people born under their polar sign of Sagittarius trip on their tongues and put their feet in their mouths with monotonous regularity, Geminis can extricate themselves like Houdini from seemingly impossible traps, thanks to their quick way with words. Like cats, Geminis always land on their feet, even when it seems as though, this time, they've got to crash.

Sagittarius is the sign of faith, but the Geminian forte is a rational approach. The only thing that Geminis, creatures of small faith indeed, believe in is the mind itself, which they worship. Sagittarians go through life as though riding stallions, given rein enough to roam and gallop wherever they please. They put their faith in the heavens above and believe in their lucky stars. After all, the horseshoe is supposed to bring luck, and the horse, which is the Sagittarian symbol, has four of them. While Sagittarians put their trust in a higher power, the sceptical Geminis trust in nothing but the superiority of the mind. So, while Sagittarians tend to be somewhat fatalistic, and don't pull on the reins of Fate too often, Geminis grip the helm with both hands, take their destinies into their own hands and proceed to steer their way through life on their own, always displaying swiftness, flexibility and great powers of improvisation in order to meet with every contingency. These people aren't likely to give chance a chance, and won't view events with a 'que sera, sera' attitude. They refuse to be ruled by Fate, and will try to control their lives, bending their destinies to their own will. For once they have reached out for the fruit of knowledge, they have already taken their fates into their own

The meteoric rise to fame of Brooke Shields while still in her early teens is typical of Gemini, the sign of youth. Gemini is the Sun sign of this beautiful actress who, incidentally, is the daughter of a tennis player, tennis being the Geminian sport – the Sun and the sign it is in also signifies the personality of one's father.

Tennis star Bjorn Borg (Sun sign Gemini) is seen here engaged in another typically Geminian activity – talking on the phone.

hands. Sagittarians, playing the poker game of life, trust they will receive the high cards — and usually do. Geminis, on the other hand, will ensure that the high cards make their way to their side of the table, at times employing questionable means. Sagittarians put all their cards on the table — not so Geminis, who like to keep an ace or two up their sleeves, just in case!

Geminis can't be called unworldly. They adapt themselves to any situation, manage in life, improvise, get to know the right people, pull the right strings and always tilt their sails to the wind. They generate momentum and glide on it, using every wave and taking every ride going in their direction. Their wheels not only turn on the road but also — ceaselessly — in their brains, which work overtime. No wonder that typical Geminis aren't content with one way of life, but prefer two-way streets. They often amuse themselves with the thought that those who meet them on the highway of life have no idea that their other Gemini self roams different paths, perhaps even straying from the straight and narrow. For example, I heard of a holy man who, although forbidden any relations with women by his religion, made a pass at a young lady. The shocked woman said 'What would your believers say?', to which he

Gemini, the sign of youth, was the Sun sign of John F. Kennedy – the youngest man ever to be elected president of the United States.

The versatility of the dual Air sign, Gemini, finds expression in the twin careers of Sir Arthur Conan Doyle – a physician by profession, who was also the creator of the immortal Sherlock Holmes. Conan Doyle was a 'double' Gemini – Gemini being both his Sun and Ascendant sign.

replied, with a twinkle in his eye, 'My believers? They wouldn't believe it!' You've guessed it — he was a Gemini!

Not only are Geminis men and women of the world, they are also true cosmopolitans who feel at home in any city. They can adapt to any situation, as they absorb the prevailing atmosphere and react accordingly. Twins have no problems when it comes to integrating. In fact, when in Rome, they'll be better Romans than the Romans themselves, getting to know the city (in the very short time they are likely to stay there) like the backs of their hands. They may even, without any problem at all, act as tour guides, not just to tourists but to locals as well, to whom they will show and explain the sights in colloquial Italian (the Gemini grasp of language is amazing — they seem to inhale it with the very air they breathe). They may even manage a phrase or two in Latin, although the Classics aren't exactly their cup of tea (far too old-fashioned).

But not only do ancient languages fail to excite Geminis. Anything even remotely connected with the past leaves them cold, being wholly absorbed by the here and now. Nor does the past have any sentimental hold on them, because it's of less interest to them than the snows of yesteryear. As far as Geminis are concerned, the past is like an old newspaper. They're fascinated by the brand-new, by front-page news whose ink has barely dried. They strive to be up-to-date in everything, and will listen to the news every hour on the hour. At times it seems as though Twins feel that they owe it to themselves to 'know it all'. This is especially true of the type of Gemini who says, in response to almost any comment, 'Oh, I know that', or 'You've really discovered America, haven't you?' The following joke perfectly illustrates the Gemini know-it-all type. The neighbours of a village's know-it-all decided to tease him, so cried to him in mock excitement 'There's a horse in your bathtub!', only to receive the stock Geminian reply — 'I know, I already know!'

Geminis live in the realms of the spoken and written word, and judge many situations on the basis of whether or not they will make a good story. Events take shape for Twins only through words — as far as they're concerned, if something isn't reported, then it didn't happen. In the beginning was the word, but for Geminis, the word is also the end. They truly have a way with words, and treat them with great respect. In return, words pave Geminis' way through life, and many Twins go far in professions associated with communication, especially in journalism, which deals with the immediate and transient. Journalism also suits the inherent Geminian desire to keep everyone informed, to transmit information and to give wing to every rumour. Other Gemini occupations are anything associated with teaching, transportation, and traffic, vehicles, mail, telephones and any kind of brokerage, mediation and commerce. Hardly surprising when you consider that Mercury, the messenger of the gods and ruler of Gemini, is said to be the patron of merchants. Geminis are extremely shrewd in business — glib talkers who will even manage to sell ice to the Eskimos. Quite a few of those born with Gemini as their Sun or rising sign have a tendency to get involved in flimsy business deals, bubble schemes and castles in the air.

Sharp, canny and clever Geminis don't live in a fool's paradise, but one type of Twin finds their paradise wherever not only many fools reside, but where a new sucker is born every minute. This kind of Gemini is cynical, unfeeling, cold and utterly merciless towards mugs. Stupidity, all Geminis believe, is worse than crime — they don't suffer fools gladly. But woe betide those whose only sin is naïvety, and whose only crime is a lack of intelligence, because these sly Twins will take every possible advantage of them. The sort of Gemini who is underhand loves nothing better than to make dupes of people and expose their stupidity.

People much younger than themselves fascinate and attract Geminis, who share a common language with them. They skip nimbly, with typical Geminian ease, over the generation gap just like Errol Flynn (a Gemini, of course!) The Twins often form romantic ties with much younger members of the opposite sex, because they believe in gathering their rosebuds while they may, even when they're in the November of their lives. (The serpent is tempting them with unripe fruit, through which they hope to rediscover their lost Garden of Eden.) Thanks to their light-hearted charm and good looks, Geminis are very successful with the opposite sex. They're witty and amusing, many-faceted and constantly changing, as enigmatic as riddles and as unpredictable as the weather. When making a date with one of these charmers, one never knows who to expect — Dr Jekyll or Mr Hyde — if they show up at all! Sometimes, the Twin will conveniently forget an appointment although, to be fair, that can occasionally be a genuine excuse.

Variety is definitely the spice of life for Geminis, and the turnover of the cast starring in their emotions is accordingly high. The statute of limitations is soon applied to any relationship — partners are like paper plates, good for one use only. Geminis establish easy-going, undemanding relationships, with no strings attached. They wear their hearts on their sleeves at the same time as twisting everyone around their little fingers. Emotionally, they're as light as feathers, feel as free as birds, and delight in spreading their charms around. They don't put all their eggs in one emotional basket, nor do they brood over them in one nest. They really aren't particularly attached to their families, and won't let family obligations clip their wings. But there is another type of Gemini who goes further than that. Like the cuckoo, these people will lay their eggs in a strange nest, leaving the job of bringing up the chicks to others while they resume their free-as-a-bird way of life.

Whether male or female, Geminis have a youthful, slim appearance. They are usually short, and their movements lithe and graceful. The Geminian flexibility is reflected in the plasticity of their faces, which means they are excellent imitators. Gemini women are as light and delicate as lace, and many of them are not only very beautiful, but endowed with feline grace too. There are at least two women inside every female Twin, so it's no wonder that the typical Gemini woman is forever changing the style of her clothing, and the cut and colour of her hair. The man who likes variety will discover to his delight that she's many women rolled into one. In fact she can, at will, embody the entire gamut of feminine roles, from the geisha girl to the amazon. He will never tire of her company, because she always keeps him guessing, and bubbles over with life. It's as though Geminis, male and female alike, had been flavoured with a range of exotic spices. Yet, in some cases, this only masks a watery broth. Small wonder that, seasoned with such heavy doses of pepper, many Geminis suffer from frequent bouts of sneezing, as well as from various allergies and many kinds of disturbances to the respiratory system . . .

FAMOUS PEOPLE BORN UNDER GEMINI

GEMINI AS THE ASCENDANT

Neil Armstrong (Sun sign Leo)
Joseph Conrad (Sun sign Sagittarius)
Arthur Conan Doyle (Sun sign Gemini)
Johannes Kepler (Sun sign Capricorn)
Henry Kissinger (Sun sign Gemini)
Jack London (Sun sign Capricorn)
Sir Laurence Olivier (Sun sign Gemini)
Dante Gabriel Rossetti (Sun sign Taurus)
George Bernard Shaw (Sun sign Leo)
Alfred Lord Tennyson (Sun sign Leo)
Giuseppe Verdi (Sun sign Libra)
Jules Verne (Sun sign Aquarius)
Queen Victoria (Sun sign Gemini)
Richard Wagner (Sun sign Gemini)
Orson Welles (Sun sign Taurus)

GEMINI AS THE SUN SIGN

Arthur Conan Doyle (Ascendant Gemini)
Clint Eastwood (Ascendant Scorpio)
Ian Fleming (Ascendant Aquarius)
Errol Flynn (Ascendant Aquarius)
Paul Gauguin (Ascendant Leo)
Che Guevara (Ascendant Aquarius)
Aly Khan (Ascendant Libra)
John F Kennedy (Ascendant Libra)
Henry Kissinger (Ascendant Gemini)
Thomas Mann (Ascendant Virgo)
Marilyn Monroe (Ascendant Leo)
Laurence Olivier (Ascendant Gemini)
Rasputin (Ascendant Capricorn)
Jean-Paul Sartre (Ascendant Scorpio)
Brooke Shields (Ascendant Virgo)
Robert Schumann (Ascendant Capricorn)
Richard Strauss (Ascendant Cancer)
Queen Victoria (Ascendant Gemini)
Richard Wagner (Ascendant Gemini)
Walt Whitman (Ascendant Taurus)

and the following people whose Ascendants are unknown: Dante Alighieri, Bjorn Borg, Albert Dürer, Thomas Hardy, Paul McCartney, Franz Mesmer, Alexander Pushkin, Marquis de Sade, Françoise Sagan, Oswald Spengler, Igor Stravinsky, W B Yeats

CANCER — THE CRAB

Symbol — The Crab

Ruling planet — The Moon, representing sensitivity

Element — Water

Quality — Cardinal

Anatomical area under Cancer's influence — The chest, womb and stomach

Polar sign — Capricorn

The first of the emotional Water signs, Cancer can be said to embody all feeling. The Crab's delicate feelers pick up nuances and moods, noting subtleties that elude less sensitive souls. Cancerians absorb impressions just as a sponge soaks up water, and are extremely susceptible to the world around them, impressions of which seep into their consciousness as if by osmosis. It's no wonder that Cancerians are in a constant state of stimulation, because everything affects them emotionally, gladdening, exciting or saddening them. The Moon, which rules this sign, symbolizes man's primary and most atavistic feelings, the emotions and impressions that form his existence before consciousness takes over. In astrology, therefore, the Moon represents infancy and the feeling of security a baby receives at the mother's breast.

Being sensitive and emotional, those ruled by this sign are vulnerable and afraid of getting hurt. They have a deep need of emotional and physical security, like the crab sheltering within its armoured shell. Capricorn, the polar sign of Cancer, also signifies a longing for security, but while Capricorns build their security on their achievements in the outside world, Cancerians seek theirs on their own turf. They take refuge in the warm, cushioned family nest, under the protective family wing. The homes of these people are definitely their castles, and their families are their fortresses. They're nurtured by their close family ties, and draw strength from familial roots. Their multiple bonds to their parents are strong, though they are particularly attached to their mothers. Even adult Cancerians sometimes seem to be almost umbilically connected — they may sail far and wide on the sea of life, but they will always seek to return to the calm shores of their mother port, to cast anchor where childhood memories lie. The home port shelters and protects them from the tempests and torrents of life and, safe in this haven, the only waves that can engulf them are those of emotion. Each wave carries its own memory, every rock of the breakwater murmurs its own story. Cancerians cling to their memories and are lulled by the gentle rocking of the harbour waters, which soothe them to sleep. Like the foetus curled in its mother's womb, they coil themselves crab-like within their shells, clinging to the rich satisfaction they derive from such emotional security.

The past exerts such a strong influence over Cancerians because, unlike the future, which they see as unknown, strange and menacing, it is familiar and secure. These people are therefore sentimental and nostalgic, and their yesterdays (though they may not have been so wonderful at the time) glow brilliantly in retrospect. They reach out longingly to the past in an attempt to hold on to it forever. In their attempts to preserve fragments of time and keep them from being lost, many Cancerians turn to photography as a favourite hobby, while others take to writing their memoirs. They have excellent memories, which allow them to recall experiences, impressions and images from their earliest childhoods, all in extraordinary detail. The finest nuances imprint themselves on the minds of Crabs as though they were composed of extra-sensitive film. Their sentimental attitude to the past can also be seen in their strong attachment to objects that have long been in the family, treasuring them in their private museums. As far as they're concerned, these aren't inanimate objects, but rather living things, each with a tale to tell. One Cancerian friend of mine is so wrapped up in the past that he dates all cheques and documents with the correct day and month, but with the year of the last decade!

The atmosphere around them strongly influences Cancerians, and is reflected in their moods, which are as changeable as the weather and their ruler, the Moon. Indeed, the periodic changes of the Moon are reflected not only in the ebb and flow of the seas but also in the emotional state of Cancerians themselves. The reasons for their emotional ups and downs are as puzzling to themselves as they are to their nearest and dearest. These people are completely ruled by their emotions, tossed about by them for no apparent reason. Even the weather affects them emotionally, and they are sometimes extremely tense when the Moon is full. Certain types of lighting may affect them too, and they can become depressed at sunset. A Cancerian acquaintance of mine often feels as though 'the streets themselves are hostile', at which point she curls up into her own little shell and even draws in her feelers. Very often, in fact, those born under this sign are adept at generating anxieties and self-pity. Once they sink into one of their black moods, they give in to it completely, and bury themselves in bed, where they can nurse their sorrows in comfort! Cancerians are easily moved to tears, and even male Crabs have confessed to needing handkerchiefs when watching emotional scenes in films. Both sexes tend to swim in a sea of sorrow, but when it seems that they're about to drown, their wonderful sense of humour will come to the rescue and a smile will shine out of the blues, like a rainbow emerging in the middle of a summer storm. No wonder it's sometimes hard to tell if these people are laughing or crying, for they may laugh from pain or cry for joy. Either way, their emotions are constantly excited.

Like an onrushing wave, this Water sign surges forward and then recedes; like the sea itself, it bestows its riches on the shores only to draw them back into its vastness; like the water smashing the coast full of sound and fury, it retreats in dim murmurs. Here, where oceans engulf the land in their embrace, where waves caress the golden sands, at the meeting point of the sea of emotions and the shores of safety, lies Cancer's domain.

Cancer, the first of the Water signs, symbolizes the initial contact with the element of water — with the emotional, mysterious and unknown. And Cancerians dip cautiously into the water, yet are quick to retreat into their sandy tunnels, before re-emerging for another go. For Crabs need the feeling of solid land under their feet, preferring to anchor safely in harbour so as not to be swept away by waves of emotion and be tossed about helplessly on the high seas. The heaving ocean of all-encompassing passion is ruled by the second Water sign, Scorpio. But emotional tempests are inimical to Cancerians, who crave security in their personal lives. Emotions centre on the home and family, to which they return time and time again, curling themselves up in its safe, protective bosom. (Cancerians dwell spiritually in the Garden of Eden, before the fall.)

This sign stands for the primal, most ancient, basic and instinctive emotions — the love of the infant for the mother, which ripens in maturity into the parent's love for the child. The monthly cycle of the Moon, ruling the sign of Cancer, is reflected in the woman's cycle of fertility. So, although Cancer is the sign of fertility, Cancer's love is devoid of all sexuality. This is the love between mother and child, and the mother figure (forgetting Freud, for the moment!) is seen as sexless. Even though she may be a very ordinary woman indeed, her children will see the Holy Virgin in her.

The Moon symbolizes the nurturing, ever-loving mother, whose sole reason for existence is the welfare and happiness of her children. In its most exalted form, the Moon-ruled sign of Cancer represents the Great Mother whose all-embracing love encompasses the whole of creation — men, beasts and plants. They are all her children. But how are these characteristics expressed in men whose Sun sign or Ascendant is Cancer? How does a man identify with the concept of the Great Mother? He may choose to remain the eternal child, hiding in the folds of his mother's apron; on the other hand he may develop a very confident personality which dares to expose his emotional, sensitive aspects. He may then become a particularly well-integrated man, willing to protect not only his immediate family but also anyone else seeking help, support and a sense of security. This type of man will often hear the calling of one of the caring professions, whether it be medicine or any work that protects nature and wildlife. Alternatively he may choose a career in the defence forces or the security services.

Because they recognize the intrinsic value of every living thing, Cancerians love and cherish nature, and take great pains to preserve it. They will even appreciate the inanimate, and value the merest scrap of paper, because it was once part of a living tree. Many Cancerians develop relationships with household objects and attribute human qualities to them. One Crab I know gave a name to every item in her house, and called her washing machine Sammy, an armchair Cuddly, and christened the oven Granny. Those close to Cancerians certainly can't complain of not receiving enough personal attention!

The characteristic Cancerian need for security and their innate hate of waste expresses itself in a tendency in many of them to become inveterate hoarders. Just as chipmunks store away nuts for the winter, so Cancerians save every scrap for that rainy day. These people are gifted and successful in business, making money and keeping it, forever saving and hoarding, conserving and salting something away for the future. Like the crab, once Cancerians have something in their claws, they don't let go. They cling to the people around them, to money, objects, and to their much-cherished memories. They may keep the most trivial of objects, even those devoid of any sentimental or monetary value. I know one Cancerian who saves empty plastic yoghurt containers. After all, they may come in handy one day . . .

Food is something else that Cancerians stash away. Seeing a larder that is almost at bursting point gives them a comfortable, safe feeling. They associate food with love, and eating endows them with a deep sense of security, such as an infant experiences while suckling at the mother's breast. Motherly love, represented by this sign, is also expressed through breast-feeding and nurturing. These feelings all come to the fore in the Cancerian's kitchen, where each dish becomes a love potion. It isn't only women who adore cooking, because many Cancerian men are also

The sense of caring, so typical of Cancer, is expressed in the profession chosen by Princess Diana (Sun sign Cancer) before her marriage to the heir to the British throne – she worked in a nursery school. Princess Diana's personality also reflects Cancerian shyness and introversion.

Salvador Dali (Ascendant sign Cancer) demonstrates the typical Cancerian desire to retreat into oneself and return to the womb.

excellent cooks, and may even take over from their wives in the kitchen!

There is a strongly sentimental side to Cancerian men, who will fondly remember their very first love for that little girl in pigtails, back in kindergarten. Subsequent loves will fail to dim his memory of her, and many years later, even after his temples have begun to grey, her image won't have faded. One Cancerian man, well into his fifties and very rich, successful and handsome, managed to track down his childhood sweetheart, although she lived overseas. One day, he appeared on her doorstep, like the Prince Charming she had been dreaming of (her drunkard husband had just left her a widow), heaping love, attention and expensive gifts on her. But the honeymoon didn't last long. As romantic as Cancerians can be, their homes and families come before everything else. Think of a crab scuttling one step forwards and two steps back, and you have the secret of Cancerian men who may make a move towards love, but will soon hurry back to the safety of their home and hearth. The Cancerian Prince Charming, therefore, returned to his family. However, despite severing the romantic ties with his old-new flame, he decided to financially support her aged mother, which he does to this very day. He even finds the time to visit her regularly (show me many sons who do!), despite his hectic schedule as a VIP.

Remembrance of Things Past, the unique creation of French writer Marcel Proust, bears witness to the sensitive Cancerian attitude to the past, to childhood memories and to the Mother figure. Proust (Sun sign Cancer) spent his last years in a sound-proof room which he hardly ever left – a rather drastic example of the back-to-the-womb nostalgia characteristic of many Cancerians.

Cancerian fear of a threatening – because unknown – future finds expression in *1984*, the celebrated novel by George Orwell (Sun sign Cancer).

The Cancerian woman is definitely a homebody. Well-proportioned, somewhat rounded and comely, she radiates femininity and maternal feelings. If in a permanent relationship, she will cleave to her partner, and cling on with love and tenacity. Sometimes it can border on over-possessiveness, making the loved one feel strangled and suffocated. However, she makes the ideal mother. She will give her all to her children, twenty-four hours a day, seven days a week, year in year out — sometimes for decades. For even when her children are well into adulthood, they will still be her babies. She can be over-protective, and her all-encompassing mother love may sometimes verge on smother love. When her young ones spread their wings to leave the nest, she'll start to panic, and may pass on to her children the typical Cancerian fears of the outside world, anxieties that make her want to hide in her shell or, better still, crawl back into the womb.

In fact, some Cancerians are afraid of leaving the womb and severing the umbilical cord to become independent individuals. They tend to become dependent on someone or something larger than themselves, in the hope of overcoming the anguish of being a separate entity. They long to lose themselves in the throng, and to erase their individuality, desperately striving to swim with the tide and be just like every other drop of water it contains.

Charity begins at home, so they say, but for some Cancerians, it also stays there. However, the love these people feel for their families is not real love — it is rather a kind of extended self-love, in the sense that 'my family is me'. They form a common front with their families in order to face a threatening world in which every stranger is a potential enemy. Their view of humanity is one in which family fights family, and clan opposes clan, each one clamming up and sheltering in its own shell. As far as these Crabs are concerned, only one's nearest are one's dearest. Indeed, they believe that the clannish protection afforded by their families is all there is.

Sleepwalking is a common complaint for people with Cancer as their Sun or rising sign. This is because they are ruled by the Moon, and some of them could even be described as moon-struck (suffering from inexplicable tensions and given to bouts of hysteria). Interestingly enough, the term 'hysteria' comes from the Greek *hysteros*, meaning the womb — an organ closely connected with the sign of Cancer. Cancer's 'lunatic' inclinations can be attributed to the influence of the Moon, Luna, which is Cancer's ruling planet. Being hyper-sensitive, Cancerians are quick to take offence, and when they feel down in the dumps and have that nobody-loves-me feeling, they often console themselves by overeating. Small wonder that many Crabs are prone to ulcers and stomach ailments!

The Moon's rulership of this sign is often reflected in the facial structure of Cancerians. There are two types of typical Crab faces: one, perhaps the most common, is the Moon-like face, as round as a Chinaman's. (Traditionally, Cancer is the sign of the Chinese people. Being ruled by the sign of fertility may explain their large population.) The other is the elongated, bony type, whose jutting chin makes the profile resemble the New Moon.

Most Crabs are full-bodied, with slender limbs and small hands and feet. They have pale colouring, just like that of their ruler. Their eyes are large, somewhat protuberant, usually greenish-hazel in colour, and their hair is mousy. This nondescript colouring is almost a form of protection, like that of the crab, enabling it to blend in with sand and rocks. In other words, the average Cancerian is nothing to write home about, though some women born under this sign are stunningly beautiful, as rare as pearls and as lustrous, shimmering in any gathering of gems. Although shy and retiring, they catch the attention and warm the heart — and hearth, of many a man . . .

FAMOUS PEOPLE BORN UNDER CANCER

CANCER AS THE ASCENDANT

Alfred Adler (Sun sign Aquarius)
J S Bach (Sun sign Aries)
William Blake (Sun sign Sagittarius)
Charles Bronson (Sun sign Scorpio)
Richard Burton (Sun sign Scorpio)
Lord Byron (Sun sign Aquarius)
Marie Curie (Sun sign Scorpio)
Salvador Dali (Sun sign Taurus)
Albert Einstein (Sun sign Pisces)
Vincent van Gogh (Sun sign Aries)
Rudyard Kipling (Sun sign Capricorn)
Rainer Maria Rilke (Sun sign Sagittarius)
Arthur Schopenhauer (Sun sign Pisces)
Franz Schubert (Sun sign Aquarius)
Richard Strauss (Sun sign Gemini)
Leo Tolstoy (Sun sign Virgo)

CANCER AS THE SUN SIGN

Alexander the Great (Ascendant Libra)
Marc Chagall (Ascendant Scorpio)
Jean Cocteau (Ascendant Taurus)
Edgar Degas (Ascendant Aquarius)
King Edward VIII (Ascendant Aquarius)
Ernest Hemingway (Ascendant Virgo)
Herman Hesse (Ascendant Sagittarius)
Amedeo Modigliani (Ascendant Virgo)
John Rockefeller (Ascendant Aries)
Erich Maria Remarque (Ascendant Sagittarius)
Cecil Rhodes (Ascendant Sagittarius)
George Sand (Ascendant Aquarius)
The Princess of Wales (Ascendant Sagittarius)

and the following people whose Ascendants are unknown: Yul Brynner, Pearl S Buck, Al Capone, Leslie Caron, Erle Stanley Gardner, Franz Kafka, Gottfried Wilhelm Leibniz, Rose Kennedy, George Orwell, Marcel Proust, Rembrandt, Jean Jacques Rousseau, Isaac Stern, Natalie Wood, Yevgeny Yevtushenko

LEO — THE LION

Symbol — The Lion, king of the jungle

Ruling planet — The Sun, symbolizing vitality and strength

Element — Fire

Quality — Fixed

Anatomical areas under Leo's influence — The heart and back

Polar sign — Aquarius

Basking in the limelight is the favourite pastime of people born with Leo as their Ascendant or rising sign. The lion, the king of the jungle, is a proud and vital creature, and those influenced by the sign of Leo long for greatness, respect and fame. They aren't happy unless they're the centre of attention, and thanks to their vibrant, cordial and outgoing personalities, strong presence and dramatic sense, they usually manage to receive top billing!

Like the Sun, around which the world turns, Leos are the pivot around which lesser mortals revolve, like mere satellites. These people are kings and queens, and their word is law. This is true of every aspect of their lives, even going back to the days when the young Leo reigned supreme in the classroom. Leos naturally find themselves in positions of authority and leadership, commanding respect by virtue of their honesty and integrity, generosity and courage, loyalty and noblemindedness. What's more, born with a sense of *noblesse oblige*, their behaviour is flawless and their word of honour universally respected. These aristocratic beings are willing to compromise many things, but never their principles and honour, for they have to be able to look themselves straight in the eyes.

Everything is king-sized for Leos, who feel nothing but contempt for the petty. As a result, they behave in a grandiose, almost theatrical manner. Their vision, verve and good imaginations help them when it comes to planning, management and organization — which they think that only they can do properly! This urge to control things even extends to the lives of their nearest and dearest, who are expected to obey and admire these majestic people. In fact, adoration is their life-blood, and the most awe-inspiring Lion will turn into a pussycat on hearing even very transparent flattery. Needless to say, anyone who questions Leo's supremacy does so at their own peril, and soon finds themselves in the proverbial lion's den. In stark contrast to Aquarians, the polar sign of Leo, whose hallmark is tolerance for others' liberty and opinions, Leos are singularly intolerant of anyone who refuses to accept their rule. Being nobleminded, though, they aren't vindictive, and in victory will treat their opponents fairly.

Supreme self-confidence, and boundless vitality and *joie de vivre* characterize the Leo nature. These overgrown kittens also like to play at love. And when they love, they love with all their hearts. In fact, the sign of Leo represents the heart, and people with Leo rising are even more preoccupied with the affairs of the heart than those with the Sun in this sign. People with Leo Ascendants take everything to heart so, despite their great vitality, their hearts may be their weak spots – romantically as well as physically. When their hearts are broken, it's harder for them than for others to get over the pain and carry on with their lives.

Like the Sun itself, Leo exudes light and warmth. And just as the Sun's light is reflected by the Moon and planets, so Leos expect their love and warmth to be reciprocated by those around them. While members of their opposite sign, Aquarius, want to love the whole world, Leos need to receive the love and respect of the whole world. Such people will seek to play leading roles on the stage, or in history — after all, all the world's a stage! And thanks to their sense of the dramatic, and their rhetorical gifts, they do stand in the middle of the stage — shining examples are Napoleon and Menachem Begin (both born with the Sun in Leo), and Sir Winston Churchill (Leo Ascendant).

The self-respect so characteristic of the noble Leo can be twisted beyond recognition by some Lions, and turned into pompous pride. These

Matters of the heart are undoubtedly important to Prince Andrew, whose Ascendant is Leo – the sign of romance. When he was a bachelor the Prince's romantic adventures filled the gossip columns to overflowing.

A gift for leadership and a highly developed sense of the dramatic – typical traits of Leo – are characteristic of the personality of Israel's former Prime Minister Menahem Begin (Sun sign Leo).

people will go to any lengths to prove that they are to the manner born, and will surround themselves with luxury and splendour. But their showy behaviour merely betrays them as being *nouveau riche*, at best. These paper lions crave an admiring audience although, needless to say, they are their own greatest fans! Every night they'll run through the highlights of the past 24 hours, casting themselves in more flattering roles than was really the case. Their theatrical streak will turn the events of the day into a string of kitschy commercials with themselves in the lead. Over and over again in their minds' eyes, they'll replay the moment they left their friends open-mouthed at the sight of their fancy new car, or the time they stunned the waiter in the expensive restaurant by nonchalantly tossing him an enormous tip calculated to buy VIP service. Then there'll be a flashback to the previous evening, when they did that incredible disco solo to what they firmly believe was the enthralled gaze of all those present. But, being creative, Leos aren't content just to replay the roles of yesterday — they are already busy casting, directing and rehearsing the lead part for the next day's performance. The show must go on, for at dawn the curtain will rise on a new day in their lives. But why wait for tomorrow when the night is still young? As a young acquaintance of mine, a typical Leo, says, 'A night I don't go out is a dead loss.'

As night falls, true Leos will don their latest outfit. This will be the gala performance for their new clothes, after which they'll be cast into the outer darkness of an already overflowing wardrobe. After all, the king or queen of the jungle wouldn't want their admirers to see them wearing the same outfit twice! At last, after much preening, the Leo will be ready for the nightly prowl. Being a true romantic, however, the only objective of a nocturnal hunt is the opposite sex. Yet, even having brought their game safely home, Leos won't want to stay snugly in their dens. Instead, these fun-loving creatures need to go out and be seen in the right places. There, they can strut about as though saying 'I am seen — therefore, I am.' Never forget that Leos aren't interested in going out to look at other people — they leave that to the other members of the zodiac. As far as Lions are concerned, everyone should be looking at them, talking about what they wore and who they were seen with, and preferably reporting it in the gossip columns of newspapers and magazines. This type of Leo must be 'in', in order to feel any kind of self-esteem at all.

Another version of this boastful type of Leo is the self-important, conceited Lion, the kind who feels they've got justice and honesty all sewn up, and are forever lecturing on the subject. These people don't have conversations. Instead, they subject one to monologue after monologue, full of dramatic (and often inappropriate) emphases and rhetorical questions. The rhetorical question is, of course, their hallmark: they never expect an answer. They've already got all the answers and besides, they aren't interested in hearing anyone but themselves.

But it's by no means all bad. Leo is the most romantic and loving of the 12 signs. The Leo man is gallant and a true gentleman, and his Lion's heart is especially susceptible to female charms. His manners towards the fair sex are impeccable: he opens doors for women, and stands up when a lady enters the room. Sir Walter Raleigh's gesture of throwing his cape over a puddle for his Queen to walk on is typical of Leo. (No wonder the lion was such a popular symbol in the age of chivalry!) The romantic Leo is always looking for an enchanted princess to put on a pedestal, to whom he will willingly surrender at least half his kingdom. He's the knight in shining armour of many a girl's dreams — his only problem is that there are so few enchanted princesses left. Today's liberated woman is definitely not to his taste — he prefers his damsel to be locked up in an ivory tower . . .

Like Aries, Leo's element is Fire. But, while Arian enthusiasms are quick to die, the fire burning in the Leo's heart is an enduring flame. If a woman takes the trouble to bolster a Leo man's image while keeping up her own appearance then, like the high priestess in the temple fanning the embers of the eternal fire, she will be his flame forever. And then, as in a fairy tale, the king and his queen will live happily ever after.

Unfortunately, there is yet another type of Leo, who isn't a charming prince but a bragging Don Juan. He never wastes any time announcing his exploits (usually imaginary) at the top of his voice. There is no need for me to elaborate on the subject, because he's his own best spokesman. You'll recognize him when you hear him speak! Needless to say, this Lion owes his broad shoulders to plenty of padding, and the only leaping he does in the city jungle is from café to discotheque!

The Leo woman wants to combine love with social status and honour. If married to an important man, she will lead an active social life, entertaining VIPs in her home and queening it over her guests. If her home is really her palace, she will be happy to run an exemplary household and excel as the perfect hostess. Her table will be laden with the best of everything, and her meals will be fit for a king, reflecting the creativity and artistic sense so characteristic of her sign. She'll want to receive the admiration of her guests and the approval of her husband. As long as she feels that her home is her castle and she its lady, she'll content herself with that. If, on the other hand, her home is smaller than her royal dreams would like, she will try to achieve her wishes outside it, trying to find her kingdom in an independent career.

'Grandeur' may be the byword of most Leos, but it is rarely applied to their physical stature. There are very few exceptionally tall people in this sign, the average Leo being of medium height. However, even when short (like Napoleon, for example), a Leo's appearance is impressive, sometimes even regal. The most characteristic feature of Leos is their excellent posture. In fact, 'standing tall' is a favourite expression of Menachem Begin, whose Sun sign is Leo. Leos' chests puff out like those of peacocks, and like peacocks, they don't lack for colour. Their vitality is reflected in their ruddy cheeks and, occasionally, in their reddish hair. Their Leonine faces are broad, and their large, cat-like eyes are wide-set. Everything about Leos is on a grand scale, so when they smile (something which happens a lot), it isn't a demure gesture, but a broad, whole-hearted, Cheshire cat-like, gap-toothed grin.

Very handsome, Apollo-like men are ruled by Leo, which is hardly surprising when one considers the connections between the Sun God and Leo. Unlike the lion with his glorious mane, Leo men are rarely noted for their full heads of hair. Many Leos go bald early, some even losing their hair long before they reach the autumn of their lives. Perhaps there is some truth in the old adage that too much time in the hay causes a man's hair to fall out . . . Leo women, on the other hand, are blessed with luxuriant locks which are their crowning glories. 'Not so!' you may object, 'the Leo woman I know is decidedly mousy.' Well, there is a very rare type of Lioness who is as unglamorous as can be. This is especially true if her horoscope shows a strong emphasis on Virgo, the sign of unassuming modesty. But don't be surprised if, one day, the mousy Lioness lets out a full roar, grows her hair, dyes it blonde, and dazzles everyone with her glorious crown of gold . . .

FAMOUS PEOPLE BORN UNDER LEO

LEO AS THE ASCENDANT

Muhammad Ali (Sun sign Capricorn)
Prince Andrew (Sun sign Pisces)
Honoré de Balzac (Sun sign Taurus)
Maurice Chevalier (Sun sign Virgo)
Sir Winston Churchill (Sun sign Sagittarius)
Claude Debussy (Sun sign Leo)
Alexander Dumas, père (Sun sign Leo)
Galileo Galilei (Sun sign Pisces)
Indira Gandhi (Sun sign Scorpio)
Paul Gauguin (Sun sign Gemini)
Samuel Goldwyn (Sun sign Virgo)
Henrik Ibsen (Sun sign Pisces)
Mick Jagger (Sun sign Leo)
Martin Luther (Sun sign Scorpio)
Maimonides (Sun sign Aries)
Edouard Manet (Sun sign Aquarius)
Henri Matisse (Sun sign Capricorn)
Marilyn Monroe (Sun sign Gemini)
Roger Moore (Sun sign Libra)
Rudolph Nureyev (Sun sign Pisces)
Robert Perry (Sun sign Taurus)
Pablo Picasso (Sun sign Scorpio)
Mark Spitz (Sun sign Aquarius)
John Steinbeck (Sun sign Pisces)
The Prince of Wales (Sun sign Scorpio)
Mae West (Sun sign Leo)

LEO AS THE SUN SIGN

Emily Brontë (Ascendant Scorpio)
Fidel Castro (Ascendant Scorpio)
Claude Debussy (Ascendant Leo)
Alexander Dumas, père (Ascendant Leo)
Henry Ford (Ascendant Scorpio)
Robert Graves (Ascendant Sagittarius)
Mata Hari (Ascendant Scorpio)
Mick Jagger (Ascendant Leo)
Carl Jung (Ascendant Aquarius)
Jacqueline Kennedy Onassis (Ascendant Scorpio)
Guy de Maupassant (Ascendant Virgo)
André Maurois (Ascendant Aquarius)
Benito Mussolini (Ascendant Scorpio)
Roman Polanski (Ascendant Sagittarius)
Robert Redford (Ascendant Pisces)
George Bernard Shaw (Ascendant Gemini)
Alfred Lord Tennyson (Ascendant Gemini)

and the following people whose Ascendants are unknown: Princess Anne, Menachem Begin, Napoleon Bonaparte, Omar Khayam, Princess Margaret, Dorothy Parker

VIRGO — THE MAIDEN

Symbol — A maiden holding a sheaf of wheat

Ruling planet — Mercury, the planet of intelligence and communication

Element — Earth

Quality — Mutable

Anatomical area under Virgo's influence — The intestines

Polar sign — Pisces

As their name implies, Virgos are modest and unassuming, the epitome of neatness and cleanliness. They're introverted, quiet and discreet, and very keen on privacy. The sheaf in the Maiden's hand symbolizes the eternal triangle around which the Virgoan life revolves: work, nutrition and health. What do these three have in common? Actually, the logic connecting them is water-tight, since anything not wholly logical won't stand up to Virgo's keen critical and rational approach: those who work have food, and those who have proper nutrition are healthy. And to complete the circle, people who are healthy have the strength to continue working. But wheat doesn't grow on trees: a lot of hard work goes into sowing and reaping it, and no one knows better than Virgoans that 'By the sweat of thy brow shall thou eat bread'. The sheaf of wheat, therefore, is the perfect symbol to express this sign's practical, productive character, and Virgo's close ties with work, food and health.

Let's begin, then, with the first side of the triangle — work. Virgoans shy away from idleness. 'Go to the ant, sluggard, and consider her ways and be wise' — replace 'the ant' with 'Virgo', and you have a very accurate astrological saying. Typical Virgos also bring to mind another creature from the insect kingdom — the worker bee (a virgin in the true sense of the word), whose sole purpose in life is to make honey to feed the offspring of the Queen Bee. In fact, most Virgos are content with modest occupations, and often work in the service fields. They make perfect employees: efficient, trustworthy, systematic, meticulous and dutiful. They are wholeheartedly committed to the job at hand and try to do it as well as they possibly can. The Maiden sets high standards for herself and is forever trying to achieve perfection. On the other hand, her demands are small and she settles for very little. Virgoans, therefore, aren't very ambitious and are not particularly interested in climbing the ladder of success to achieve high positions. Typical Virgos are unpretentious and comfortable in their little niches. They don't resent being small cogs since, that way, they always know their place and will never be taken unawares. The monotonous everyday routine might be boring, but it's also safe. And as nothing frightens them more than the unknown, at least in doing a routine job, they know exactly where they stand.

Now, let's take a look at the second side of the Virgo triangle — nutrition. Proper nutrition is a subject close to every Virgo's heart, whose eating habits are suitably strict. They follow different diets, try being vegetarians or only eat natural foods, and know the exact vitamin content of every foodstuff imaginable. The typical Virgo mother will never tell her children to eat cake, even if there isn't any bread, for two very good reasons. Firstly, cake isn't good for them, and secondly, her pantry is never bare — before her stock runs out she's certain to have laid in a new supply, tidily arranged on the proper shelves. Neatness and orderliness are a Virgo's staff of life. They are also very neat when it comes to measurements. These people can fill a teapot with exactly the right amount of water for the number of cups required.

Offer Virgo's neighbouring sign, Leo, a choice between bread and games and they'll usually choose the latter. Purposeful Virgos, however, will always choose bread — and not just any old bread, either, but the wholewheat variety. Despite their best attempts to stick to wholesome food, Virgos sometimes succumb to temptation, furtively nibbling at sweets between meals. For not by bread alone — even the wholewheat kind — do Virgos live! If caught, they can always claim that snacks settle their stomachs or ease their heartburn. Not surprisingly, members of this sign suffer from stomach ailments, and fretful Virgos will eat their hearts out, not just at meal-times but round the clock, too!

And this brings us to the third side of the Virgo triangle: health. The typical Virgo is mad about health, and as well as being a nutrition expert they also know the fine differences between Asian flu and the Mediterranean strains. Those people are walking medical dictionaries! Most Virgos are proud of their healing touch and gentle hands, equally suited to soothing sore muscles and setting broken bones. In fact, they're experts when it comes to medical problems, whether their own or those of their relatives, or those that they encounter in the course of their work, which is often associated with medicine in some way. Their strong side is caring for physical ills and devotedly nursing the sick, but they are less understanding when it comes to soothing emotional troubles — their motto being 'Health above all'. Virgos in general, and particularly those who have Virgo rising, either enjoy extremely good health, hardly knowing a day's illness, or it's the exact opposite, and they are weak and sickly.

Being of service is very important to Virgos, who are always willing to lend a helping hand, especially to someone who is ill. They are often the only people in the neighbourhood to visit an unwell neighbour, make a cup of tea and offer to buy the groceries. When in need themselves, however, those born under this sign find it very difficult to ask for help, disliking the thought of being a burden. They prefer to do their own shopping, even when they've got double pneumonia, rather than ask someone else to do it for them. Besides, being perfectionists, they don't trust anyone else to pick out the best apples or tomatoes! The thought of someone bringing back a blemished fruit or vegetable literally sickens them, as does the idea that their precious money might be wasted on an ill-advised purchase. They feel that a penny saved is a penny earned, and with so many worries on their minds, it's no wonder that they prefer to do the shopping themselves, and feel all the better for it!

Mercury, the planet ruling this sign, symbolizes intelligence and the communicative skills and indeed, most Virgos are witty speakers who delight in puns and word-play. (Some, however, have a wit that borders on the scathing.) Quick to learn any subject, the in-coming information filters swiftly through their receptive brains to be stored away, neatly and efficiently, in their little grey cells. They are proud of their excellent memories, and the ability to recall any fact at a moment's notice. Ask a Virgo, for instance, what year Napoleon was exiled to Elba and they're sure to get the date right. Should they make a mistake, however, and have it pointed out to them, they'll be cut to the quick. Hardly fair, really, considering that they will always point out someone else's mistake, and won't mince their words about it, either! Virgos are teachers at heart and pretty strict ones, too. Their brains are well-springs of information that are being constantly replenished, usually through reading. These people are veritable bookworms, devouring volumes on such varied topics as medicine, history and biographies of famous people. On the other hand, they stay away from philosophy, mysticism and other abstract themes, finding security only in the concrete. Anything beyond the here and now, anything uncertain, alarms them.

Dealing with the small details of life, and doing unexciting routine jobs that require precision, give them a sense of security. The schoolchild enthralled by grammar lessons, and the accountant bent in rapture over the ledgers, are both almost certainly Virgos. Pisces, Virgo's opposite sign, feels like a fish in water in any kind of mess; Virgos, however, revere order, which represents everything known and safe. Typical Virgos feel that cleanliness — and neatness — is next to godliness, and their homes are always as neat as new pins.

'What will the neighbours say?' is the sort of question that keeps Virgos awake at night — they attach great importance to what people think and say about them. Despite the fact that Virgos are unfailingly critical of their fellow men, they find it very difficult to swallow a dose of their own medicine. They desperately need to be accepted by their peers, and are therefore polite and well-mannered, and always well-groomed. They're the sort of people who won't leave the house without a clean, starched and ironed handkerchief. Just as Virgos need to be accepted by society, society must also be acceptable to them, and they're willing to do their share in improving the quality of life. Sometimes they may even overcome their habitual timidity to give litterbugs a dressing-down. Ideally, they'd like to share their vast stores of knowledge with others, and thereby better the world at large. Virgos regard the education of the younger generation to be of the utmost importance and, like some prim Victorian governess, put great emphasis not only on teaching them the three Rs, but also on minding their Ps and Qs.

Virgos can get by on very little sleep. They're light sleepers and as soon as they wake up, they're wide awake. Unlike Pisceans who, on waking seem to be sleepwalking and can even have trouble remembering their own names, Virgos are instantly alert, with all senses honed — rather like the cook in *Sleeping Beauty* who, on awakening from a hundred years of sleep, remembered to slap his apprentice for a misdemeanour committed a century before!

Virgos may rise like the proverbial early bird, but they don't necessarily get up with a song on their lips. Quite a few of them start their days with a low but insistent hum of petty fault-finding, interspersed with biting criticism and remarks which have a sting that a wasp would envy. What sets them off? Just about anything! These carping creatures will always find (or invent) a good enough reason for a moan, being by nature pessimistic, critical and fretful, and suffering from chronic dissatisfaction. It may be said that 'Those who sow in tears will reap in joy' but, for Virgos, only the first part of that saying applies. Perhaps sheer joy goes against their grain. Even at harvest-time, they'll find something to complain about — if nothing else, last year's harvest was better! These people are in a constant state of anxiety. A typical conversation between such a Virgo and their spouse might go like this: 'I'm so worried.' 'What about? Everything's fine.' 'Exactly — that's just what's worrying me!' For Virgos believe that behind every silver lining lies a cloud!

Some Virgos are so lacking in self-confidence that even the slightest

Virgo – the sign of medicine – was the Ascendant sign of Florence Nightingale who, in the 19th century, laid the foundations of the nursing profession as it is known today.

The American multi-millionaire Howard Hughes was famous not only for his fabulous wealth, but also because of his obsession with cleanliness. Virgo – which among other things is the sign of cleanliness – was his Ascendant sign.

state of doubt or uncertainty will throw them off-course. They must know, at any given time, exactly where they stand. The trouble is that life isn't always geared to supplying the answer. And when life becomes too complex and uncertain for comfort, they'll take refuge in their work. Sailing uncharted waters is much better suited to Pisceans — Virgos like to feel solid ground under their feet. When work becomes a Virgo's escape route, it may also become their sole existence. That sane, clear-headed Virgo might easily turn into a workaholic and let life slide by without experiencing it at all, turning into a pedantic old maid or bachelor along the way. For fear of being swept away by the tides of life, these Virgos might end up being inundated by a sea of office paperwork instead.

A further distortion of the basic level-headed Virgoan characteristics is the obsessive, nit-picking, ultra-starched person. People like this are liable to fall prey to all sorts of strange and unusual fears, including bacteriophobia. The late and eccentric multi-millionaire, Howard Hughes, is an extreme example of this type of Virgo. Hughes, whose rising sign was Virgo, became a virtual recluse in his own home for fear of coming into contact with other people's germs. He even made his guests undergo a disinfection process before entering his house!

To a much lesser degree than Howard Hughes, most Virgos have a dread of anything dirty, and that includes anything sexual as well. If taken to extremes, the Virgoan attitude is somewhat twisted, and instead of eroticism, you find neuroticism. Sex both attracts and repels them at the same time. They will daydream at length about sex in the same way that the famished dream of food, often indulging in erotic fantasies and pornographic literature. But not all of them will be content to sit on the bookshelf and have a sex life by proxy — some practical, straightforward Virgos want to experience the bare, naked truth, carefully following all the instructions they've read in their sex manuals. Some Maidens aren't at all coy — they want to experience the real McCoy, betraying their symbol, the virgin, in no time at all!

The pedantic Virgoan approach to life makes some people born under this sign obsessed with petty details. These Virgos will look at everything through a magnifying glass, noticing every last blemish. But while concentrating so closely on details, they are likely to lose sight of the general picture, and don't see the wood for the trees. Such an approach may result in a distorted sense of proportion, and difficulty in telling sense from nonsense. Impaired judgement and a strange order of priorities are two results of this attitude.

Those Virgos who love minute details are rarely content to let well enough alone, and will grind their grain over and over again. They are usually male. In a small party (the bashful Virgo might not dare to open his mouth at a larger gathering), this man will go on and on about the medicinal properties of some herbal tea, displaying a phenomenal, encyclopaedic knowledge of everything connected with it, from where each and every strain is grown, to how it's stored after harvest to preserve the aroma. Just as his semi-dozing audience is relieved to discover that their ordeal of a lecture has finally come to an end, he'll suddenly remember another string of seemingly fascinating facts. His long-suffering listeners will pour themselves another cup of coffee in a desperate attempt to stay awake, solemnly swearing never to touch any type of herbal tea again!

They may have an eye for detail, but many Virgos have an inadequate sense of direction. One Virgo I knew, while on a long cruise, was unable to find her way to her cabin unaided, even after several weeks of sailing. Another Virgo of my acquaintance got lost one day, coming home from work, simply because he had decided, after many years, to try a different route!

Virgos, men and women alike, are fairly average-looking. Some, however, especially the women, are blessed with a kind of ethereal, other-worldly beauty: their complexions are unblemished, almost translucent, and their expressions serene and madonna-like. They radiate tranquillity, peace and purity. But most Virgo women have slightly elongated noses, smallish eyes and hair pulled tightly back in a bun, or cut in a very short, plain style. They pride themselves on their flat stomachs and narrow waists, which they emphasize by wearing tight dresses and belts. They are usually buttoned up to the neck — some Maidens reinforce this prim, straight-laced look by wearing silk scarves around their throats.

Although there are some very handsome men among them, the majority of male Virgos are quite ordinary-looking with long noses and narrow, pursed lips. They often perch pairs of glasses on their noses, when they will look over them with a half-ironic, half-harassed expression. They are always well-dressed, with their ties perfectly centred, and one can almost hear their starched shirts crackle as they move.

Many Virgos are short-sighted but, unlike those born under the other signs, these people don't balk at wearing glasses. The typical Virgo wants to see things the way they really are: you are hardly likely to find them looking at the world through rose-coloured spectacles. They see every fault, every wrinkle, clearly — even the ones on their own faces . . .

FAMOUS PEOPLE BORN UNDER VIRGO

VIRGO AS THE ASCENDANT

Jane Austen (Sun sign Sagittarius)
Leonard Bernstein (Sun sign Virgo)
Charlotte Brontë (Sun sign Taurus)
Albert Camus (Sun sign Scorpio)
Pablo Casals (Sun sign Capricorn)
Frederic Chopin (Sun sign Pisces)
Agatha Christie (Sun sign Virgo)
Nicolaus Copernicus (Sun sign Pisces)
Valéry Giscard d'Estaing (Sun sign Aquarius)
Charles Dickens (Sun sign Aquarius)
Marlene Dietrich (Sun sign Capricorn)
Walt Disney (Sun sign Sagittarius)
Ernest Hemingway (Sun sign Cancer)
Howard Hughes (Sun sign Capricorn)
Thomas Mann (Sun sign Gemini)
Guy de Maupassant (Sun sign Leo)
Amedeo Modigliani (Sun sign Cancer)
Wolfgang Amadeus Mozart (Sun sign Aquarius)
Florence Nightingale (Sun sign Taurus)
Richard Nixon (Sun sign Capricorn)
Franklin D Roosevelt (Sun sign Aquarius)
Peter Sellers (Sun sign Virgo)
Georges Seurat (Sun sign Sagittarius)
Brooke Shields (Sun sign Gemini)
Oscar Wilde (Sun sign Libra)
Virginia Woolf (Sun sign Aquarius)

VIRGO AS THE SUN SIGN

Leonard Bernstein (Ascendant Virgo)
Maurice Chevalier (Ascendant Leo)
Agatha Christie (Ascendant Virgo)
Johann von Goethe (Ascendant Scorpio)
Samuel Goldwyn (Ascendant Leo)
Maurice Maeterlinck (Ascendant Libra)
Peter Sellers (Ascendant Virgo)
Leo Tolstoy (Ascendant Cancer)
H G Wells (Ascendant Aquarius)

and the following people whose Ascendants are unknown: Greta Garbo, Georg Hegel, Samuel Johnson, Arthur Koestler, D H Lawrence, Sophia Loren, Paracelsus, Raquel Welch

LIBRA — THE SCALES

Symbol — The Scales

Ruling planet — Venus, the planet of love, beauty and the arts

Element — Air

Quality — Active

Anatomical area under Libra's influence — The kidneys

Polar sign — Aries

What are Librans made of? Sugar and spice and everything nice. They're considered *la crème de la crème* of the zodiac. Is it then merely a coincidence that Venus, ruler of Libra, emerged from the creamy foam of the sea?

Their paths through life are strewn with roses, and their popularity and attractive appearances work strongly in their favour. People born with Libra rising are carried on the wings of their charm, and it's not surprising that so many of them are regarded as the cream of society. Two men who rose to the Presidency of the United States, despite the fact that they were political novices, were John F Kennedy, who was also the youngest President of the Western superpower, and Jimmy Carter. Both were born with Libran Ascendants.

Librans have an inborn interest in art and culture, and rapidly absorb the rules of etiquette and good manners, so that even those born into very simple or poor families quickly climb the social ladder and find their places in the higher circles of society. Eliza Doolittle must have been a Libran!

The sign of Libra, the Scales, symbolizes justice, and people who are born with it as their Sun or rising sign strive to be objective, fair and just. For example, they can always see all the aspects to any problem. Unlike those born under the opposite sign of Aries, for whom everything is plain and obvious, cut and dried, Librans believe that life just isn't that simple. To them, things aren't merely black or white, but human experience is made up of different shades of grey (one of their favourite colours, by the way).

So, unlike the decisive Arians, Librans don't make snap judgements. Knowing how complex life is, they examine every question and weigh every problem over and over. When they finally do come to a decision, they show that they can be objective — they understand the other person's interests, even if they're in conflict with their own, and take them into consideration. Their innate Libran tact and diplomacy, and their charming manners, are part of the secret of their popularity. Their pleasant, easy-going and conciliatory natures, coupled with their ability to understand conflicting interests, enable them to bring opposing camps together and make peace between them. As Jimmy Carter said about the Camp David negotiations: 'I did what I really like doing — explaining the Israeli position to the Egyptians, and the Egyptian position to the Israelis.' An almost impossible mission that only a Libran could accomplish!

Being born under the influence of Venus, the planet of love, Librans have a strong need for close contact with other people. 'Two heads are better than one' is their maxim, and they find it hard to be alone or to function on their own, needing someone to balance and complete them. Togetherness is very important to Librans, and being involved in a marriage or a partnership is their natural state. They loathe any sort of disharmony, so always look for those things that they have in common with other people. They try to ignore any differences of opinion, preferring to give way or reach a compromise, with the result that they generally have successful marriages. A Libran and his or her spouse will bill and coo throughout their lives like a couple of turtle doves.

Their dependence on other people may prove to be a stumbling block if Librans become involved with the wrong person. But because Venus, their ruler, is the planet of love, she does her best to find Librans the right soulmate. Venus, Libra's fairy godmother, doesn't have to wave her magic wand too much: the charms of her sons and daughters, their harmonious and pleasant personalities, and their good looks, do most of the work for her – no one is more popular with the opposite sex than the typical Libran. People born with Libra rising usually get married at a very early age, and sometimes they seem to have been born married! But love isn't the only sphere in which Librans succeed without any effort. They lead charmed lives and sometimes it seems that everything comes easily to them — and that they take things too easily, as well. One Libran I knew would always say 'Take it easy', whether the topic of conversation was the danger of nuclear war or the latest improvements at the local supermarket. And he takes his own advice, living a life of ease.

A highly-developed aesthetic sense is one of the best aspects of people born under the influence of Venus. They love to surround themselves with beauty, works of art and everything which less refined souls consider to be luxuries. Not so for the children of Venus, who regard them all as basic necessities — they need beauty and culture just as they need air. What seems to be icing on the cake to others is daily bread to Librans.

Some people claim that though Librans may like the good things in life, they aren't always willing to work for them. And although some Librans are naturally calm and easy-going, Libra is an active sign — a fact which no doubt comes as a surprise to those who think of it as 'Lazy Libra'. Libra is one of the four signs belonging to the Cardinal (active) quality, but its action is mental rather than physical. Because the Sun enters Libra towards the end of September, it's an autumnal sign and, like torpid autumn (calm on the surface while seeds are sprouting underneath), ideas are taking root, shooting and flourishing in the minds of Librans. Their brains never stop working — constantly thinking and pondering, considering situations and weighing them up, making comparisons, and struggling with problems. All in all, they put in a lot of overtime! So it's hardly surprising that after all that effort, these people don't have much energy left for putting their bodies to work!

However, some Librans do illustrate the saying 'Lazy Libra' perfectly. They are always able to manoeuvre someone else into helping them with a task and then, tactfully and diplomatically, manage to get them to do the hardest part of the job. Meet one of these people and you can expect to hear something like this: 'How sweet of you to offer to help paint my room. I've got a wonderful talent for mixing paints to get just the right shade, so while I mix them up it would be lovely if you'd climb up the ladder and start painting. It's also good exercise for your arms.' But for some Librans even this is too much. Lazy Libra's natural position is horizontal — flat on their backs, surrounded by sweets and other goodies. Oblomov, the lazy aristocrat of Russian literature who didn't even sit idly by, but just lay idly by, is a caricature of the Libran who is careful to avoid any superfluous motion while always making sure of being clad in an elegant silk robe. Sometimes there is a decadent side to Libra. These people behave like the descendants of an old aristocratic family in its decline and fall, like an autumn leaf about to drop off the family tree. But even if they're going to the dogs, Librans always do it in style!

At the same time, most Librans are willing to be harnessed to some

Brigitte Bardot is undoubtedly the personification of Venus – the goddess of beauty and love. Small wonder, then, that the beautiful star was born with her Sun in Libra, ruled by Venus.

Ali Khan, the international playboy and heir to millions, lived 'La Dolce Vita' to the hilt – as befits one whose Ascendant sign was Libra. He was married to the beautiful star Rita Hayworth whose Sun sign, like that of Brigitte Bardot, is Libra.

task, but only on condition that either it's as part of a team, since they like to do everything with other people, or that it at least benefits someone close to them. A Libran man, for instance, will always be willing to make an extra effort in order to give his wife an expensive present. But even when Librans are at their most active, they always know how to temper physical activity with rest, unlike Scorpios, their astrological neighbours, who never know when to stop!

Because Librans are noted for their love of beauty, art and culture, you may well expect to find many artists and composers born under this sign. Oddly enough, that isn't the case, and surprisingly few artists were born under Libra. This may be because in most cases creativity is the expression of a stormy spirit, whereas the evenly-balanced scales of Libra do not, as a rule, sway in the storm — their natural state being one of spiritual balance and equilibrium. The vast majority of Librans aren't passionate enough about anything to be truly creative, and the birth charts of those few Librans who do have creative ability show a strong emphasis of either Leo or Scorpio. But although the creative muse doesn't usually touch them, Librans do appreciate the creativity of others, and are very successful in fields connected with the arts, such as running an art gallery or being a lecturer on artistic subjects.

Most Librans may not be creative artists, but you can be sure that they have turned public relations into an art form. They are popular, well-liked by everyone, avid party-goers and are always to be seen at social events attended by the rich or well-known. Librans often choose careers in public relations, or in some other field requiring close contact with the public.

Unfortunately, there is one type of Libran whose strong urge to be popular turns what should be a strength into a weakness. These people need to fit in with all kinds of people — sometimes, at almost any price. If, for instance, they meet some people who want to sniff cocaine, these Librans will join in, even if personally they are turned off by drugs and their only 'trip' is to the bathroom to throw up. For them, the important thing is to be 'in' — the idea of being 'out' is unendurable to them.

Librans are often known for their indecisiveness. The Scales keep tipping one way and another, and they can't seem to come to any decision. To be or not to be? (Obviously Hamlet was a Libran!) They keep wavering: tea or coffee? According to an old joke, the late Israeli Premier, Levi Eshkol (a typical Libran) solved that dilemma by ordering half and half! But, as a rule, the most that these unsure Librans are willing to do is to decide not to decide. They'd rather let someone else make the decision for them.

These people are very gentle, always worrying about hurting other people's feelings and creating unpleasant situations. But sometimes it is this very gentleness of theirs which causes the problems in the first place. They find it hard to give a definite 'no' to anyone, and they may complicate their lives as a result, getting themselves into hot water and confusing the other person, simply because they haven't made their position clear.

Despite the Libran gentleness and sympathetic understanding of other people and their problems, the Scales is not a particularly sensitive sign. Libra is the only sign in the zodiac symbolized by an inanimate object and, like the scales in their sign, Librans are well-balanced and even-handed. Yet some people claim that behind their veneer of poise, friendliness and politeness they are really cold and calculating. Indeed, there are some Librans who can be the most charming and amusing friends in the world when everything's going well but who, at the first hint of trouble, simply vanish into thin air. These fair-weather friends are like prettily-wrapped packages, done up with lots of ribbons and decorations, but which contain nothing but air — the element to which this sign belongs.

Venus, the planet of beauty and love, bestows great beauty on those who have Libra as their Ascendant. Nature has given the daughters of Venus all the characteristics necessary for beauty: a well-proportioned body, an oval face and lovely, delicate features, as well as dimpled cheeks. The female Libran tries to make her home a true love nest, creating a pleasant and cultured atmosphere. She is a first-rate homemaker and, even though she takes regular breaks to rest and relax, her excellent sense of timing and organizational abilities enable her to get as much housework done as three other women — and she does it efficiently and without fuss. With fairy-like lightness she glides from one household task to another, and with a wave of her magic wand creates order out of chaos and harmony out of confusion wherever she goes. She's perfectly co-ordinated, physically as well as mentally, and would never clumsily spill anything. She has a wonderful sense of timing and can cook several dishes at the same time without letting anything burn or boil over. There is always a well-balanced and varied menu, and she likes to serve something different every day. Her dishes are never too spicy, too salty or too sweet. She knows the golden mean and, as a woman who sees the role of wife as her mission in life, she will choose the path that leads to a golden wedding anniversary. The role of a married woman was made to order for the Libran female, and her husband knows how to appreciate her virtues. On the other hand, there are some Libran women who fear that motherhood won't agree with their slender figures, and many of them are unable to breast-feed their babies. This type of woman feels that her husband is the sun around which she revolves, and he will always overshadow their children in her affections. There are some people — men and women alike — born with this sign rising who find the role of a parent a difficult one: those Libran scales are built to handle only featherweights, and it is very hard for them to bear the responsibilities and self-sacrifice which raising children entails. They love to lean on other people, but find it rather difficult to be props themselves.

Usually, the Libran man is good-looking and has a highly-developed sense of dress. He likes the company of beautiful women and enjoys impressing them with his stylish clothes and flamboyant manners. For example, I know one Libran man who, when offering a woman a light, pulls his lighter out of his inside pocket with an elaborate gesture, which shows off his jacket's elegant crimson lining to perfection. Although most

Libran men are very popular with women and like to flirt, they are also rather vulnerable and fear rejection. Libran men will, therefore, never court a girl seriously unless she's given them the green light. She has to drop her handkerchief first — preferably a lace-edged, silk one. Not only are these men unable to bear hearing the word 'no', they can't even utter it themselves — and many women have taken advantage of this to drag these men to the altar.

Once married, even the most faithful Libran husband usually flirts with other women. He doesn't really mean anything by it, he simply can't resist beauty in general, and the charms of the female sex in particular. These flirtations are always lighthearted, with no obligations — on his side, at least. So, he doesn't feel any sense of remorse, nor does he let these flirtations go to his head like champagne. Over-indulgence in the real bubbly, however, may cause him health problems, because the sensitive body areas for both male and female Librans are the kidneys.

FAMOUS PEOPLE BORN UNDER LIBRA

LIBRA AS THE ASCENDANT

Jimmy Carter (Sun sign Libra)
Dwight D Eisenhower (Sun sign Aries)
Uri Geller (Sun sign Sagittarius)
John F Kennedy (Sun sign Gemini)
Ali Khan (Sun sign Gemini)
Arthur Miller (Sun sign Libra)
Louis Pasteur (Sun sign Capricorn)
Albert Schweitzer (Sun sign Capricorn)
Rod Stewart (Sun sign Capricorn)
Elizabeth Taylor (Sun sign Pisces)
Harry S Truman (Sun sign Taurus)

LIBRA AS THE SUN SIGN

Brigitte Bardot (Ascendant Sagittarius)
Jimmy Carter (Ascendant Libra)
F Scott Fitzgerald (Ascendant Aquarius)
Mahatma Gandhi (Ascendant Libra or Scorpio)
John Lennon (Ascendant Libra)
Roger Moore (Ascendant Leo)
Friedrich Nietzsche (Ascendant Scorpio)
Juan Perón (Ascendant Scorpio)
Margaret Thatcher (Ascendant Scorpio)
Giuseppe Verdi (Ascendant Gemini)
Oscar Wilde (Ascendant Virgo)

and the following people whose Ascendants are unknown: Julie Andrews, David Ben Gurion, Levi Eshkol, Graham Greene, Rita Hayworth, Lord Nelson, Shirley Temple

SCORPIO — THE SCORPION

Symbol — This sign has two symbols, a Scorpion (sometimes a snake) and an Eagle

Ruling planets — Pluto, the planet of depths and regeneration, and Mars, the planet of war

Element — Water

Quality — Fixed

Anatomical areas under Scorpio's influence — The reproductive organs

Polar sign — Taurus

By nature passionate creatures, the uncompromising personalities of Scorpios are much given to extremes. These people don't do anything by halves, and they are either wholly good or wholly evil — never average, ordinary, lukewarm, watered-down or temperate. It's no coincidence that this is the only sign which has been given two symbols: the Eagle, symbolizing the higher type, and the Scorpion (sometimes a snake instead), which represents the insidious, poisonous members of this sign.

While Taurus, Scorpio's polar sign, stands for the good, fertile earth and pastoral serenity, Scorpio symbolizes all that is hidden under the surface — subterranean caverns, and depths of unplumbed passions. And, in contrast to Taureans, who are content as long as their grass is green, Scorpios don't accept anything at face value, and won't be content until they discover what goes on beneath the surface. As befits those whose ruling planet is Pluto, the planet of abysses and depths, Scorpios go right down to the very bottom in their attempts to reveal the truth. They will leave no stone unturned in their unrelenting search, yet the truth they finally do expose is not always agreeable. (Turn a stone over, and you might well be confronted by a seething nest of scorpions.) But these people prefer the truth — bitter as it may be — to any illusion. They will almost invariably choose the harder path, one which is strewn with brambles rather than rose petals. But Scorpios, who see themselves as warriors, accept all this stoically, as something inevitable that life serves up, and which one has to accept with dignity. Therefore, even though Scorpio is one of the Fixed signs — thus denoting a great need for stability — the lives of people born under this sign are rarely peaceful, and they often find themselves at the centre of storms and subject to crises. Entire periods of their lives may end with a bang, but they pick themselves up, dust themselves off and start all over again. In this, they resemble the phoenix, the fabled bird that rose from its own ashes.

Nothing but sheer perfection is good enough for Scorpios. Things have to be absolutely faultless, or they'll be torn down and rebuilt from scratch. They don't whitewash the cracks or sweep anything under the carpet, and this holds true in even the most prosaic, everyday details. A Scorpio child may one day discover that the paint is peeling in one of the furthest reaches of the house. (Don't worry, they'll find it! Nothing escapes the Scorpio's spying eye.) True Scorpios won't rest until they've peeled down all the paint from that wall: this is an irresistible, internal urge which no parental scolding can restrain. And so, exposing an inch here and an inch there, this child will soon uncover the wall of its treacherous, superficial paint.

In their search for truth, Scorpios don't burrow only in the affairs of others: they are equally relentless with themselves, and their search for self-knowledge is unending. More so than any other sign, Scorpios are aware of the dark and hidden side of man's nature, and of the seething cauldron of urges and passions that boil in their own subconscious. As well as Pluto, Mars, the planet of war, is Scorpio's ruling planet. The combination of combative Mars with Scorpio's sensitive Water element produces constant emotional strife. It is as if the souls of Scorpios were battlefields where good and evil engage in eternal combat, where the decisive battle between the Sons of Light and the Sons of Darkness will take place. Positive Scorpios, represented by the Eagle, succeed in raising themselves above their baser desires and can soar to great heights. But there are also those children of Pluto (the planet named for the ruler of the mythological underworld) who give in to temptation, sell their souls to the devil and plunge into the depths of sin. These people can fall to the very bottom of the abyss, until the only way open to them is the way up. From the depths of the abyss, they call out for help from on high, but the way to salvation is fraught with difficulties, as though the devil himself were standing in the way of those newly repentant, waiting to ensnare them in his net again by setting every conceivable temptation, trap and stumbling block in their way.

The emotional lives of Scorpios can be so intense that even if you greatly diluted them, they'd still be too strong. Scorpios embody a strange duality: despite being introverted, even secretive, they have an almost compulsive desire to confess, indulging in Dostoyevsky-like confessions, breast-beating and verbal self-flagellation. Many Scorpios feel the need to reveal the most intimate experiences, usually in writing. They have to let off some steam, to relieve the incredible pressures building up in the boiling cauldrons of their inner lives. Anyone who believes that a Scorpio has wholly revealed himself, and can now be read like an open book, is sadly mistaken. Scorpios always hide more than they show: as with an iceberg, much more lies under the surface than meets the eye.

Despite the fact that they conceal certain aspects of their lives — even going so far as to bury them completely underground — in their professional lives, Scorpios are hardly shy or diffident. As a result, many Scorpios are in a dilemma: their desire for privacy tugs them one way, while their career, which often puts them in the limelight, pulls them in the opposite direction. People whose rising sign is Scorpio are usually outstanding members of their professions and end up taking centre stage, while those whose Sun sign is Scorpio are mostly attracted to the performing arts, the worlds of entertainment and show business. People running nightspots usually have the Sun in Scorpio — in nature, the scorpion is greatly attracted to lowdown dives!

Much has been said of Scorpio's deadly nature, lying in wait ready to strike the intended victim. Indeed, there are some Scorpios who make J R Ewing (the power-hungry, vengeful character in the American television series *Dallas*) look as harmless as a pussycat. The poisonous side of Scorpio's nature is most likely to emerge when the Sun is in this sign, towards the end of October and in early November. But not all Scorpios are poisonous by any means. I know at least three Sun sign Scorpios whom I wouldn't trade in for anyone else. (Scorpio is extreme in good as well as evil.) Always remember that our characters are symbolized by our Sun signs, whereas our Ascendants or rising signs express themselves to a great degree through events and circumstances. So, when Scorpio is the rising sign, its poisonous sting is often externalized, and expresses itself in chance circumstance rather than through character. What's more, many of those with Scorpio Ascendants are sometimes even rather naïve. Yes, strange as it sounds, there are indeed such creatures as naïve Scorpios.

Margaret Thatcher's Ascendant sign – Scorpio – reflects the strong character and determination of Britain's Prime Minister, the 'Iron Lady'. Incidentally, iron is ruled by Mars, one of the rulers of Scorpio.

Another Scorpion 'strongwoman' was Indira Gandhi – the late Prime Minister of India (Sun sign Scorpio). If Margaret Thatcher is the 'Iron Lady', Indira was undoubtedly the 'Steel Lady' – steel being ruled by Pluto, one of the two rulers of Scorpio.

And the more naïve, the more poisonous the circumstances they are likely to encounter. For example, the only 'dangerous' element in a young girl whose rising sign is Scorpio may be her sex appeal. Yet what trouble it can cause her! The very air around her may seethe with jealousy, plots and malicious gossip, compared to which the serpent's hiss sounds friendly. Even her mother's rather mature lady friends will scheme to snatch her school-boy sweetheart from her. It will seem as though the stocks and bonds of any suitor of hers skyrocket, with the women's market registering 'Buyers only'. Getting him is a real challenge, and they don't sit about idly waiting for him to fall into their laps like a ripe fruit. Instead, they stir their witches' brew, concocting all kinds of poisons for her, and love potions for him. Pretending to be well-intentioned friends, they try to poison her mind against him. They also make every possible attempt, by resorting to all kinds of wiles, to lure him into their beds. All the infamous Scorpio traits — insatiable sexual appetite, jealousy, intrigue, plots, sub-plots and venomous hate — are exposed here in all their ugliness, not in the character of the girl with the Scorpio Ascendant, but in the circumstances surrounding her.

This sinister aspect of Scorpio is admirably illustrated in the two fairy tales, *Snow White and the Seven Dwarfs* and *Sleeping Beauty*, in which evil women attempt to destroy the young innocent heroines. In *Snow White*, the poisoned apple symbolizes Scorpio's venom, while the poison-tipped spindle in *Sleeping Beauty* represents its sting. But don't worry. As in the fairy tales, naïve Scorpio girls finally awaken from their sleep, usually before a hundred years have gone by, although not to the chime of wedding bells, but rather to a ringing slap in the face. The rescuing prince, whose kiss puts an end to innocent slumber, is in reality Scorpio's own psychological insight, awakening at long last. Even the most innocent Scorpios have this gift, which gives them an insight into their enemies' deepest, darkest motives, and thus can save themselves — sometimes at the very last minute.

However, most Scorpios are far from having been born yesterday and their keen insight is honed to a sharp edge, enabling them to see through smoke screens and masks. Their still waters run deep indeed, uncovering the hidden motives and secret niches of the mind. Not surprisingly, Sigmund Freud, the father of psychoanalysis, had Scorpio as his rising sign. But the better the Scorpio understands his or her fellow men, the more difficult it is (for even the most observant Scorpio-watchers) to understand the Scorpio. After all, they are adept at concealing their motives and feelings. Thus they keep a tight lid on their seething emotions, steadily growing hot under the collar, until they finally explode with rage. Unfortunately, they make no warning sounds before they strike, nor do they attack immediately. If they're hurt or abused, they may decide it was an accident, and see if it happens again. Their initial lack of response doesn't act as a warning, so people may repeat their mistakes, for few pass the Scorpio test. They can appear to be a victim time and time again, and just when the unsuspecting perpetrator feels they've got away with it, the Scorpio will strike with sudden, swift and deadly accuracy.

Scorpios don't bark, they simply bite!

The willpower and self-control of these people is extraordinary, and they will determinedly carry on in the face of the most adverse conditions. They never lose sight of their goals, and achieve their objectives in spite of any obstacles and setbacks that are in their way. Their spiritual fortitude becomes most apparent under pressure — they are ready to go through hell or high water for a person or cause they are wholly devoted to, risking their own lives if necessary. Dauntless Scorpios seem to be made of steel, the metal associated with their ruling planet, Pluto. Their other ruling planet, Mars, the planet of war, is connected with iron. But while iron rusts, enduring stainless steel best symbolizes the mental and spiritual strength of this sign.

Scorpios rely on their abilities to such an extent that they are often unaware of their limits — or that they have any at all. When they devote themselves to a cause they do so wholeheartedly, never resting till the task is completed. They won't desert their posts, convinced that they are irreplaceable. As a result, they are very reluctant to delegate their authority, and prefer to carry the burden of decision alone, while pushing themselves far beyond the point of exhaustion. Luckily for them, their powers of recovery are remarkable and they are soon on their feet again. The trouble is that they never learn from experience, and as soon as they're up and about, they allow themselves to be swept away by a new idea or job — and they're back at square one.

The activities of cold-blooded reptiles slow down during the winter, and it's the same with Scorpios. In spite of their legendary Stainless Steel Stamina, their life forces seem to wither in the winter, especially if they have passed the spring and summer of their lives. As the years go by, Scorpios increasingly feel the need for sun and warmth. They drink them in greedily, like an iguana sprawled out on some rocks absorbing every last ray of the setting sun.

Extremists by nature, Scorpios are especially so when it comes to cleanliness. Some of them scrub and scour every hidden nook and cranny, as though their cleaning were an act of spiritual purification. But not all Scorpios are compulsive cleaners — in fact, some of them seem to suffer from hydrophobia, running away from soap and water like a vampire fleeing from garlic!

I have already compared the sign of Scorpio to an iceberg, the most dangerous parts of which are all underwater, and scheming and plotting are indeed characteristic of the negative Scorpios who delight in intrigue and subterfuge, stirring up trouble and wallowing in the mud. These venomous Scorpios are subtler than the proverbial snake and, like him, will crawl on their bellies, fawning and grovelling, to achieve their despicable ends. They are jealous, coveting their neighbour's house, home and spouse. A Scorpio woman of this type is likely to become involved with married men, men who 'belong' to other women, making her conquest all the more delicious — stolen apples taste so much sweeter!

Magnetism is the reason so many people are attracted to Scorpios. No one can remain indifferent to Scorpios who are either the object of great love and intense admiration or, less frequently, the target of unbridled hate. There is something bewitchingly fatal about this sign as far as the opposite sex is concerned. Many fall victim to Scorpio's magnetic attraction, getting ensnared in the net of their complicated personalities, sinking deeper and deeper into the turmoil of their being. Some never come up for air . . .

But they don't just attract members of the opposite sex. Strange as it may sound, Scorpio draws to itself property and money too. Pluto, ruler of the underworld and subterranean riches, represents fabulous wealth. But unlike Leos, who tend to indulge in *la dolce vita*, whatever the cost, Scorpios prefer to lead spartan lives. The greatest delight that their money affords them is the feeling of power inherent in their wealth.

There's a trace of the exotic in these people's appearances, and their slightly slanted eyes and Sphinx-like expressions evoke the mysterious East. In many cases, the jawline is square and wide, and the nose unusual — pointing off-centre, being otherwise asymmetric, or marked by a mole, scar or other identifying feature. Quite a few Scorpios are thickset, yet some Scorpio women are slight and delicate to the point of fragility, and move with sinuous grace. Both sexes have deep, somewhat husky voices, the women sounding like snakes gliding softly over rustling autumn leaves. Scorpios have a tendency to hoarseness, since the influence of their polar sign, Taurus, gives them sensitive throats. But, as befits this sign's secretive nature, the sensitive parts of Scorpios are private indeed — the private parts!

FAMOUS PEOPLE BORN UNDER SCORPIO

SCORPIO AS THE ASCENDANT

Emily Brontë (Sun sign Leo)
Maria Callas (Sun sign Sagittarius)
Paul Cézanne (Sun sign Capricorn)
Marc Chagall (Sun sign Cancer)
Charlie Chaplin (Sun sign Aries)
James Dean (Sun sign Aquarius)
Clint Eastwood (Sun sign Gemini)
Thomas Alva Edison (Sun sign Aquarius)
Gustave Flaubert (Sun sign Sagittarius)
Henry Ford (Sun sign Leo)
Sigmund Freud (Sun sign Taurus)
Johann von Goethe (Sun sign Virgo)
Victor Hugo (Sun sign Pisces)
John Milton (Sun sign Sagittarius)
Benito Mussolini (Sun sign Leo)
Friedrich Nietzsche (Sun sign Libra)
Alfred Nobel (Sun sign Scorpio)
Jacqueline Kennedy Onassis (Sun sign Leo)
Juan Peron (Sun sign Libra)
Edith Piaf (Sun sign Sagittarius)
Edgar Allen Poe (Sun sign Capricorn)
Raphael (Sun sign Aries)
Ronald Reagan (Sun sign Aquarius)
Jean-Paul Sartre (Sun sign Gemini)
Rudolph Steiner (Sun sign Pisces)
Stendhal (Sun sign Aquarius)
Margaret Thatcher (Sun sign Libra)
Henri de Toulouse-Lautrec (Sun sign Sagittarius)

SCORPIO AS THE SUN SIGN

Charles Bronson (Ascendant Cancer)
Richard Burton (Ascendant Cancer)
Richard Byrd (Ascendant Capricorn)
Albert Camus (Ascendant Virgo)
Marie Curie (Ascendant Cancer)
Feodor Dostoyevsky (Ascendant Sagittarius)
Indira Gandhi (Ascendant Leo)
Grace Kelly (Ascendant Aquarius)
Martin Luther (Ascendant Leo)
André Malraux (Ascendant Aries)
Alfred Nobel (Ascendant Scorpio)
Pablo Picasso (Ascendant Leo)
Auguste Rodin (Ascendant Capricorn)
Erwin Rommel (Ascendant Capricorn)
Jonas Salk (Ascendant Capricorn)
Robert Louis Stevenson (Ascendant Aquarius)
The Prince of Wales (Ascendant Leo)

and the following people whose Ascendants are unknown: Georges Bizet, Charles de Gaulle, Chiang Kai-shek, Robert Kennedy, Theodore Roosevelt, Friedrich von Schiller, Leon Trotsky, François Voltaire

SAGITTARIUS — THE ARCHER

Symbol — The Centaur, a mythological figure of a half-horse, half man

Ruling planet — Jupiter, the planet of abundance and expansion

Element — Fire

Quality — Mutable

Anatomical area under Sagittarius' influence — The pelvis and lower vertebrae

Polar sign — Gemini

Luck often seems to follow Sagittarians wherever they go, which is hardly surprising when you consider that they are ruled by Jupiter, the planet of good fortune. People who are lucky enough to be born under this sign are brimming over with vitality, optimism and the joy of living. The horse in the Archer's symbol implies that Sagittarians are born to be free, and freedom and the wide, open spaces are as vital to them as the air they breathe. Sagittarians won't easily agree to being harnessed in any way and, as in a rodeo, people who try to ride them will have to be good enough sports to put up with the Archer's tendency to fling them off the saddle and bolt away. The only way to tame Sagittarians is to snare them with lassos which are long enough to let them gallop off, and sometimes even graze in distant fields. A typical Sagittarian believes that the further the pasture, the greener it is.

Adventure is the spice of life for these people. Their roaming spirits wander far and wide. The Sagittarian motto, 'The further the better', is best seen in their attraction to far-away places and people of foreign extraction, nationalities or different faiths. Their lives revolve around travel to such an extent that they refer to fateful events in their lives as having occurred 'two months after I came back from India', or they'll say 'I met him about a year before my walking tour of America.' Archers love change and adapt quickly to new places, people and circumstances. In fact, there's something of the gypsy about them, as they wander from place to place, job to job, and from love to love. Feeling fenced in by the very idea of marriage, they do their best to avoid it, or at least put it off for as long as possible!

Even the stork finds it difficult to track Archers down, and often visits people with Sagittarius rising when they are nearing thirty. But even bringing a child into the world (the stork usually catches up with them only once) doesn't necessarily turn the merry Archer into a family man or woman. Very often, they simply hand over the care of the child to others, so that they can continue to enjoy their freedom unhampered. After all, life has so much in store, and these people haven't even begun to exhaust all the delights it has to offer. Even though they become parents at a relatively mature age, Sagittarians still feel like children who haven't played enough. And they know how to be happy, joyful and high-spirited, as only children can be — their laughter often echoing the neighing of horses. Didn't someone say that life wasn't a picnic? Well, whoever it was, they should know that Sagittarians don't agree one bit!

Typical Archers are believers, and have faith in the future and in themselves. They gallop ahead, seeking challenges, and even though they may sometimes stumble and fall, they won't let such bumps trouble their spirits or hinder their progress, and in a relatively short time they'll be riding high again. There must be some truth in the belief that a horseshoe brings luck — remember that Archers have four of them!

Intuition and foresight are two of the gifts with which Sagittarians are blessed. The gypsy in their souls has no need of a crystal ball and, even without laying out the cards, knows that life has dealt them a winning hand. Remembering that 'no one is a prophet in his own land', Archers wander far and wide seeking their fortunes — and they usually find them. They succeed thanks to their intuition, good judgement, imagination and vision. And who said that vision and success don't go together? The spiritual and the worldly blend harmoniously in these people, like the bow-shaped line of the horizon, where earth and sky meet. It takes a visionary like Walt Disney, who had the Sun in Sagittarius, to turn the fairytale world of childhood into the reality called Disneyland. His success was due not only to his enormous talents, but also to his Sagittarian love of animals: his great empire had its beginnings in his kindness to a little mouse with whom, as a penniless young student, he shared his room and meagre meals. The mouse, whom he named Mickey, repaid young Disney handsomely for the cheese and sympathy by becoming his inspiration for Mickey Mouse.

Sagittarius is also the sign associated with spirituality and philosophy. Even rather simple, uneducated Archers have relatively wide horizons and a certain philosophical attitude to life. The horizons of Sagittarians are broadened not only by actual travel, but by flights of fancy as well. An unusual mixture of animal vitality (the horse in the sign's symbol) and spiritual aspiration (the Archer aiming his bow at the heavens), Sagittarians are a constant source of surprise to those who find it hard to believe that the very same sportsman who is the life and soul of every party, while not being above engaging in horseplay and childish pranks, has a doctorate in law or philosophy. The lively, outgoing personalities of Sagittarians are in stark contrast to the popular image of intellectuals as boring and sickly bookworms.

Their cheerful, generous natures make Sagittarians very popular. But the secret of their popularity lies also in the fact that there is never a dull moment when they're around, and there's a feeling of 'Join the Archer and see the world' about them. It's as though Archers were bearing the horn of plenty, while those around them enjoy the overflowing surplus. A Sagittarian girl, for example, is usually very popular with men who, attracted by her gaiety, amiability and love of life, swarm around her like bees round a honey pot. Needless to say, she will gladly donate the surplus to her less popular girlfriends. Archers are perhaps the most friendly of all the signs, always willing to help a friend in need, sometimes even at risk to themselves. One Sagittarian acquaintance of mine, upon learning that a friend of his was afraid to take his maths exam, offered at once to take the exam in his stead. He presented his friend's identity card at the entrance of the examination hall and, although any resemblance between him and the picture on the card was purely coincidental, his Sagittarian luck saw to it that he wasn't caught, and managed to pass the exam with flying colours. Archers are lucky at the gaming tables too, although Lady Luck may one day turn against them.

The families of Sagittarians are often heard to complain that the Archers are willing to do more for their friends than they are for their own flesh and blood. And they could be right, because Sagittarians do tend to prefer friendship to family ties. After all, they're free to choose their friends — and they believe wholeheartedly in freedom of choice. On the other hand, they weren't free to choose their nearest and dearest, and

Love of animals, a natural appearance, wind-blown hair – all are characteristic of Sagittarius, Brigitte Bardot's Ascendant sign. Jane Fonda is also a famous Sagittarian. But the two stars have another lucky star in common – both were discovered by the French director Roger Vadim and subsequently married and divorced him.

Jane Fonda's highly developed sense of justice – so characteristic of her Sun sign, Sagittarius – inspired her to go to Vietnam in order to alleviate the suffering of the Vietnamese. This politically orientated actress recently won fame as the bestselling author of health and exercise books – physical culture, incidentally, is typically Sagittarian.

quite often feel like strangers among them.

Claustrophobia often plagues people with Sagittarius rising. Many of them find themselves in constant conflict between their desire to travel and their terror at being confined to a small space on a boat or plane. Even being in a closed room or lift makes them feel suffocated, and some can have problems breathing. Typical Sagittarians insist on sleeping close to an open window in all weathers, so as to ensure plenty of fresh air, and a Sagittarian friend of mine has been known to wake up in the middle of the night buried under a blanket of snow!

Even the negative Sagittarian traits spring from overactive good natures and unbounding optimism, which is sometimes not so much imprudent as completely unbridled. Overflowing with goodwill, Archers try to help all and sundry, taking upon themselves more than they can cope with. But their wild optimism and bonhomie are quite often justified, and they succeed in helping their friends in need, putting them back in the saddle again.

Despite their highly-developed sense of justice (or perhaps because of it), a certain type of Sagittarian tends to break the law, especially when

The uniquely Sagittarian blend of imagination, vision and inspiration characterizes the personality of Walt Disney (Sun sign Sagittarius), who brought children's fables to life, first in his films and then in his most fabulous creation – Disneyland.

The vision and inspiration of Sagittarius found expression in the uncanny intuition of Benjamin Disraeli, novelist, statesman and Prime Minister who shrewdly acquired shares in the Suez Canal for Britain. Disraeli was a 'double' Sagittarian – both his Sun and his Ascendant signs were in Sagittarius.

they believe that justice is on their side. These people have a Robin Hood complex. (Robin Hood, by the way, must have been born under the sign of the Archer — remember his expertise with a bow and arrow?) In less idealistic cases, it is the Sagittarian sense of adventure and thirst for new experiences which makes them gallop past the sign reading 'Stop! Danger ahead'. These people may even welcome a jail sentence as a rather interesting experience, but only if it's going to be a short one — Archers do worship their freedom. Like those born under Gemini, their polar sign, Archers are rather loquacious. But, unlike Geminis whose glib tongues will get them out of the trickiest situations, Sagittarians' tongues usually trip them up. One of their biggest stumbling blocks is their frankness, because they believe in putting all their cards on the table. They do whatever they feel like and say whatever crosses their minds, acting on the spur of the moment. They're proud of their frankness, which they feel proves what splendid and decent people they are. However, such sentiments aren't always shared by others, who may feel that the Archers should learn to bridle their tongues, or even, at times, muzzle their big mouths! Not that they bite (they're much too easy-going for that), but they bark too much, being often unnecessarily offensive. But even this unpleasant trait doesn't spring from malice: they're only saying what's true, and don't see how anyone can find fault with that.

Impulsiveness is another trait which can plunge Sagittarians into embarrassing situations, like the girl who happily informed her colleagues at work, 'You won't be seeing me for much longer in this stifling office — I'm going to marry a millionaire!' The only problem was that before announcing the glad tidings, she had forgotten to check one small detail — whether the man in question was serious or not. As it turned out, he wasn't, and she felt too humiliated to face all her colleagues again. But letting their mouths run away with them isn't the only problem that Archers have — some of them stutter, lisp or have some other peculiarity of speech. Even that past-master of rhetoric, Sir Winston Churchill (Sun in Sagittarius), spoke as though he had pebbles in his mouth. Archers express themselves in a very free, idiomatic way, full of the latest slang. Some of them also have the irritating habit of latching on to a silly saying, such as 'It's fantastic, absolutely elastic!' and using it every few minutes.

There's something about the typical Sagittarian that's evocative of a fresh breeze. These people have tall, lithe bodies, sunny expressions and there is a youthful aura about them. Sagittarian women wear their hair long and windblown, although Sagittarian men tend to go bald relatively early. But in their youth, male Archers let a lock of hair fall over their foreheads, and will shake it back with a toss of their heads, like spirited colts. Both the male and female Archers prefer to wear their shirts open, since a buttoned collar makes them feel suffocated. When it comes to their appearances, they often have the air of a pure-bred horse. Most of them have high foreheads and fairly long, straight but slightly arched noses. 'Abundance' is a Sagittarian byword, and some Archers are living examples of this, since their abundant love of food and drink leads them to become overweight.

The vulnerable parts of the Sagittarian body are the lower vertebrae — the very part of the centaur at which the human torso grows out of the horse's body . . .

FAMOUS PEOPLE BORN UNDER SAGITTARIUS

SAGITTARIUS AS THE ASCENDANT

Hans Christian Andersen (Sun sign Aries)
Brigitte Bardot (Sun sign Libra)
Marlon Brando (Sun sign Aries)
Lewis Carroll (Sun sign Aquarius)
Neville Chamberlain (Sun sign Pisces)
Charles Darwin (Sun sign Aquarius)
Bette Davis (Sun sign Aries)
Feodor Dostoyevsky (Sun sign Scorpio)
Paul Getty (Sun sign Capricorn)
Robert Graves (Sun sign Leo)
Katharine Hepburn (Sun sign Scorpio)
Herman Hesse (Sun sign Cancer)
Rock Hudson (Sun sign Scorpio)
Charles Lindbergh (Sun sign Aquarius)
Roman Polanski (Sun sign Leo)
Erich Maria Remarque (Sun sign Cancer)
Leonardo da Vinci (Sun sign Taurus)
The Princess of Wales (Sun sign Cancer)
Raquel Welch (Sun sign Virgo)
Emile Zola (Sun sign Aries)

SAGITTARIUS AS THE SUN SIGN

Jane Austen (Ascendant Virgo)
Ludwig van Beethoven (Ascendant Taurus)
William Blake (Ascendant Cancer)
Willy Brandt (Ascendant Aries)
Maria Callas (Ascendant Scorpio)
Sir Winston Churchill (Ascendant Leo)
Joseph Conrad (Ascendant Gemini)
Walt Disney (Ascendant Virgo)
Gustave Flaubert (Ascendant Scorpio)
Uri Geller (Ascendant Libra)
John Milton (Ascendant Scorpio)
Edith Piaf (Ascendant Scorpio)
Reine Maria Rilke (Ascendant Cancer)
Georges Seurat (Ascendant Virgo)
Frank Sinatra (Ascendant Aries)
Alexander Solzhenitsyn (Ascendant Aquarius)
Henri de Toulouse-Lautrec (Ascendant Scorpio)

CAPRICORN — THE MOUNTAIN GOAT

Symbol — The Mountain Goat

Ruling planet — Saturn, the planet of limitation

Element — Earth

Quality — Cardinal

Anatomical area under Capricorn's influence — The knees

Polar sign — Cancer

The last of the three Earth signs, Capricorn is also possibly the most materialistic. Rational and realistic, Capricorns are well aware — more so than anyone else — of limitations and restrictions, and this creates in them a strong need for security and safety. Capricorn's polar sign, Cancer, shows the same craving. But while a Cancerian's idea of safety is to take refuge in the family nest and within their own four walls, Capricorns, who are more aware of the outside world, are busy erecting a thick wall meant to protect them from that world. People born under Capricorn spend their entire lives building and fortifying their strongholds and their positions, while every new accomplishment represents another layer of stones in their fortresses. An enduring ambition for more and greater achievements, position and respect are the most outstanding Capricorn characteristics. Practical and clear-eyed Capricorns see things as they are, and calculate accordingly; they aren't people who indulge themselves in daydreams. On the contrary, their expectations are firmly rooted in reality, and they expect to go far!

The summit holds a special fascination for Capricorns, who know no fear of heights, in all senses of the word. Appropriately enough, the symbol of this sign is the Mountain Goat, and as far as the Goat is concerned, life is one long struggle to the peak. But it's not that simple, because Capricorn's ruler, Saturn, the planet of restrictions and limitations, prevents their rapid rise to the top. At the start of the race, Capricorns are not among those out in front. Their progress through life is fraught with difficulties and stumbling blocks, but by virtue of hard work, perseverance, patience and circumspection, they often manage, slowly but surely, to reach that yearned-for summit.

'All beginnings are difficult' is a phrase that has particular relevance for this sign. Many Capricorns are weak and sickly early in life, looking much older than their years suggest. But time is kind to them, and the older they get, the more likely they are to succeed. Young, vulnerable kids who mature into goats are more self-confident, since experience has taught them that they really can rely on themselves. Their health improves, and their Capricorn seriousness is tempered with a delightfully ironic sense of humour, as subtle and dry as a smooth Scotch (a drink beloved of

Capricorns, by the way!). By the time they reach their forties, Capricorns who have always looked older than they really are, will have begun, for the first time in their lives, to look their age. And from then on, the older they get, the younger they look. Capricorns, like good wine, definitely improve with age!

Speaking of wine, many Goats are fond of alcohol, especially if, for one reason or another, they aren't lucky enough to be able to get drunk on that heady mountain air. And there are those Capricorns who manage to reach their coveted, snow-covered pinnacle only to find it a forbiddingly cold, isolated and lonely place. These people hold a pessimistic view of life, which they call simple, clear-eyed realism. For example, they always describe their whisky glasses as being half-empty, never half-full!

Like a grandfather clock ticking away the minutes and chiming out the hours, Capricorns are intensely aware of the inexorable march of time. They're constantly thinking about how old they are, and worrying about the possible advantages held by their younger competitors in the race to the top. Fear that the sand in the hourglass is running out intensifies their over-achieving and ambitious approach. Their awareness of time can also be seen in their deep-rooted feelings for the past and for their heritage. They appreciate the conservative aspects of religion, tradition and ceremonies, which go very well with their need for security and stability. They're also capable of learning from the past, and aren't likely to repeat old mistakes. But Capricorns don't find only their own pasts instructive — they are always willing to accept advice from older people, as they respect their rich experience of life. This is a very conservative sign, and Capricorns are wary of anything new-fangled. They're perfectly content to tread the safe, beaten track, because for a mountain climber, the smallest stumble could prove fatal. Typical Capricorns are neither very brilliant nor astoundingly original — instead, their strength lies in their wise and reasonable attitude.

Well aware of strictures and limitations, Capricorns are always careful never to cross the invisible red line. Everything they do stays firmly within the bounds of good taste, and everything is done in its proper proportions, carefully measured and calculated to the last drop. These people are never wasteful, never spendthrifts. They don't gamble, and place no trust in sudden windfalls. (All those jokes about mean Scotsmen could easily be applied to careful Capricorns!) They also save their breath, speaking only after some deliberation, and then with just a few well-chosen words. (Capricorns whose horoscopes are strongly influenced by Gemini or Sagittarius may be slightly looser-lipped.) They don't pledge themselves to grandiose things, but when they do promise something, they deliver. Compliments are far from two-a-penny with these people, either, and to be on the receiving end of a Capricorn's appreciation is a rare and honoured privilege indeed! Responsibility and duty are the cornerstones of their existences, and they won't abandon them even in the face of the most attractive alternatives. A positive Capricorn is a person of unusually tough inner fibre, as though their core were weighted down by a heavy load. Small wonder, then, that lead, one of the heaviest metals, is associated with this sign. Such a Capricorn arouses admiration and respect, and is a rare find indeed.

The sign of Capricorn represents status and duty — *noblesse oblige*. Very often, people with Capricorn rising are scions of titled aristocrats or of a strictly religious family, who feel that their fulfilment as human beings is superseded by a code of ethics dictated by the family's status. From an early age, they have been aware of the expectations and the load of duty and responsibility soon to be placed upon them by their heritage. Despite receiving this heavy burden of duty while still young, they will continue to bear it stoically, because they have great appreciation of their heritage and want to enjoy the many advantages that their status will ultimately bestow on them. Capricorns are loyal to their family names, and would never dream of changing their surnames, even if it would be to their advantage to do so in certain circumstances. Their respect for their elders, as well as their ancestors, wouldn't allow them to do such a treacherous thing, and they will continue to bear the name proudly.

Status and class are very important to Capricorns. They look up to people in high positions and act in appropriately humble ways when they

The serious and responsible personality of Queen Elizabeth II is characteristic of Capricorn, her Ascendant sign. From childhood she was aware of her burden of duty as the future Queen of England.

Richard Byrd (Ascendant sign Capricorn) was the foremost antarctic explorer of his day and the first man to fly over the Arctic Circle in 1926. In his autobiographical book *Alone*, he describes his loneliness at the snow-covered top of the world. The concept of 'loneliness at the summit' is closely associated with the symbol of the Mountain Goat.

deal with them. By the same token, they expect their own inferiors to give them the proper respect. An authoritarian manner is natural to them — they aren't democratic people! Their world is definitely divided into masters and servants, and they, of course, make every attempt to belong to the former category. But if they should find themselves in the latter, they will still stick (with an almost religious fervour) to the old class distinctions, willingly accepting the haughty attitude of so-called masters as their prerogative. They will expect their bosses to enforce rigorous discipline, and won't be impressed by an employer who treats them kindly or as an equal. In fact, this sort of behaviour confuses them, because it upsets all their ideas of hierarchy.

Saturn, their ruling planet, is the planet of restriction, and some Capricorns seem to have an exaggerated awareness of limitations. This can result in chronic pessimism and a belief that everything in this world, except evil, is limited. These people believe that there is only a certain amount of wealth, happiness, good jobs, suitable spouses and the haves (as opposed to the have-nots, who abound). They will make every attempt to be among the haves, simply because there are only so many pieces of

Richard Nixon fought for years against great odds in his efforts to become president of the United States. Such amazing perseverance and ambition are characteristic of Capricorn, Nixon's Sun sign.

'The end justifies the means' – the famous maxim of Niccolo Machiavelli (Ascendant sign Capricorn) – accurately reflects the harsh philosophy of life often so characteristic of this stern Earth sign. The adviser of princes and kings, Machiavelli's name became synonymous with political intrigue and conspiracy.

cake to go round. No new members must be admitted to the elite group who are playing pat-a-cake, because then, of course, their own piece would be that much smaller. Better yet would be to weed out some of the old players. Their advice to those who get no cake at all is 'Eat bread', and if there isn't any, then it's 'Starve'! 'Live and let live' is hardly the motto of these people! According to them, life is a see-saw, and if you want to stay up, then you've got to make sure the other side stays down — both can't be in the air at the same time. Other people must know their place and not try to climb up and compete with these haughty Goats. If they do, such Capricorns will mercilessly trip them up, and when they fall, the Goats will unhesitatingly step over their bodies to continue their march to the top. They know the rules of the game, and treading on bodies is one of them — that's crystal clear to these Capricorns, who feel that only romantic fools or dreamy idealists would disagree. Indeed, the very concept of idealism arouses their scorn and contempt: let those misguided idiots go on their merry fools' way, let them waste time and lag behind in the great race. So what if there's injustice in the world? Some suffer by it, while others benefit. These people have no desire whatsoever to better the world. The world will turn as it always has, and they will make very sure that they know what the rules are, and will play accordingly!

Another, thankfully rare, breed of Goat is narrow-minded and jealous, and their only joy lies in being malicious. Their highly developed herd instincts, and desire to identify with something larger and more powerful than themselves, extinguishes the last flames of individuality from their souls. These people love uniforms, and as far as they are concerned, it's the uniform that makes the man. While Cancerians, the opposite sign to Capricorn, find their security in being tied to their mother's apron strings, that same need to feel secure is expressed in Capricorn's search for a powerful, authoritarian father figure. These Goats adore a dictator, someone who, through complete identification and total submission, will relieve them, once and for all, of all the insecurities and self-doubts eating away inside them.

Beautiful bone structures can make some Capricorns extremely attractive. Less handsome Capricorns have elongated noses, pursed lips and disapproving expressions. Whether male or female, Goats aren't particularly romantic, being married, very often, to their careers. A female Capricorn will abandon her career for marriage only if she's dazzled by the social status of her future husband, in which case the marriage itself will become her career. Capricorns are often attracted to partners much older than themselves, with whom they have much more in common than with their contemporaries. They get along especially well with people born under Libra, the sign of the Scales, who in turn are much taken with Capricorns. And it's no wonder that Capricorns, who measure every last ounce, could certainly use a pair of scales!

FAMOUS PEOPLE BORN UNDER CAPRICORN

CAPRICORN AS THE ASCENDANT

Richard Byrd (Sun sign Scorpio)
Sean Connery (Sun sign Virgo)
Queen Elizabeth II (Sun sign Taurus)
David Lloyd George (Sun sign Capricorn)
Paul Getty (Sun sign Sagittarius)
William Gladstone (Sun sign Capricorn)
Maxim Gorky (Sun sign Aries)
J Edgar Hoover (Sun sign Capricorn)
Rex Harrison (Sun sign Pisces)
James Joyce (Sun sign Aquarius)
Edward Kennedy (Sun sign Pisces)
Niccolo Machiavelli (Sun sign Taurus)
Yehudi Menuhin (Sun sign Taurus)
Paul Newman (Sun sign Aquarius)
Aristotle Onassis (Sun sign Capricorn)
Auguste Rodin (Sun sign Scorpio)
Erwin Rommel (Sun sign Scorpio)
Helena Rubinstein (Sun sign Capricorn)
Jonas Salk (Sun sign Scorpio)
Mao Tse Tung (Sun sign Capricorn)
Joseph Turner (Sun sign Taurus)

CAPRICORN AS THE SUN SIGN

Konrad Adenauer (Ascendant Pisces)
Muhammad Ali (Ascendant Leo)
Marlene Dietrich (Ascendant Virgo)
Federico Fellini (Ascendant Virgo)
David Lloyd George (Ascendant Capricorn)
William Gladstone (Ascendant Capricorn)
Gurdjieff (Ascendant Libra)
J Edgar Hoover (Ascendant Capricorn)
Howard Hughes (Ascendant Virgo)
Johannes Kepler (Ascendant Gemini)
Rudyard Kipling (Ascendant Cancer)
Jack London (Ascendant Gemini)
Henry Miller (Ascendant Aries)
Richard Nixon (Ascendant Virgo)
Aristotle Onassis (Ascendant Capricorn)
Louis Pasteur (Ascendant Libra)
Edgar Allan Poe (Ascendant Scorpio)
Elvis Presley (Ascendant Taurus)
Helena Rubinstein (Ascendant Capricorn)
Albert Schweitzer (Ascendant Libra)
Mao Tse Tung (Ascendant Capricorn)

and the following people whose Ascendants are unknown: David Bowie, Carlos Castaneda, Simone de Beauvoir, Cary Grant, Garcia Lorca, Moliére, Gamal Abdel Nasser, Isaac Newton, Anwar El Sadat, Joseph Stalin

AQUARIUS — THE WATER BEARER

Symbol — The Water Bearer, a man pouring water from an overflowing jug

Ruling planets — Uranus, the planet of originality and inventiveness, and Saturn, the planet of limitations

Element — Air

Quality — Fixed

Anatomical area under Aquarius' influence — The bloodstream and thighs

Polar sign — Leo

The last human symbol in the zodiac, the sign of Aquarius the Water Bearer, represents man at his most noble. The image of a man pouring clear, quenching waters from an overflowing jug signifies the Aquarian dream of contributing to the welfare of all humanity and furthering the cause of social justice. Aquarians want to leave the world a better place than the one they were born into. The signs of Aquarius and Pisces represent the idealists of this world, but while Aquarians are deeply involved with social problems and strive to reform existing conditions, Pisceans prefer to retire from the world, believing in redemption through spirituality.

Aquarius is ruled by two planets: Saturn, traditionally the ruler of this sign, and Uranus, a relative newcomer to the Solar System, discovered only in 1781 and named after the Greek god of the star-studded sky and father of the other gods. Greek mythology has it that Uranus was the ruler of the entire universe until his son, Saturn, castrated him and took his place. Now that Uranus is considered the chief ruling planet of Aquarius, and Saturn has been relegated to secondary status, one can't help feeling that Uranus has finally got his sweet revenge . . .

Not only have Uranus and Saturn been sworn enemies and rivals from the beginning of time, but they are also in diametric opposition, which explains the many contradictions in the Aquarian character: the waters in the jug are calm, but that may simply be the calm before the storm. And a storm in the Water Bearer's jug is no mere tempest in a teacup, but a real thunder-and-lightning affair. When an Aquarian bursts their dam, don't just expect floods, but be prepared for high tension and electrifying atmospheric changes, too. In fact, the discovery of Uranus heralded the age of great technological inventions, including that of electricity. (Interestingly enough, the inventor of the electric light bulb, Thomas Alva Edison, was born with the Sun in Aquarius!)

Uranus represents the light of reason illuminating man's conscious mind, and signifies individualistic man born out of the vast ocean of collective consciousness where each drop is identical. Born into the world, he severs the umbilical cord by virtue of his ability to reason for himself. So, perhaps Aquarius, the last of the signs to be symbolized by a human, is really the first truly human sign, in the fullest meaning of the word. The first planet to be discovered beyond Saturn, which is the planet of restrictions, Uranus symbolizes the breaking of the bonds of convention and a striving for freedom and liberty. And indeed, the discovery of Uranus came hot on the heels of the Declaration of American Independence (1776), a document dedicated to human liberties, and of the French Revolution (1789), which cried out for Liberty, Equality and Fraternity. Saturn is content to leave well enough alone and follow convention, while Uranus, always open to change and progress, represents man's desire to circumvent the restrictions of the past — and soar into the future.

Most Aquarians are truly astronauts of the soul who feel at home in the upper spiritual strati. For this type of Aquarian, floating somewhere in outer space, even the sky itself isn't the limit. Yet, there is also the earth-bound Aquarian, the kind who suffers from a fear of heights, because Saturn still has a certain hold on this sign. The planet of limitations may clip the wings of those born under its rulership, and Saturn-bound Aquarians will impose on themselves the rigid, frozen rules that this planet represents. The flowing waters of life in Aquarius' jug may freeze into ice cubes in the Saturnian ice tray. And, like the cube, these Aquarians are super-squares, who make the traditional square of the zodiac, Capricorn, look like a wild trapezium. But sometimes the distinction between Uranus-ruled and Saturn-ruled Aquarians isn't so cut and dried. The Uranian Aquarian may unexpectedly react in a Saturn-like way, while the Saturnian Aquarian might one day stun everyone (and most of all themselves) by reacting like a typical Uranian, suddenly jumping like a jack-in-the box.

As well as being the last of the Air signs, Aquarius is also the most spiritual and intellectual. Aquarians float somewhere in the upper stratosphere of the abstract. Their horizons are wide, spanning many worlds, and their spirits, to freedom born, range in all directions, freed of all restrictions and prejudices. Aquarians always view everything from a certain distance, which is necessary for anyone wanting to find the unbiased, objective truth. They have no patience with anyone who believes that they have a monopoly on the absolute truth. The typical Aquarian is too independent a thinker to identify with any ideology, and much too individual to allow themselves to be defined, labelled and catalogued as belonging to any particular camp. The strife and rivalry between the various groups seem petty and absurd to Aquarians, who sometimes feel like Gulliver listening to the Lilliputians arguing about which end of the egg to crack.

Leos, the polar sign of Aquarius, want the whole world to love them, whereas Aquarians love all of mankind, regardless of race, creed or sex.

Being progressive, liberal and tolerant, they are willing to listen to any idea, and are true democrats willing to fight for man's inalienable right to express his opinion — even should it be opposed to their own. They don't force their own ideas on anyone, their attitude being 'If they want it, they can have it'.

Just as Aquarians respect the right of other people to do as they please, so do they insist on the right to go their own way. Public opinion is not a factor in their decision-making, and they don't play according to the accepted rules of society. As a result, they are often regarded as strange and eccentric. Not that that bothers them in the least, since what's important to Aquarians is to live according to their own values and to be true to themselves. They refuse to participate in social games and it seems that they are the only ones who see the naked truth hiding behind the external lie of social norms. Like the little boy in *The Emperor's New Clothes*, they are the only people courageous enough to speak the truth and shout that the king is naked.

And, as one king leads to another, let's get back to the king of the jungle. Leos, Aquarians' opposite sign, are very particular about the external trappings of honour, and dearly love to clothe themselves in royal raiments — even though they may be paupers. Aquarians, on the other hand, won't dress up no matter what their social standing, and would have no qualms in exchanging clothes with a pauper, for they fear no loss of status. They want to be judged by what they are, not by what they wear. As far as they are concerned, anyone who thinks that clothes make the man is sadly mistaken. The Aquarian attitude is 'Take me as I am — or leave me'.

In the eyes of an Aquarian, all men are equal, whether poor, humble, rich or titled. Aquarians neither grovel nor show off — instead, they stand as tall as trees. Their natural place, it seems, is at the top and they often find themselves there, even though they aren't ambitious. Aquarians are uncomfortable in any authoritarian role, since they hate to tell people what to do, just as they themselves hate to be given orders. They feel nothing but contempt for any hierarchical structures and are embarrassed by any honours lavished on them, even though they may be richly deserved.

Uranus' glyph (♅) resembles a tree. Gemini, the first of the human signs, seems to represent the temptation to taste the fruit of knowledge which caused man's eternal expulsion from the Garden of Eden. If so, Aquarius, which is the last of the human signs, would appear to represent the desire to find the tree of life through the tree of knowledge, thereby recreating the Garden of Eden here on earth through wisdom and knowledge. Uranus was discovered at the dawning of the new age of science and technology and, strangely enough, its symbol somewhat resembles an antenna, which picks information out of the air — a man-made tree of knowledge planted on every rooftop. Aquarians much prefer a real forest to an antennae jungle, and try to escape from the rush of modern, big-city living. They heed nature's call, for isn't man likened to a tree in a field? Aquarians love nature, and ecology is a subject close to their hearts — they are convinced that the tree of life is only to be found in nature.

The only tree scorned by Aquarians is the family tree. Far from being snobs, they are truly democratic, and have no fear that it will be overcrowded up there at the top. In any case, they soar in skies huge enough to encompass countless stars. Aquarians are free of jealousy and other negative feelings, these being emotions that they know of only theoretically, as strange phenomena not taken from real life but from some peculiar anthropological study. Base emotions are alien to Aquarians, who will therefore have trouble recognizing them in others. Not a single drop of suspicion muddies the clear waters of Aquarius, since these people believe implicitly in the human spirit. Being pure themselves, they attribute pure and high-minded motives to others. Every time reality proves them wrong, they are aghast all over again. It's no wonder that their eyes are perpetually wide open in surprise, astonished at the strangeness of the world — Aquarians are usually very innocent and unworldly, like visitors from outer space.

The clean, clear, pure waters in the Aquarian jug are untainted by even one drop of dishonesty. Some feel that these waters are too bland, and would prefer something more sparkling, even at the cost of stirring up

Abraham Lincoln (Sun sign Aquarius) was the president of the United States who liberated the Negroes from slavery. His fight against slavery reflects the humanitarian ideals of Aquarius, and the readiness of those born under this sign to fight for justice.

Rebellious Aquarius is the Ascendant sign of Edward VIII who stepped down from the throne of England in order to marry his great love, Mrs Simpson, an American divorcee.

some spicy mischief in the jug. Aquarians are leisurely in an aristocratic manner, their blue blood flowing languidly through their veins. (Usually, by the way, these people have very low blood pressure, and tend to be anaemic.) Some even speculate that this bluish fluid is not blood at all, but water, and only wish it were a bit more bubbly and lively . . . For their part, Aquarians prefer the relaxed, horizontal position. They'd rather not stand if they can sit, and if it's possible to lie down — well, so much the better! Lying prone is their most natural position. In this, they seem to be identifying with their ruling planet, Uranus, which leans so much on its axis that it almost seems to orbit on its back. The Tower of Pisa must have been born under Aquarius!

Like the Tower of Pisa, Aquarians usually lean one way or the other — but usually to the left. However, there are also some who argue hotly over tea (coffee is too strong for them) about the need to save the working class from its oppressors. All this will be expounded in their drawing room; meanwhile, back in the kitchen, they'll be keeping the maid slaving away. This type of Water Bearer bubbles over when speaking of problems that beset humanity — but, when it comes to deeds, won't give a single drop to those in need.

Although Aquarians are overflowing with goodwill towards the whole world, as far as some of them are concerned, charity not only doesn't begin

The originality of Aquarius finds expression in the brilliant creations of Lewis Carroll (Sun sign Aquarius), the author of *Alice in Wonderland*.

Charles Dickens made the British people conscious of the cruel exploitation of child labour in the 19th century. His fight for social justice is characteristic of Aquarius, his Sun sign.

at home, but it isn't even invited to visit. These people will tell you that they neglect their family because they are too busy saving the rest of the world. The personal problems of those close to them shrink in importance when compared to the troubles taxing the world. These Aquarians are insensitive to the woes of the individual, and seem to forget that humanity is really made up of many individuals. This attitude is especially prevalent among Aquarian men.

The men born under this sign have a computer-like grasp of things and a knack for inventions. They seem to have been equipped with mental antennae which pick up brilliant ideas out of thin air, flashing like lightning in their brains. The Aquarian man is like a tree whose branches reach the clouds — but, alas, he himself often fails to take root. So, sometimes you get an Aquarian who, despite (or rather, because of) his many gifts and talents, is disconnected, uprooted and floating, seeking — but not always finding — himself. If, however, he should turn to humanitarian or idealistic pursuits, or to a career in electronics, computers, electrical engineering or aeronautics, he might well discover his true self after all.

The Aquarian man, with his air of quiet, restrained masculinity, and high moral stature, is attractive to many women. Physically, he's usually tall, once again suggesting a tall tree towering above the bushes of the

The cool and pure beauty of Grace Kelly is characteristic of Aquarius – it was the Ascendant sign of the famous actress and Princess of Monaco.

Grace Kelly's daughter, Princess Caroline, has her Sun in Aquarius – her mother's Ascendant sign. Indeed, 'astrological heredity' is noticeable in most families – a parent's Sun sign appearing as the Ascendant sign of the child, or vice versa.

world. (This is a distinct advantage when playing basketball, his favourite sport.) He is like the evergreen tree which keeps its leaves throughout the year — in fact, most Aquarian men don't shed their hair even in the autumn of their lives. The Aquarius woman stands as straight and tall as a date palm, is as tender and willowy as a young sprig, and as rare as an orchid. Hers is a dreamy soul, forever floating off somewhere, and even while engaged in something as prosaic as the washing up, she might take off after a soap bubble, float along the Milky Way and slide down a rainbow. There is a heavenly-angelic quality about her; her head seems ringed by a halo like those wonderful coloured northern lights, the aurora borealis. The sign of Aquarius is associated with the north, and many Water Bearers have a tall, Scandinavian blond look. Even among the darker races, those born under Aquarius are comparatively fair.

Aquarians are usually clean-living, abstaining from drugs, cigarettes and alcohol. If they are hooked on anything at all, it's milk! Their natures are not carnal, and they live on a vegetarian diet — morally if not physically. Spiritual and physical purity and cleanliness are important to them. In fact, they are obsessed by cleanliness and, with the exception of Virgos, are the cleanest of all the signs. But when it comes to neatness, Virgos still have the upper hand! True, there are a few extraordinarily pedantic Aquarians too (some of the women of this sign even iron their underwear!), but on the whole, both the men and women look very rumpled. It's not unusual to run into an Aquarian who has managed to put their jumper on both inside out and back to front, with the label waving merrily under their chin. Aquarian men seem to have been born in their jeans — they go in for T-shirts in summer and for heavy fatigue jackets and woolly scarves in winter, but the jeans go everywhere, whatever the season. Aquarians don't dress up for even the most important functions!

Women born under this sign also prefer the rumpled look. In contrast to that rare Aquarian woman who irons everything she can find, many don't even bother to press their dresses. The creased look must have been invented by an Aquarian, and indeed, many women of this sign are gifted fashion designers, coming up with original, even revolutionary, styles. There is also a type of Aquarian woman, who prefers the naked truth to any tale, will often bare not only her heart but also her breast. Joining a nudist colony might simply be an expression of her need to be different at any price, to astonish and shock — something typical of some Aquarians. On the other hand, dressing like Eve could simply be her way of recreating the Garden of Eden here on earth . . .

FAMOUS PEOPLE BORN UNDER AQUARIUS

AQUARIUS AS THE ASCENDANT

Robert Baden-Powell (Sun sign Pisces)
Che Guevara (Sun sign Gemini)
King Edward VIII (Sun sign Cancer)
F Scott Fitzgerald (Sun sign Libra)
Ian Fleming (Sun sign Gemini)
Errol Flynn (Sun sign Gemini)
Dame Margot Fonteyn (Sun sign Taurus)
Carl Jung (Sun sign Leo)
Immanuel Kant (Sun sign Taurus)
Grace Kelly (Sun sign Scorpio)
Karl Marx (Sun sign Taurus)
André Maurois (Sun sign Leo)
Karl May (Sun sign Pisces)
Auguste Renoir (Sun sign Pisces)
Maximilien Robespierre (Sun sign Taurus)
George Sand (Sun sign Cancer)
Alexander Solzhenitsyn (Sun sign Sagittarius)
Dr Benjamin Spock (Sun sign Taurus)
Robert Louis Stevenson (Sun sign Scorpio)
H G Wells (Sun sign Virgo)

AQUARIUS AS THE SUN SIGN

Alfred Adler (Ascendant Cancer)
Humphrey Bogart (Ascendant Gemini)
Lord Byron (Ascendant Cancer)
Princess Caroline of Monaco (Ascendant Aries)
Lewis Carroll (Ascendant Sagittarius)
Charles Darwin (Ascendant Sagittarius)
James Dean (Ascendant Scorpio)
Charles Dickens (Ascendant Virgo)
Thomas Alva Edison (Ascendant Scorpio)
Valéry Giscard d'Estaing (Ascendant Virgo)
James Joyce (Ascendant Capricorn)
Charles Lindbergh (Ascendant Sagittarius)
Norman Mailer (Ascendant Pisces)
Edouard Manet (Ascendant Leo)
Wolfgang Amadeus Mozart (Ascendant Virgo)
Anna Pavlova (Ascendant Pisces)
Ronald Reagan (Ascendant Scorpio)
Franklin D Roosevelt (Ascendant Virgo)
Franz Schubert (Ascendant Cancer)
Mark Spitz (Ascendant Leo)
Stendhal (Ascendant Scorpio)
Jules Verne (Ascendant Gemini)
Virginia Woolf (Ascendant Virgo)

and the following people whose Ascendants are unknown: Tallulah Bankhead, Bertolt Brecht, Martin Buber, Benjamin Franklin, Clark Gable, Charles Lamb, Abraham Lincoln, Felix Mendelssohn, Thomas More, Jeanne Moreau, Boris Pasternak, Romain Rolland, Gertrude Stein

PISCES — THE FISHES

Symbol — Two fish swimming in opposite directions

Ruling planets — Neptune, the planet of dreams, and Jupiter, the planet of plenty

Element — Water

Quality — Mutable

Anatomical area under Pisces' influence — The feet

Polar sign — Virgo

There are many fish in the sea: goldfish and carp, dolphins and sharks, plankton and whales, fish of prey and preyed-upon fish, clear-water fish and fish in mud-ponds, flying fish and deep-water fish. There are fish who camouflage themselves, pretending to be something else — a plant or a rock. The sea is a vast world of its own, and it's no easy task writing about the many, many kinds of life it holds under one single heading — Pisces.

The one feature common to all those born under Pisces is a sensitivity that knows no bounds. They absorb the innermost feelings of others like a sponge and have no need of words to be able to understand the inner workings of the heart. Pisceans have the capacity for perfect empathy, as though they were stepping into another person's shoes. Who knows — perhaps they wore them in a previous incarnation? The mystic school of astrology holds that the soul begins its earthly journey by being born in Aries, the first of the zodiac signs, and progresses through the other signs until the final incarnation in Pisces.

Perhaps this is why the last of the 12 astrological signs is so multi-faceted and complex. Pisceans contain something of each of the other signs, thus encompassing the entire zodiac: they have the Arian pioneering spirit, the Taurean love of comfort, the Geminian flexibility, the Cancerian sensitivity, the Leonine love of the stage, the Virgoan modesty, the Libran need for harmony, the Scorpionic secrecy, the Sagittarian desire for freedom, the Capricorn gift of organization, and the Aquarian love for mankind. The Water sign of Pisces blends together all these opposites while smoothing away the blunt edges of the contradictions.

Aquarius and Pisces are considered to be the highest-minded of the signs. Why, then, after the Aquarian peak of evolution, represented by man pouring forth life-giving water, does there come a sign symbolized by fish, definitely primary creatures on the evolutionary scale? It might seem like regression. Mystery surrounds the last of the signs and its symbol, as though saying that Creation is a mystery, and what we cannot understand we mustn't attempt to fathom. Perhaps the fish symbol reminds us of our destiny: we emerged from the sea (in an evolutionary sense, too) and shall return to that vast ocean of souls, just as all rivers flow to the sea. Indeed, the strictures of the ego break down in the sign of Pisces, where the Piscean soul merges with that of his fellow man; not surprisingly, the Piscean feeling of separateness is so frail that these people are hardly aware of any barrier between themselves and others. The Piscean 'I' is very fluid, taking on different shapes as he or she easily identifies and empathizes with others.

Poetic and romantic, Pisceans soar on the wings of their imagination, letting their spirits float far beyond the misty horizon. In complete contrast to Virgoans, Pisceans' astrological opposites, who need to have their feet firmly planted on the ground and know just where they stand, Pisceans aren't afraid to be carried along by hidden currents, swimming in a sea of uncertainty just like a fish in water. The two fish in the Pisces symbol, which are swimming in opposite directions, represent the contradictions inherent in this sign. A typical Piscean seems to float in a fog of confusion, yet has remarkable organizational and planning skills. They seem open and outgoing, though they are really very secretive. There's an air of poetic sadness about them, but they know joy as well; and sometimes, when it seems that they are most likely to drown in a sea of tears, the sun breaks out of the clouds and plays merrily on the shimmering water. They are lofty even in humility, free even when enslaved. When distancing themselves from the vanities of the world they are close to Nirvana, when declining honours they win eternal grace, and their crown is a crown of thorns.

Many Pisceans are unworldly and lost in this materialistic world — their emergence into reality is no easy birth. Their gills aren't suited to earthly breathing, and they feel suffocated on land. They believe that in order to survive they have to link themselves to a sublime, ethereal infusion of another reality — one that is other-worldly and spiritual. The essence of that other reality is the oxygen that will sustain them. No wonder that with all the artificial respiration the typical Piscean needs in order to survive in the materialistic world, he or she doesn't feel like a fish in water in these mundane surroundings . . .

Each Piscean trait encompasses its contradiction as well. So, this sign's spiritual strength could also be its earthly weakness. The Piscean psychological Achilles' heel is their almost complete lack of ego (they're like jellyfish, with no protective shell or skeleton), their fluid, vague 'I' overflowing with empathy for their fellow men. They understand only too well the other's point of view, even at the expense of their own, giving right of way to the desires of others. They sacrifice their own best interests for the sake of others — who see these Fish as hapless victims, Dostoyevskian Idiots. Pisceans certainly have scales, but these are rarely tough enough to repel others from trying to bite them. And indeed, people are often tempted to hurt Pisceans who, being naïve and unworldly, seem willing victims. Most Pisceans never forget a hurt or insult and, holding a grudge, are capable of planning their sweet revenge for years. Yet there are also some Pisceans who will always rise above themselves, understanding and forgiving those who have hurt them. Sometimes they'll even go so far as to turn the other cheek. Some say that these people enjoy playing martyred saints, others that they're just masochistic. Be that as it may, these golden fish have one golden rule: they'd rather be preyed upon than do the preying.

The goldfish, then, must be declared a protected species. Otherwise, it might become extinct. If some rare specimens of this unusual creature have somehow managed to survive, it's thanks to their uncanny intuition and sixth sense which help them sense the traps, nets and bait others have set out for them, so they can avoid them. At the same time, Pisceans are very clever at concealing their own intentions, and can confuse their enemies, all the while playing the fool. Indeed, their only defence is camouflage.

Just as you can't hold a fistful of water, you'll find it hard to get hold of elusive, slippery Pisces. It seems sometimes as though this watery sign simply evaporates into thin air. Those close to Pisceans often feel it necessary to moor their ship of life to earthly reality with a heavy anchor, and to bind the slippery Fish with ropes and knots to stop them slipping out of reach, never to be seen again. Entangled in all those ties and knots, Pisceans really do feel like netted fish. Earthly commitments weigh them down like heavy chains, while reality closes in on them like prison walls, within which they must serve a life sentence. Yet, even though their bodies are imprisoned, their souls long for freedom — to be as one with the patch of sky visible through the narrow prison window. Their imaginations set sail beyond the horizon, transcending the boundaries of time and space. They contemplate even the most abstract questions of philosophy, mysticism and the inner nature of earthly existence. They wonder whether the material is an illusion, and the spiritual the true reality. The truth, they believe, hides behind the myriad mocking veils which merely give the illusion of reality. Nothing is certain, not even their own existence. Perhaps they've dreamt everything up — even themselves. Perhaps they've invented reality, spun their being, entwined their personalities, and woven an insubstantial web of dreams? Do they exist, or are they only a dream themselves? The Chinese philosopher, Chung-Tse, once dreamt that he was a butterfly. On awakening, he mused, 'Now I do not know whether I am a man who dreamt he was a butterfly, or a butterfly dreaming it is a man.'

Pisceans are not quite sure who or what they are. It is as though the outlines of their identities were blurred by their empathy for others. Their souls reach out to their fellow men, and they are swept along by overflowing emotion. Just as water assumes the shape of whatever container it happens to be in, so does the fluid Piscean personality take on different shapes. The leopard may not be able to change his spots, but the Fish continually sheds and replaces his scales. There are some Pisceans who want to be all things to all people, and end up changing costumes and masks at a dizzying rate. One Piscean girl would ask her mother, before every date, 'How should I behave? Be dramatic and mysterious? Bubbly and cheerful? Or quiet and pensive?'

Being able to soak up their surrounding atmosphere, Pisceans can subconsciously assimilate the collective expectations of society, even if they're hidden. Pisceans with a particularly changeable personality may be so influenced by social needs that they become moulded into society's ideal shape as if they were made of clay. For instance, in a society demanding that men should be macho, a Piscean man may make Clint Eastwood look like a mummy's boy. But it may cost him dearly: being caught in a mould which distorts his Piscean quality, playing a role entirely foreign to himself which demands that he destroy the delicate fabric of his personality and deny his sensitive side could all mean that mentally, something has got to give. A nervous breakdown, or a nervous tic, are both warning signs when something in the Piscean personality begins to unravel.

The illusory, mirage-like quality of reality is familiar to Pisceans. To them, the world seems like a stage on which a mock play is taking place, earthly reality being just a backdrop. They may then simply decide to quit the game, especially if they feel that the cards have been marked, and will content themselves with watching from the sidelines. Some Fish may decide to retire from the vanities of this world, but there are also Pisceans who decide to join in the game wholeheartedly, just for the fun of it. They won't be content to stay mere players, but will take upon themselves the parts of playwright and director too, as well as proving themselves to be masters of design and illusion. And then there are the fishy Pisceans who, when participating in the vanities of the world, spread a fog of illusion.

The ideas of Professor Albert Einstein (Sun sign Pisces) were influenced to a great degree by his intuitive/mystical grasp of the secrets of the universe. Mystical intuition is characteristic of Pisces.

The elegiac music of Frederic Chopin (Sun sign Pisces) reflects the poetic melancholy of Pisces.

Hiding behind smokescreens of their own design, while spinning yarns and fabricating fabulous fables, they pull the strings, manipulating the other players as though they were mere marionettes.

It can be hard to decide at which end of the fishing rod a Piscean can be found: is he or she a fish, dangling helplessly from the fisherman's hook, or the fisherman himself? Perhaps the Piscean is a fish dressed like a fisherman, or a fisherman masquerading as a fish? Or maybe both situations apply? Because there are certain Pisceans who, in the same way that they fall into the nets spread out by others, are equally adroit at setting traps themselves. In playing the fisherman's role, Pisceans are very dangerous indeed. After all, who knows better than they, which bait is most likely to appeal and what the web of lies looks like when viewed at close range? The Piscean can then turn into a shark devouring other fish. But many lesser Pisceans, rather than resembling sharks, remind one of those dangerous and slippery poison fish, lurking in muddy waters. Masquerading as harmless, these fish of prey hunt in secret, under the guise of friendship. Such creatures may even pretend to be poor fish themselves in order to play on the feelings of their intended victims.

Some Pisceans would like to taste all kinds of earthly bait without getting hooked. But once caught, the more they wriggle to get free, the more hooked they become — especially if caught in a drug-dealer's net. The temptation-prone Pisceans have a strong tendency to become addicted, whether to food, sex, alcohol or drugs. They have no critical faculty and no sense of proportion, gulping everything down like whales, and drinking like fish. Their ship of fools is buffeted hither and thither by every current, drunkenly bobbing like an empty shell at the mercy of the waves. By giving in completely to their addictions, to the point of oblivion, they hope to lose themselves and gain the illusion of being free of their earthly prisons. But the more they let themselves go, and the more rope they allow themselves, the more hopelessly entangled they get, enslaved by a false sense of liberty, trapped by an illusion of boundless freedom. These people distort the idea of the high-minded Piscean yearning to rise spiritually above crass reality, by escaping from that reality. These poor Fish are not really alive: they exist in a world of illusion, imagining that they can rise on the fumes of incense to the summit of happiness, to a synthetic Garden of Eden created instantly out of thin air. It's a dream which is bound to end in self-destruction, since in the alcohol-induced haze and drug-created smoke, they not only lose their way but might lose themselves as well.

Many Pisceans, even those who don't drink or take drugs, are confused and scatter-brained, particularly in the mornings. In contrast to Virgoans, who rise with the early bird, Pisceans find it uncommonly difficult to shake off the cobwebs of sleep that spun them an enchanted dream world, and return to reality. Virgoans may be early risers, who hop out of bed bright-eyed, fully awake and ready to go, but typical Pisceans crawl out of bed closer to noon, and even then need several cups of coffee and half a packet of cigarettes before they have the faintest notion of who and where they are. The morning mists and blurriness of the waking hours so typical of those born under this sign may be because the Piscean consciousness, hovering in some other plane during sleep, finds it difficult to re-enter the body again.

Most Pisceans differ from Virgoans in their attitude to neatness, as well. Virgoans are the most pedantic of creatures, while Pisceans only seem to be able to function in a clutter. One Piscean told me that ever since her Virgoan friend persuaded her to tidy up her wardrobe, she hasn't been able to find a single thing! When her wardrobe used to be in a mess, she had no trouble at all — she'd stick a hand into the jumble and always manage to fish out what she needed!

Paperwork is one of the areas in which the Piscean muddle reigns supreme. These people can only stare and sigh when faced with a growing heap of papers, threatening to overflow its banks like a swollen river. If a fish can drown at all, it's in a sea of papers! They tend to turn blind eyes to petty, everyday bureaucratic annoyances, such as misunderstandings with the Inland Revenue, until these assume gigantic proportions, growing into a rising tide which threatens to pull them under. Some Pisceans get into fishy deals which may culminate in bankruptcy, self-destruction, and even imprisonment.

The arts, and especially music, are environments in which Pisceans feel most at home. They excel in any pursuit that has an illusory quality, such as the cinema, stage and acting. Pisceans can be superb set decorators or make-up artists, and are truly gifted with cosmetics. They also do well in costume design, fashion and textiles, and everything connected with the shoe industry. Also, they are often associated with closed institutions such as monasteries, hospitals and prisons. Many Pisceans choose careers in medicine, nursing, social work or other occupations that involve caring for people. On the other hand, there are also those Pisceans who, rather than do the looking-after, choose to be the ones who have to be looked after, and lead the lives of professional parasites. In typical slippery fish-like fashion, they glide away from any real work and use their skills by pulling the wool over everyone's eyes. Many people do indeed fall prey to their charms and swallow their yarns wholesale, yearning to follow them to their never-never land and believing in the soap bubbles they blow. These Pisceans may not be masters at creating something out of nothing but, on the other hand, they do excel at creating nothing out of something . . . They weave tangled webs of enchanted illusions like the spider spinning his web. Every insect knows there's no use trying to escape once it has been trapped.

Many Pisceans look as though they're not altogether here, as though some part of them is off floating elsewhere. Typical Pisceans have large eyes, round facial features and small noses. There is another type of Fish (especially when Pisces is the Sun sign) which has sharp, shark-like features. And some are the jellyfish type — one almost expects their bodies to overflow the moulds in which they were formed. Both male and female Fish are noted for their fine, beautiful hair, which is usually wavy like the waves of the sea. The men retain their glorious heads of hair even late in life. Many of them grow beards and moustaches, but their bodies are usually as hairless as those of fish. The feet of Pisceans are their Achilles' heels, being weak or flat. Sometimes, this leads to more serious complaints, which may cause difficulties in walking. In some cases, Pisceans not only have a strange gait, but a peculiar stance as well, holding their heels together while turning their feet out, like a ballerina's feet in the third position, giving the impression they're standing on a fish tail.

A noticeable Piscean feature is their eyes, which are usually beautiful, with a somewhat dreamy expression. Screened by their long lashes, they seem to be looking at some far-off vision. Many of them are short-sighted but, unlike Virgos who must see the world for what it really is and therefore wear glasses to see each detail clearly, Pisceans prefer to gaze at a misty, hazy world, like an Impressionist painting in which the soft pastel colours merge and blend. Pisceans believe that, without glasses, the world is a much more beautiful place!

FAMOUS PEOPLE BORN UNDER PISCES

PISCES AS THE ASCENDANT

Konrad Adenauer (Sun sign Capricorn)
Alexander Graham Bell (Sun sign Pisces)
Henry Fonda (Sun sign Taurus)
Norman Mailer (Sun sign Aquarius)
Zubin Mehta (Sun sign Taurus)
Anna Pavlova (Sun sign Aquarius)
Robert Redford (Sun sign Leo)

PISCES AS THE SUN SIGN

Prince Andrew (Ascendant Leo)
Robert Baden-Powell (Ascendant Aquarius)
Alexander Graham Bell (Ascendant Pisces)
Neville Chamberlain (Ascendant Sagittarius)
Frederic Chopin (Ascendant Virgo)
Nicolaus Copernicus (Ascendant Virgo)
Albert Einstein (Ascendant Cancer)
Bobby Fischer (Ascendant Leo)
Rex Harrison (Ascendant Capricorn)
Victor Hugo (Ascendant Scorpio)
Henrik Ibsen (Ascendant Leo)
Edward Kennedy (Ascendant Capricorn)
Karl May (Ascendant Aquarius)
Michelangelo (Ascendant Sagittarius)
Rudolf Nureyev (Ascendant Leo)
Auguste Renoir (Ascendant Aquarius)
Arthur Schopenhauer (Ascendant Cancer)
John Steinbeck (Ascendant Leo)
Rudolf Steiner (Ascendant Scorpio)
Elizabeth Taylor (Ascendant Libra)
George Washington (Ascendant Taurus)

and the following people whose Ascendants are unknown: Yuri Gagarin, Thomas Masaryk, Liza Minnelli, Vaslav Nijinsky, Samuel Pepys, Valentina Tereshkowa

THE SECOND HOUSE

Finances; Possessions; Internal resources; Proprietary feelings

ARIES — THE RAM

Fire, Cardinal, Mars

Self-sufficiency, economic independence and a do-it-yourself attitude to money all characterize people with Aries in their Second House. Even when severely handicapped or ill, people with this placing will make every conceivable effort to remain self-supporting, and will hate to be dependent on others. Usually, however, there will be no need to rely on anyone else, because initiative and resourcefulness will always stand these people in good stead.

Aries, symbolized by the Ram, the leader of the flock, is a sign that strives to be first at all times — a quality that can be a mixed blessing! Daring may turn into foolhardiness, the desire for quick profits may lead to investing in risky ventures, and get-rich-quick schemes can swiftly backfire and send any capital up in smoke. Although these people seethe with truly original ideas, the heat of their fervour may burn holes in their pockets. Their cheque books and credit cards are always at the ready, and often they spend first and wonder if they can afford it later. Very often, they can't!

Anything connected with warfare, including the armed forces, will have a great bearing on their money, as will machinery, metals and mechanics. Fire may be a hazard, and these people should insure all their property with that consideration in mind.

TAURUS — THE BULL

Earth, Fixed, Venus

People with this placing have a realistic, practical and logical attitude to finances. They have a healthy respect for the value of money and a highly developed business sense and, as befitting an Earth sign, will want to feel that their finances are rooted in firm foundations. Flights of fancy, pipe dreams and castles in the air will all be spurned in favour of no-nonsense, solid and straightforward schemes that seem foolproof. These people are literally down to earth — anything linked with land or real estate will make them feel safe, because they know what they are dealing with.

Seeing is believing for people with this placing, and being able to touch or see what they own (especially property and valuables) fills them with a tremendous sense of security. Despite a certain weakness for a sybaritic existence, people whose fundamental attitude to money is Taurean will first secure the essential, everyday necessities of life, and only then turn their attention to its luxuries.

They are excellent at spotting bargains, and instinctively know the worth of each item. They always manage to buy the right thing at the right place and at the right time. As well as having a pronounced proprietorial sense ('What's mine is mine'), they have remarkable sensitivity to the needs of others, and warm and generous natures. They will happily help others less fortunate than themselves.

Agriculture, real estate and anything related to land will all influence the monetary affairs of these people. Likely sources of income come from concrete occupations such as construction, architecture and banking.

GEMINI — THE TWINS

Air, Mutable, Mercury

All the quick thinking and mental mastery of Gemini comes to the fore in the financial ability of people with this placing. They can easily invent brilliant money-spinning schemes, and have first-class minds when it comes to business. Such people are constantly thinking about ways of making money, and everything related to property and finance stimulates them intellectually. This Geminian attitude to money can be rather too flexible at times, and some people born with the lively Twins in the Second House may be financial tricksters or wheeler-dealers going in for fly-by-night business schemes, which border occasionally on the shady, or are even downright illegal! Fortunately for these people, their clever way with words and gift for inspired improvisation usually comes to their aid, neatly extricating them from all sorts of sticky situations.

The Geminian approach to money is a dual one, as befits the sign of the Twins. These people always recognize that there are two sides to every coin, they like to have fingers in every pie, dabble in all sorts of projects and, in most cases, draw their incomes from several different sources at the same time. Their financial situation is constantly changing, fluctuating between feast and famine. Money seems to come and go and, since Gemini is an Air sign, in some cases it can even be gone with the wind! It will just vanish into thin air, but that is mainly due to bad judgement and a poor sense of priorities. For those with Gemini in the Second House, their handling of finances is often influenced by a complete mixture of hard facts, rumours and hearsay. Brothers, sisters, cousins and neighbours will also have a great influence on their money.

Very often, people with this placing earn their incomes through their gift of the gab. Possible sources of money include anything to do with buying and selling, and commerce, or occupations connected with agency work, transport, the media, teaching and literature. Paperwork is usually in evidence somewhere, and if any investments are to be made, they will be in stocks and shares. People with Gemini in the Second House should insure their property against theft, and keep a wary eye open for con men and anyone out to make money at their expense.

CANCER — THE CRAB

Water, Cardinal, The Moon

A deep need for financial security is the driving force behind people with this placing, and they have an extremely cautious attitude towards anything connected with property, plus a tendency to hoard as much money as they possibly can. (Squirrel-like, they are nuts about saving.) Even when surrounded by wealth, they find it hard to shake off their nagging fear that a rainy day is just around the corner, and will plan accordingly. Despite what can be, at times, an exaggerated thriftiness, they can be very generous with money when their emotions are involved, especially when it comes to helping members of their family.

People with Cancer in the Second House have strong sentimental feelings about family heirlooms, childhood possessions and personal memories. They find it extremely difficult to part with anything, and cram their cupboards and attics with momentoes. Not surprisingly, this makes them inveterate collectors, and sometimes if they can't afford to buy expensive objects, they'll collect something small, such as matchboxes, instead. Whether rich or poor, they also tend to stockpile food, and their kitchen cupboards will be groaning with supplies of groceries for every conceivable occasion — it makes them feel secure.

People born with this placing will find that their family — and their mother in particular — will have a great influence on their finances.

Money-making ventures stand a good chance of succeeding if they are linked to catering or real estate. Since Cancer is a Water sign, professions connected with liquids, or the sea, are also suitable.

Taking out insurance policies is usually second nature to these people, because they instinctively want to protect all their possessions. Amongst the clauses, they should make sure they are well-insured against floods and water damage of all kinds.

LEO — THE LION

Fire, Fixed, The Sun

Love and money walk hand in hand for these people. In most cases, they simply love to make money, and usually do so quite easily! They manage their financial matters very ably, and with the utmost honesty. Sometimes Leo, being the sign associated with gold, bestows the Midas touch and, like the fabled Greek king who turned everything to gold, people with this sign in the Second House cannot help making a fortune!

In other cases, there can be a certain confusion between the concepts of love and money. For example, there may be an exaggerated need for wealth to compensate for feeling unloved; an ostentatious flaunting of money designed to buy admiration; or the kind of self-esteem that increases in direct proportion to their bank balance. But, however it is shown, there is always an intense relationship between love and money, often expressed through presents given to loved ones. Very insecure people may even attempt to buy love through gifts.

These people enjoy living in true regal style, indulging in grand, sometimes ostentatious, gestures, and spending exorbitant sums on luxuries, the high life, gambling and *objets d'art.*

Love and children both have a profound financial effect, and gold can also exercise a powerful influence. These people are very creative, so should choose jobs that harness that talent, and many are attracted to the entertainment business. Politics and banking are also good — back to gold again! Hobbies can also turn into hard cash for these people, so they should explore ways of making money from pastimes. For some of them, the mere making of money will be their favourite hobby!

VIRGO — THE MAIDEN

Earth, Mutable, Mercury

Money doesn't grow on trees for these people, and if they sit waiting for it to land in their laps they will be deeply disappointed. However, they are usually all too well aware that it's hard, responsible work that pays dividends — and the bills. This placing signifies a realistic and cautious attitude to money, which can sometimes be taken to extremes. The main worry of people with Virgo in the Second House is of being taken ill and therefore being unable to work, and they should insure themselves against such an eventuality.

These people run their financial affairs like clockwork, and are highly organized, practical and efficient when it comes to managing their money. They'll go over their bank statements with a fine toothcomb, and pay all bills promptly. Sometimes, however, they become so absorbed in obsessively counting every penny that they forget about the pounds, and run into exactly the sort of trouble they were trying to avoid.

Nursing, medicine and the caring professions are all likely to attract those with Virgo in the Second House, as are the food industry, agriculture, education, communications and any work that requires a critical sense and a good eye for detail.

LIBRA — THE SCALES

Air, Cardinal, Venus

The Libran love of harmony and balance can be seen in the easy-going, relaxed and moderate attitude of these people towards money matters. They try at all times to tread the middle path, being fair, generous and willing to compromise for the sake of peace. Nevertheless, they are not perplexed strangers to the world of finance, but are often extremely successful, because they believe that, in order to succeed in business, everyone must be happy.

The less positive side of this placing is the tendency to be financially dependent on others, becoming at times a burden, or even an outright parasite. Such people will do all they can to tip the balance of the scales in their favour, helping themselves to the resources of others, as though saying 'What's mine is mine, and what's yours is mine, too'. However, even the exploitation of others is usually performed in an engaging and charming way! They can get away with murder!

The last thing these people want is a hard life, and they'll long to live in comfortable circumstances, surrounded by luxury on all sides. They'll also be very generous, and will always want to give presents that bring real joy to their recipients. Their finances are affected by those of other people, and especially a spouse or lover. Working in any sphere connected with the law, diplomacy and the beauty business can be very profitable.

SCORPIO — THE SCORPION

Water, Fixed, Mars and Pluto

Secrecy surrounds the money matters of people with Scorpio in the Second House, and sometimes even their main source of income is not generally known. The fact that Scorpio is a Water sign does not necessarily mean that these people keep on an even keel. Usually, the reverse is true, and their financial situation might become stormy, tempestuous and turbulent.

Very often, these people attract money and possessions like magnets, but sometimes they do it so well that the division between their property and that of others becomes blurred until it is quite impossible to tell which is which. They can also borrow and lend money to such a degree that at times it seems that all their possessions — perhaps even themselves — are out on permanent loan. These people run the risk of sinking dangerously into a state of debt which, like a treacherous bog, threatens to pull them under.

Other people's property, especially that of their spouse or partner, greatly influences the financial situation of people born with Scorpio in the Second House. They will do best in jobs connected with mining, or secrecy, such as detective or secret government work.

SAGITTARIUS — THE ARCHER

Fire, Mutable, Jupiter

Optimism colours the financial attitude of these people, and they generally have every reason to look on the bright side. Lady Luck appears to smile benevolently on them, and money just gravitates towards them. It may look like luck, but it is also a finely-honed intuition, combined with a sound economic vision, which play a part in making these people successful.

Their sanguinity and faith in providence expresses itself in their tremendous magnanimity and liberality, and many people with this placing are benefactors and philanthropists. However, even if they aren't rich, people influenced by this fiery sign behave as though they had money to burn. 'Easy come, easy go' is their motto, and signing cheques can be second nature to some of them. Nevertheless, they long for enough money to give them the freedom and independence they crave.

These people don't bother with trifles, but go for the jackpot every time, and the bigger the better. They believe that if they shoot their arrows into the air, by the time they return to earth they'll be gold-plated. Unfortunately, this optimistic attitude can lead to problems, as it changes from a feeling of confidence to one of complacency. The spinning wheel of fortune might change direction and they may find themselves playing Russian roulette.

Legal matters, travel and foreign countries all have a material effect on people with Sagittarius in the Second House, but professionally they will enjoy earning a living from a wide variety of occupations. They will be attracted to anything relating to higher education, the law, religion and publishing, or connected with sports, horses, dogs and gambling.

Sagittarius, the sign of plenty, in Jacqueline Kennedy Onassis' Second House is a fitting expression of her wealth.

Leo – the sign of theatre and love affairs – is in Richard Burton's Second House. Indeed Burton earned huge sums as an actor, only to spend most of his fortune on women.

CAPRICORN — THE MOUNTAIN GOAT

Earth, Cardinal, Saturn

Prudence and frugality characterize the Capricorn attitude to money and property. People with the Goat in the Second House do not believe in the horn of plenty, or finding gold at the end of the rainbow. Instead, they prefer to take things slowly but surely, and will invest in long-term insurance policies and pension funds that offer safe and secure rewards.

When Capricorn is found in this House it accentuates the feeling that self-esteem is associated with status, and these people strive for impressive achievements. As far as they are concerned, money is synonymous with status, so they try to prove themselves financially. However, they may confuse the terms 'status', 'self-esteem' and 'money', and consider a blow to their bank balances to be equally damaging to their pride. Their attitude to finance is far from frivolous — instead, it is somewhat calculated, and they expect full value for their money. The lesser type of people with this placing will do their best to give the minimum, while demanding the maximum in return.

Those with Capricorn in the Second House have a worrying, pessimistic attitude towards their money, and always have a gnawing fear that disaster is about to strike. Being aware of the problems of elderly people, they do their utmost to ensure that they will enjoy their last years in comfort. No matter how rich they become, they will continue to save, in order to stave off their terror of the vicissitudes brought by old age.

Their monetary position is always greatly affected by the status of their fathers, and also by their own prestige. Real estate, agriculture, administration and geology are all possible sources of income for those with Capricorn in the Second House.

AQUARIUS — THE WATER BEARER

Air, Fixed, Saturn and Uranus

The Aquarian attitude to money and property is an interesting blend of opposites — an originality and a taste for innovations and changes, combined with a practical, cautious attitude to money matters, and the tendency to follow the true, tried and tested path. These conflicting viewpoints are not only a constant surprise to the friends of those with Aquarius in the Second House, but they repeatedly come as rather a shock to the people themselves. They are very much like the water jug that symbolizes Aquarius — at times it is so full that it brims over, and at others it is hermetically sealed, so that not a single drop can escape.

Although these people seem capricious and even totally unpredictable, it is still possible to foresee when their generosity will overflow, and they will invariably be magnanimous towards any friends in need, and subscribe to any charity that seems worthwhile.

Acquaintances and friends will greatly affect the wealth of these people, but their finances are still liable to swing from one extreme to the other. Large organizations and corporations are possible sources of income, as well as anything related to aeronautics, electronics, computer science, electricity, radio and television.

PISCES — THE FISHES

Water, Mutable, Jupiter and Neptune

The Water sign of Pisces in the Second House denotes very fluid finances, with money seeming to evaporate into thin air. People with this placing don't take to the material sphere like fish to water, and their attitude to property and money matters is generally erratic, hazy or other-worldly. At times, Pisces gives an idealistic attitude to money, and a readiness to contribute to altruistic causes. Such people may, in some cases, even give away their property, believing it to be too weighty a load for them to shoulder on their path towards spiritual advancement. In other cases, however, these people long to make some easy money and, consequently, tend to get caught up in tempting offers and apparently water-tight deals. Needless to say, these schemes usually leak badly. More often than not, they turn out to be nothing but bait set out by shady characters fishing in muddy waters, who reel in unsuspecting victims and trap them in their nets. If these people are gullible they should steer clear of dubious situations and strive, instead, for the utmost clarity and unambiguity where their money is concerned.

The financial situation of those with Pisces in the Second House is often unclear. They usually receive money from various sources at one time, some of which are obscure, or shrouded in mystery. Amongst likely and profitable occupations for people with this placing are maritime matters, oil, music, the law, the cinema, and the textile and shoe industries.

THE THIRD HOUSE

Mentality and self-expression; Learning; Siblings; Neighbours; Immediate surroundings; Short trips

ARIES — THE RAM

Fire, Cardinal, Mars

When Aries, the first of the Fire signs, is ablaze in the Third House, it denotes a typical Arian mentality: someone who is impulsive, tempestuous, volatile and enthusiastic. People with Aries in the Third House are quick on the uptake but tend to arrive at hasty conclusions, and they rely on their own judgement too much, ignoring the advice of friends. Their unbounding Arian enthusiasm prods them on constantly to learn as much as possible as fast as possible, but they lack consistency and perseverance. They can easily be carried away by a new hobby, subject or idea, but their new-found interest doesn't last for long, and usually fads pall within a relatively short time.

People with the Martial sign of Aries in their Third House are good at studying military science. Other subjects that appeal include those requiring physical fitness, or a technical aptitude and mechanical ability.

The frank, straightforward mentality of these people means that they don't hesitate to call a spade a spade. However, this candour doesn't only border on downright tactlessness, but sometimes scathing comments can leave long-lasting scars.

As a rule, people with this placing don't enjoy harmonious relationships with their siblings. Often, there is a very strong element of rivalry.

TAURUS — THE BULL

Earth, Fixed, Venus

Commonsense, a mentality as solid as an ox, and a practical, down-to-earth attitude to life are all signified when Taurus is in the Third House. Unlike people with Aries in this House, who merrily jump to conclusions in a jiffy, those with the careful, considering Bull in the Third House tend to ruminate and ponder on all the pros and cons before reaching a decision. But when they finally make up their minds, they won't be swayed from their viewpoints. So, it's hardly surprising that they are often described as stubborn, or even plain obstinate!

Although people with this placing have calm, patient and tolerant mentalities, don't be lulled into a false sense of security and take them for granted. Their tempers operate on slow-burning fuses, and if you goad them too far, they'll act like real Bulls, start to see red, put their heads down and charge!

Taurus is the sign associated with property, and when it is found in the Third House it denotes people who like to acquire knowledge. They regard their educations as assets in the literal sense of the word, and so will try to find practical uses for their learning. These people are capable of sustained intellectual effort, concentration, and perseverance in their studies. Being an Earth sign, Taurus in the Third House gives a type of mentality well-suited to studies in practical matters such as economics or agriculture. And because this sign is ruled by Venus, it often bestows success in the arts, as well.

These people enjoy harmonious and stable relations with their nearest and dearest, and there will be a mutual willingness to lend support and financial help, whenever it is needed.

GEMINI — THE TWINS

Air, Mutable, Mercury

People who have Gemini, the sign of the Twins, cavorting in their Third House, are endowed with versatile, highly intelligent, multifaceted and alert mentalities. There is hardly a subject under the sun which doesn't arouse the interest of these mental magicians. But although admirable in itself, these wide-ranging interests make those with Gemini in their Third House spread themselves rather thin, intellectually. They will flit like butterflies from one Tree of Knowledge to another, gathering snippets of information as and when the fancy takes them. Is it any wonder, then, that even their nearest and dearest consider them to be quite shallow and superficial?

But not to worry — even when their knowledge of a particular topic is flimsy, to say the least, they will still succeed in holding forth on the subject like true experts, thanks to their extraordinary gift of the gab. And as if that weren't enough, they also show a certain duality in their mental make-up and can express ambiguous or equivocal opinions. Don't be surprised when these people argue cleverly for one view, and then suddenly switch viewpoints and begin brilliant counter-arguments.

The chameleon-like mentalities of people with Gemini in their Third House means that they find it easy to adapt themselves to new surroundings and fresh ideas. And, very often, they have a quick grasp of languages as well. Self-expression comes easily to people with this placing, and they enjoy any work connected with oral or written communication, such as journalism or teaching. They often study two or more subjects at the same time, or will change topics halfway through a course, seemingly without missing a beat.

They may have ambivalent relationships with their brothers and sisters, and there can be many ups and downs.

CANCER — THE CRAB

Water, Cardinal, The Moon

People who have Cancer in the Third House are overly introverted, with sensitive mentalities. Ruled to a great extent by their emotions and feelings, they tend to be far too subjective for their own good. Because these people are very impressionable, they absorb — like extra-sensitive film — the subtlest shades and nuances of a situation, and store them in the archives of their memories forever. And their memories are excellent — sometimes photographic — enabling them to recall, in extraordinary detail, experiences which go back to their early childhoods. These people are very much aware of the past, and will go over it again and again, brooding upon it and taking great interest in their family histories. The attraction that they feel for the past is sometimes expressed by writing memoirs, and very often in a marked interest in history and archaeology.

Since those with Cancer in their Third House are deeply aware of their need for security, they do their utmost to be on the safe side, keep out of harm's way, and see how the land lies before committing themselves. Being always on their guard, they carefully plan their moves ahead of time, and advance slowly, step by tentative step. They are often so cautious that, like the crab, they seem to take two steps back for every one they take forward.

Not only is their approach to the basic problems of life greatly influenced by their families but, in most cases, their interest in, and choice of studies is strongly influenced by the general attitudes of their families. They tend to study subjects related to the caring professions, such as nursing and nutrition and they are also attracted to hotel management, cooking, interior design and real estate.

As you might expect, people with Cancer in their Third House are very warm and affectionate towards their families, who mean a great deal to them. Although they feel caring towards all members of their families, they are especially protective towards their younger relations.

LEO — THE LION

Fire, Fixed, The Sun

Leo always thinks big, which is why people with the Lion roaring in their Third House look for wide horizons and have all-embracing outlooks on life. Only king-sized matters appeal to these kings, or queens, of the jungle. They resent pettiness and pedantry, and prefer to grasp the essentials while ignoring the details. (They are far too trifling to bother with.) People with this placing have a gift of self-expression that is dramatic, impressive and convincing. In many cases, they are also blessed with creative talent in the field of writing.

People with this placing have a love of knowledge, and greatly enjoy reading. They are very proud of their erudition, and often lay claim to possessing the crown of wisdom. Sometimes, unfortunately, they can become intellectual snobs, and will speak in a conceited, arrogant or pompous manner.

Theatrical and artistic studies often appeal to people born with Leo in their Third House, as do any spheres connected with children. In fact, these people share a common language with children, attracting them by their vitality and warmth. Other possible fields of study are organization and management.

When it comes to family matters, these people enjoy remarkably good, warm relationships with their siblings and close relations.

VIRGO — THE MAIDEN

Earth, Mutable, Mercury

Virgo in the Third House denotes a methodical, orderly, analytical and logical way of thinking — people with this placing pay a great deal of attention to details, and they tend to be as meticulous as possible in everything they do. These people are endowed with an excellent gift for self-expression, in both writing and speech (although they can be far too critical, sometimes), and a quick grasp of details and facts. There's no doubt that they have a deep thirst for knowledge, and every drop of information they absorb quickly penetrates their minds and is stored away efficiently in the filing systems in their brains. The sign of Virgo may suggest those who are shy and hide their light under a bushel, but these people forget all about modesty when it comes to revealing their own knowledge. They are often walking, talking encyclopedias and if there's anything you want to know, you can be fairly certain that someone with Virgo in the Third House will be able to supply the answers, in great detail, and off the tops of their extremely knowledgeable heads. However, people who have this Virgoan way of thinking can pay too much attention to details, and at times it seems as though they are looking at the world through a microscope, focusing only on the smallest, most trivial things in life. They are shining examples of people who can't see the wood for the trees.

Virgo is the sign of work, so people with this placing are more than happy to invest a lot of time and effort in study. They also often find that there is a strong link between their ability to communicate through speech and writing, and their choice of profession — many of them work in education, or the communications and media industries. They will do best when concentrating on subjects which require a great deal of precision, and the ability to focus on small details.

They get on well with their relations, but they tend to behave in a rather critical and reserved manner.

Leo, the sign of drama and creativity, is found in George Bernard Shaw's Third House.

Virgo in Marie Curie's Third House reflects the systematic way of thinking of this great woman of science, as well as the strenuous work she put into her studies when she was young and penniless.

LIBRA — THE SCALES

Air, Cardinal, Venus

When Libra, the sign of the Scales, is in this House it indicates a balanced, composed and objective mentality, an understanding of the other person's point of view, and an ability to influence people, albeit in a very diplomatic way. (This is the sign of the iron hand in the velvet glove!) Those with Libra in their Third House are also often great conversationalists. Listening to them air their views is a fascinating experience — it's not the weight of their arguments which tips the scales over to their side, but the charm of their silver tongues which enchants their listeners.

However, there is also a less positive side to Libra in the Third House, and people with this placing find it difficult to reach decisions. Those inner sets of scales tip up and down for a very long time before these people can allow them to settle.

Interesting and intelligent people attract those with Libra in the Third House, because they need strong intellectual ties and joint interests in their close relationships. They want to share their thoughts and ideas, and to exchange viewpoints, with people close to their hearts. In many cases, the life-partner, or a close friend, will influence these people's choice of studies. They are drawn to subjects which require a balanced and objective judgement, a diplomatic and tactful approach, or an appreciation of beauty or culture. A harmonious atmosphere in their immediate surroundings is as vital as the air they breathe to people who have Libra in their Third House, otherwise they feel unsettled, unbalanced and unhappy. As might be expected from these born diplomats, they get on very well with all their relations.

SCORPIO — THE SCORPION

Water, Fixed, Mars and Pluto

An uncanny intuition, and an enquiring intellect which is quick on the uptake, are the chief mental characteristics of people born with Scorpio in their Third House. They don't accept things at face value, and instead, they analyse and examine everything first. Their keen psychological insight pierces through disguises, masks and smoke-screens, revealing any hidden, secret motives that lie beneath someone's outward behaviour. People with Scorpio mentalities, being introverted and secretive, keep their opinions to themselves, and drop only the barest hints here and there, never revealing the full story. Even though they use their words sparingly, the little they do say will often seem like highly concentrated venom, which has to be diluted at once in order to make it bearable. And as if that weren't enough, these people have a tendency to stubborness and a suspicious and subversive turn of mind!

Many people who have Scorpio in the Third House tend to be preoccupied with the eternal mysteries of life, death and sex. They often take an interest in other people's money, too, though not always out of mere curiosity or greed. Purely objective reasons may force them to give a great deal of thought to the finances and property of others, and they often find themselves managing the financial affairs of others.

Very often, people with this placing are the lucky recipients of a scholarship, which enables them to further their studies when they might not have otherwise been able to do so.

These people's relationships with their families are not necessarily as they appear to be on the surface. There may be undercurrents of rivalry or jealousy, which will go undetected for years, before they finally make their presence felt.

SAGITTARIUS — THE ARCHER

Mutable, Fire, Jupiter

People who were born with the sign of Sagittarius in the Third House have a remarkably wide range of interests, above-average intelligence, wide mental horizons, highly developed intuition, a well-spring of ideas and excellent judgement. This sign's attitude to life is positive, hearty and highly optimistic. In fact, these people can spot the rainbow in a sky that seems to be full only of dark thunderclouds. It sometimes seems that, as far as they are concerned, the sun is always shining and roses are forever in bloom. Small wonder, then, that their unbounding sense of optimism borders sometimes on complacency.

When people are born with this placing they are eager to expand their horizons, and are intellectually tolerant, being always open to new ideas. They travel extensively, adapt themselves with ease to every new situation and manage to find a common language with all and sundry. They are remarkably frank and honest, yet even when they put their cards on the table, they will do so with care. These people are plainspoken — often downright blunt! — and their barbs, although they are usually honey-coated, land squarely on target.

Sagittarius in the Third House gives a desire for higher learning and a tendency to study several subjects at once. These people are usually attracted to the study of law, philosophy, theology, foreign relations and languages. With their love of travel, there is also a possibility of them studying abroad. Their relationships with their families are usually conducted on a warm, hearty and generous basis.

CAPRICORN — THE MOUNTAIN GOAT

Earth, Cardinal, Saturn

A serious, logical and practical mentality, and a realistic approach to life, typify those with Capricorn in the Third House. They have the ability to concentrate deeply and to express themselves clearly — they may not say a lot, but when they do speak it is to the point. People with Capricorn, the sign of the Mountain Goat, climbing through their Third House tend to equate social status with education, aspire to academic achievements and will cram and grind their way to attaining the highest marks possible. Being extremely ambitious, they devote a great deal of thought to their careers, and will gladly spend many hours reading all sorts of professional literature in order to get ahead. Some setbacks on the way to the top are possible, but thanks to the Capricorn ability to concentrate on the task in hand, these people are certain to make up for lost time, and can even come out on top. In some cases, they may gain an impressive reputation as a result of their intellectual achievements.

These people always seem to be more mature mentally than their years would suggest, and even when they were children, they would have acted and thought in an adult way. But no matter what age, people with a Capricorn mentality are drawn to the company of their elders, often preferring it to their peers, and being keen to learn from their experiences. They have a deep sense of the past and of their family roots, and they admire and respect tradition, historical sites, antiquities and period furniture — anything that has an old atmosphere will appeal to them.

Their choice of studies may well be influenced by their father, or some other authoritarian figure. Unfortunately, the subject chosen can seem rather conservative because it takes into account the wishes of their families.

These people may not have particularly warm relationships with their families, but they will be dutiful and mature. What they lack in cordiality will be made up for in responsibility.

AQUARIUS — THE WATER BEARER

Air, Fixed, Saturn and Uranus

Individual, independent and original are just some of the qualities of people born with Aquarius in their Third House. They have remarkably quick, almost electronic, perceptions and ideas flash through their brains like sparks from a high-voltage wire. People with this airy sign blowing through their Third House have ideas that seem revolutionary for their day, and they themselves seem to have been born before their time. It's no wonder, then, that anything to do with the future (such as science fiction and futuristic sciences) fascinates them, as well as anything to do with the out-of-the-ordinary, such as research into the paranormal and supernatural.

Sometimes, the Aquarian originality will express itself in an urge to be different, or in a chronic state of disagreement with the world at large. In extreme cases, there is a tendency towards unexpected behaviour and erratic whims. Is it to be wondered, then, that these people can be regarded as rather strange and eccentric — and that their friends and family long ago resigned themselves to expecting the unexpected where they are concerned?

The Aquarian mentality is well suited to the study of unconventional subjects, and everything from aeronautics, astronomy or astrology, to electronics, computers, radio and television will appeal. In spite of (or perhaps, because of!) their unorthodox mentalities, these people get on well with their close relations.

Aquarius in Emile Zola's Third House indicates the French writer's sense of social justice, as expressed in his book *J'Accuse* in which he came to the defence of Alfred Dreyfus – the Jewish army officer wrongly accused of treason.

Scorpio in Agatha Christie's Third House perfectly reflects the famous detective writer's secretive and mysterious creations.

PISCES — THE FISHES

Water, Mutable, Jupiter and Neptune

'An enigma' is the way to describe people with Pisces in their Third House. They have finely-honed intuition, a strong sense of empathy with others, and a refined sense of humour. But because their Ascendant is Capricorn, the reserved side of that sign clashes with the soft, dreamy mentality of Pisces, making these people a mystery to themselves, as well as to those who know them. Their basically Capricorn natures may make them seem outwardly too rational, cold and calculating, while the Piscean influence induces in them a tendency to flights of fancy, daydreaming, and even writing poetry in secret. These people are very introverted and secretive, wanting to keep silent on their private feelings. When they do choose to reveal something of the workings of their minds, there is good reason to believe that they are not telling the whole story!

People with the Fishes swimming in their Third House tend to express themselves ambiguously, and they don't always strive for maximum accuracy. Instead, you can expect a good measure of poetic licence! Their vagueness often stems from confused, befuddled thinking and bad memories. Very often, however, the Fishes in the Third House denotes a literally fishy mentality: deliberately creating a smoke-screen, in order to throw others off the scent. In such cases, people with this placing turn into fishermen bent on fishing in muddy waters — only to get lost in a Piscean fog of their own making and become entangled in the net of their own lies.

With all that, the Pisces mentality is well-suited to studies relating to philosophy, religion and mysticism. Many people with this placing get their elementary education in closed institutions, such as boarding schools or convents. Their attitude towards their brothers and sisters, and close relations, is very loving and altruistic.

THE FOURTH HOUSE

Parents; Family; Home life; Twilight years

ARIES — THE RAM

Fire, Cardinal, Mars

Aries in the Fourth House is an indication that the parents and childhood circumstances have encouraged independence from a very early age. Such people devote a lot of energy to their homes and families, and invest their all in their home lives. Unfortunately, they can get carried away, and tend to interfere too much, trying to force their wills on their nearest and dearest.

People with Aries in their Fourth House develop a strong sense of self at a very early age, which often expresses itself in a series of arguments, or differences of opinion, with their parents. They are then likely to challenge the authority of their parents while they are still youngsters, confronting them head-on and insisting on what they regard as their rights. Such children may be constantly battling with their parents, contesting and fighting for control and the right to have the last word. So, it's very important that their energies should be channelled into outdoor activities, to stop the atmosphere at home getting too heated. After all, Aries is a Fire sign!

Mars, the planet of war, rules Aries, and in extreme cases the home lives of people with the Ram in their Fourth House resemble battlefields. In other examples, this Martial connection may not necessarily result in a combative atmosphere at home, but rather in a member of the family having a strong connection with the army possibly the father was in the service at the time of the child's birth. Events pertaining to war will often have a fateful influence on this family's life.

The Fourth House also represents the final years of life. A dynamic sign like Aries in this House shows that people with this placing will retain their youthfulness into old age, continuing to face new challenges even in the twilight of their lives.

TAURUS — THE BULL

Earth, Fixed, Venus

A stable and peaceful family life is signified for people born with Taurus in the Fourth House. Very often, their parents are financially well off, but even if that is not the case, they do their best to give their children everything they can, and instil in them good, sound values which provide a stable moral base. These people know how to appreciate everything their parents have given them and will support them in their old age and keep in close, warm contact with them until the end of their lives. When it comes to their own family lives, they will try to build them on the firmest material foundations, and to create the same emotional stability that they were given from their parents. As a result, they will have peaceful, constructive and uplifting family lives. Sometimes, this constructive element finds concrete expression in the building of their homes with their own hands. Such a house is usually out in the country or in a quiet, leafy suburb. However, even if circumstances force them to live in a city, their flats or town houses will seem at one with nature, as they will overflow with plants. And once they have created homes they like, they will be unlikely to move — people with the Earth sign Taurus in their Fourth House tend to put down roots. They have a deep need to stay in one place, living and flourishing in that home happily ever after.

People with this placing can expect the last years of their lives to be spent in peaceful, comfortable circumstances and surroundings.

GEMINI — THE TWINS

Air, Mutable, Mercury

There are frequent moves and many changes of residence for people born with this placing. They may even live in two, or sometimes three, different places at the same time! Their home atmosphere is one of mobility — here today, gone tomorrow — and they may even live in some sort of vehicle, such as a caravan, at one stage in their lives.

The atmosphere at home will be buzzing with activity. Relatives, friends and neighbours will come in and out constantly, and the home will resound with lively conversation from dawn to dusk. The shelves will be crammed with books and magazines, and the home life will centre around the telephones (there's bound to be more than one), radio and television. For those with Gemini in the Fourth House, home is not some quiet corner, impervious to the tumult of life. Instead, there will be an abundance of information constantly pouring out of the latest technological gadgets, such as mini television sets, which never seem to be turned off.

It's perhaps hardly surprising that family life for these people isn't always stable. One of the parents may be away from home a lot, and often an older brother or sister steps in to fill the missing parent's role. The parents will place great stress on their childrens' intellectual development, encouraging them to speak and read at an early age and developing their interest in studies. The profession of one of the parents will be in the fields of communications, education, or connected in some way with commerce.

Since the Fourth House also represents old age, people with the sign of the Twins in this House will preserve their intellectual awareness and interests until their dying days. They will continue to be interested in a wide variety of subjects, not being content just to rest on their laurels and stagnate.

CANCER — THE CRAB

Water, Cardinal, The Moon

The homes of these people will be more like nests, being cosy, comfortable and warm. Relationships between the family members will be charged with emotion, and the ties to the parental household will be lifelong. The further these people may range in adulthood, the stronger their need to return again and again to their home ports, for only there can they recapture the childhood memories so dear to their hearts.

When people with Cancer in their Fourth House start their own families, they will do their utmost to ensure that the same snug, homely atmosphere pervades their households. For them, home is a safe harbour, a refuge from the storms of life and the sound and fury of the outside world. Their homes are their castles and, if they can't surround them with high stone walls and deep moats, they'll find other ways of preventing the outside world from intruding upon the warm nests they've built.

These people like to stress the contrast between the softness and snugness of their home-sweet-homes, and the rough and tumble of the great wide world. The interiors of their homes seem to be padded with shock absorbers — the floors with carpets and rugs, the walls with wallpaper and the ceilings with rafters. Everything that can possibly be padded will have been so, including doors and window sills. Even the light switches are often covered with some ornamental plastic, and not infrequently the lavatory seat will be swathed in frilly covers. This exaggerated need to emphasize the difference between indoors and outdoors expresses itself quite often by heating the home on days which are not particularly cold, and then running the air-conditioning unit full blast even on mildly warm summer days. Their home manner, too, is quite different from their behaviour elsewhere — though they may be pussy-cats at home, they can turn into tigers when venturing beyond the confines of their own four walls.

Another characteristic of people with Cancer in their Fourth House is that they love keeping family memories by recording everything on film, whether video or photographs, and by adorning their walls and shelves with treasured family pictures.

Astrology indicates a peaceful old age for those born with this placing, because Cancer in the Fourth House shows that, barring unexpected events, such people will spend the end of their lives in the loving, caring bosom of their families.

LEO — THE LION

Fire, Fixed, The Sun

Home isn't so much a castle as a kingdom for those born with the royal sign of Leo majestically reclining in their Fourth House. They will do their utmost to have homes as grand as possible, in which they can live like kings (or queens) and throw lavish parties. The creativity of these people is often linked to their homes, and sometimes they will have an artistic hobby which they pursue at home. In other cases, the home itself will serve as a creative outlet for their artistic leanings. They will design, furnish and sometimes even build their own homes, and planning the interior decoration will become a fascinating hobby. Every so often they will redecorate the whole house, as though making set-changes between the acts of a play. (You don't need me to tell you who has the starring role!) Although these people can change the interior, what they won't do is change their place of residence — people with Leo in the Fourth House are happy to stay in the same home for years at a time.

There is a sunny and happy atmosphere to these people's homes. They like the company of children — their laughter, their jokes and the patter of little feet. They take pleasure in their games, even joining in now and then. The home usually has a playroom or games room — at the very least, it has a corner where one can have fun without disrupting the household routine. Very often, there is a playground, swimming pool or sports field in the neighbourhood.

The Fourth House symbolizes the end of one's days, and this placing promises that these people will enjoy the company of their children and grandchildren, sharing their enjoyment of life, despite the generation gap, in a happy and creative old age.

VIRGO — THE MAIDEN

Earth, Mutable, Mercury

People with this placing have rather modest starts in life, and in some cases, even deprived childhoods. This is often because of the ill health of a member of the family, or of the person themselves. Alternatively, Virgo in this House might signify that the parents were engrossed in their work to such an extent that the people with this placing felt that they were neglected.

The parents will be very conscious of health, proper nutrition and hygiene. One of them may be a doctor or nurse, or serve in some other medical capacity. Quite often, one parent is a teacher or journalist. The home will be neat and clean, although sometimes it can be too much so, giving it the atmosphere of a clinic.

Virgo is the sign of work, and when placed in this House it symbolizes a strong connection between work and the home, such as a career that is run from home. In other cases, the work will be connected with the residences of other people, through such jobs as those of doorman, housekeeper, home help, or any profession or job in the hotel business. Another example of the Virgo-Fourth House connection is work done in co-operation with other members of the family. In some cases, people with this placing may have to move to another city because of the demands of their jobs, or even live on the premises where they work — for example, doctors who have to live in the hospital grounds, lecturers who live on campus, military personnel who have to live on army bases, and so on.

The sign of Virgo has a strong connection with health, and in certain cases health problems, such as asthma, may force these people to move elsewhere, if only for a short time. I would suggest that they don't live in the vicinity of the sea, or in locations where the humidity is high, if they have difficulties with their breathing.

These people get on perfectly well with their families, but the relationships may not be particularly warm, and sometimes they will be tinged with a slight atmosphere of disapproval. When Virgo is found in the Fourth House, it suggests that people with this placing will continue to work late into their lives.

LIBRA — THE SCALES

Air, Cardinal, Venus

Life at home is a calm, peaceful oasis imbued with a cultured, aesthetic atmosphere, when Libra is in the Fourth House, and family relations will be good, too. People with this placing shy away from strong contrasts in colour in their homes, preferring a harmonious blend of subtle, gentle pastels, that induce a serene feeling and bring peace of mind. In such homes the emphasis is very much on togetherness. These people find it very difficult to live alone and if they don't live with a lover or spouse, will seek to share their homes with a friend or flatmate.

For people with Libra in the Fourth House, marriage is synonymous with domesticity. Their urge to marry usually stems from a need to settle down, rather than from any particularly romantic reasons. Their model of married life is patterned after that of their parents, who lived like a pair of turtle doves. When children, these people probably expressed a wish to marry the parent of the opposite sex. In adulthood, this parent will serve as the role-model in the choice of spouse, and people with this placing often marry an older person who represents the father or mother figure.

Libra in this House ensures harmony and tranquillity at the end of one's days. 'And they lived happily ever after' is a phrase that can certainly be applied to couples when one of them has Libra in the Fourth House.

SCORPIO — THE SCORPION

Water, Fixed, Mars and Pluto

The Water sign of Scorpio in the Fourth House denotes a stormy family life. Relationships between family members tend to extremes: there is often fierce loyalty and a readiness to face hell or high water for the family's sake, while in other cases, it seems that unmentionable subjects flow like hidden currents under the surface, eating away at the foundations of the family structure. The atmosphere will be charged with tension, suspicion, intrigue and jealousy. Time and time again, bitter arguments will flare up over money matters, casting their shadows over complex family interrelationships which at times resemble a nest of vipers.

Being a Fixed sign, Scorpio in the Fourth House denotes a strong tendency to permanence in family life, but not at all costs. When the turbulent waters of family strife threaten to inundate people with this placing, they may react either with violent outbursts or sudden departures.

Scorpio in this House often suggests the early death of a parent, or a separation from one of them at a young age. This placing also symbolizes a strong link with other people's money. And in many cases indeed, the family homes of these people will have been bought with money that was inherited or privately loaned. There is another possible link between the homes of people with this placing and other people's money; they may discover a treasure buried in their back gardens, or hidden in a wall, or be told that an old painting gathering dust in the attic is a valuable masterpiece.

Bearing in mind that the Fourth House represents the final years of life, Scorpio in this House indicates a considerable inheritance, or an impressive grant, received late in life.

Scorpio in Marilyn Monroe's Fourth House indicates the secrecy and mystery surrounding the origins of this glamorous star (who tried throughout her life to trace her father) as well as reflecting her separation from her mother at a tender age.

Taurus in Grace Kelly's Fourth House represents the stable and affluent family background established by her father, a building contractor. Taurus also symbolizes everything associated with building.

SAGITTARIUS — THE ARCHER

Fire, Mutable, Jupiter

People with Sagittarius in the Fourth House enjoy warm, friendly and open family lives. Their parents will always do their utmost to shower them with the best of everything, to widen their horizons and to instil in them high moral values. The openness, so typical of this sign, expresses itself both in the openmindedness of the family and in the door-is-always-open policy of the household — guests will be warmly welcomed at all hours. A sense of freedom and open spaces is of great importance to these people, so that even if they live in small flats, they will use every interior design trick to make them seem more spacious.

Those with Sagittarius in the Fourth House tend to move house frequently, and many of them live in foreign countries for fairly long periods at a time. Very often, they have to live for some time with their spouses' relations, too. In many cases, there are legal problems connected with the purchase or leases of their homes.

Sagittarius in the Fourth House, which represents the last years of one's life, indicates that people with this placing will strive to widen their mental and physical horizons even late in life, and may even embark on long journeys in their old age.

CAPRICORN — THE MOUNTAIN GOAT

Earth, Cardinal, Saturn

When people are born with Capricorn in the Fourth House, they will experience a conservative atmosphere at home, and a somewhat strict (often religious) upbringing. They are frequently well-born, so have an innate sense of *noblesse oblige*. Yet, when the family strictures are too severe, and the demands to fulfil their duties become too overbearing, these people's illustrious links with the past and family traditions may turn into chains. In many cases, one of the parents will be an authoritarian figure who has high hopes of his or her offspring, so that the people with this placing feel duty-bound to justify those expectations, doing everything in their power to prove their mettle.

People born with Capricorn in their Fourth House not only devote much time to their careers, often at the expense of their families, but often turn their homes into extensions of their offices. In spite of that, they are very responsible towards their families and parents, deciding sometimes to postpone having families of their own out of an overriding sense of duty towards a sick parent for whom they have to care.

Capricorn in this House, which rules the last years of life, suggests that people with this placing will be very active in their careers late into their lives.

AQUARIUS — THE WATER BEARER

Air, Fixed, Saturn and Uranus

There is an original, often intellectual, home atmosphere when the sign of the Water Bearer is found in the Fourth House. People with this placing draw ideas and social ideals from the fountainhead of their parents' homes, which often serve as socio-ideological meeting places. Their parents will be progressive and individual, in many cases devoting more time to social issues than to family matters. The family backgrounds are somewhat unusual or bohemian, and the homes are always open to guests, even at what to others would be the most ungodly hours.

Once they have created their own families, these people try to base their relationships with their partners and children on high-minded ideals, such as friendship and equality, while not foregoing their own freedom and individuality. As one of the Fixed signs, Aquarius induces a desire for stability in family life, yet such people's family lives are often far from being placid! The atmosphere at home can be tense and charged with electricity, especially when family members show too much independence. There are unexpected upheavals in their family lives for those with Aquarius in their Fourth House.

People who have this placing can expect to spend the ends of their lives in a friendly and uplifting atmosphere, surrounded by their friends. If they feel disappointed early in life, they should bear in mind that many of their wishes may come true as they become older.

PISCES — THE FISHES

Water, Mutable, Jupiter and Neptune

A deep, warm and highly emotional attitude towards family members is characterized by Pisces in the Fourth House. These people are prepared to make far-reaching concessions for the sake of their families.

The Fishes swimming in the Fourth House of these people indicates that there is something hidden or confused in their parents' lives. In extreme cases, they may even feel a concealed hostility directed towards them by one of their parents.

Their tendency to assume too many family responsibilities will gradually make them feel trapped, as if not only their numerous duties, but the very walls, were closing in on them . . . Sometimes, such a claustrophobic feeling is caused by living in truly closed-in places, such as army barracks, convents or hospitals. Also, people born with this placing often spend many years in boarding schools when children. Sometimes, they will keep their addresses secret for a time — a symptom of the mysterious nature of Pisces in the Fourth House. Many of them live close to the sea, or another body of water, such as a lake or river. Quite a few of them even find themselves living aboard a ship for a while.

The Fourth House also rules the closing years of life. Pisces in this House denotes deep mystical experiences and spiritual journeys in the twilight years of people who, in their youth, underwent adventures and experiences of a far more earthy kind!

THE FIFTH HOUSE

Love; Children; Creativity; Pleasures; Hobbies; Gambling

ARIES — THE RAM

Fire, Cardinal, Mars

The fiery sign of Aries burning in the Fifth House denotes a hot temperament, excitability and a dynamic love life. These people are by no means wallflowers sitting on the sidelines, waiting for romance to land in their laps. Their approach to love can be summed up in three little words — 'Veni, Vidi, Vici' ('I came, I saw, I conquered')! Setting out on the chase, they often initiate romantic encounters too hastily. The adventure, challenge and novelty of the experience spark their fire of love, but those who want to keep this flame burning brightly have to present these people with a constant challenge, because their ardour might cool down as soon as the spice of novelty wears thin. Still, the embers need only be lightly fanned, for as soon as the old flame is extinguished a new one is sure to set the Arian emotions ablaze again. However, people with this flirtatious placing can often be attracted to someone new, who will provide that dash of novelty they were looking for. In extreme cases, every reasonably attractive person these people meet will present them with a fresh amorous challenge, so that they leave behind them a trail of scorched and broken hearts on their victorious march of conquests. Needless to say, people whose emotional lives are influenced by Aries love playing with fire.

'Dans l'amour que dans la guerre' ('in love as in war') is another saying that accurately describes the Arian attitude (a sign ruled by Mars, the planet of warfare) to romance. Aggressive Mars indicates strife in these people's love lives which, in many cases, resemble battlefields.

Those with Aries in their Fifth House can hardly be described as perfect parents. Usually, they lack the necessary patience and expect their children to become independent quite early in life. They are bent on having fun, rushing from one party to the next, from one entertainment to another. Many of them indulge in those sports which have a strong competitive element and entail certain risks, because risk is the spice of life for them. It's not surprising, then, that a lot of them have a strong gambling streak — with a particular weakness for long shots!

People born with Aries in this House have a strong urge for creative self-expression. This creativity needn't necessarily find an artistic outlet, but whatever the chosen subject, these people will throw themselves into the effort wholeheartedly, leaving their personal stamp on their work. In many cases they will be the first in their chosen field, while others attempt to imitate them, and even to steal the show. When their creativity does find expression in the arts, a quality of invigorating, charming freshness is readily apparent, appealing primarily to children and young people.

TAURUS — THE BULL

Earth, Fixed, Venus

Frank, stable emotions, and the desire to establish a romantic relationship on a firm, permanent basis, characterize those born with Taurus in the Fifth House. Because they are influenced by an Earth sign, these people tend to express their emotions in an earthy manner. Mere platonic relationships are not for them — they need to express their love on the physical plane, first and foremost. People who have Taurus in their Fifth House are attracted to people they can admire, those they feel are 'worth much', and worthy of their attentions and emotional efforts. Consequently, their attitude to their beloved is rather proprietorial. Tending as they do to identify the concept of love with that of property and money, they long to bestow every kind of material comfort upon their loved one. Sometimes, however, the presence of Taurus (the sign of property and money) in the Fifth House implies that love is conditioned by financial considerations.

Most people with Taurus in their Fifth House have a loving, devoted attitude to their children, investing much time and money in them, and showering them with the best they can afford. They want to give their offspring a feeling of material security and a solid financial standing, thereby enabling them to blossom and mature without a care in the world.

Although prepared to spend a lot of money on enjoying themselves, those with this placing know how to get the most out of the simple pleasures of life, too. Taurus in this House often signifies a talent for music and singing, but the creative urge usually finds expression in more physical forms, such as sculpture. Yet just doing sculpture — art for art's sake — might seem pointless to those with practically-minded Taurus in their House of creativity. They may prefer to make useful objects in ceramics or wood, and they often choose carpentry, or something similar that involves construction, as a hobby. (As children, their favourite toys were often sets of building blocks.) These people may make a profit from their creative talents, hobbies or gardening, which is another activity that they love. In some cases, the mere making of money becomes a hobby in itself!

GEMINI — THE TWINS

Air, Mutable, Mercury

People with Gemini in their Fifth House find romance not only dear to their hearts, but to their minds as well. Gemini is an Air sign, and the feelings of these people shift with the wind, their emotional weather-vanes being subject to frequently changing moods. They have a Geminian attitude to love, believing that variety is the spice of romance, and so flit from one romantic flower to another like butterflies. Sometimes, these light-hearted creatures can carry on two or more affairs at the same time!

Gemini in Errol Flynn's Fifth House reflects the famous movie actor's astounding agility. Light-hearted and airy, Gemini also hints at Flynn's many romantic escapades and his fascination with young girls which, on occasion, landed him in trouble with the law.

Gemini in Ian Fleming's Fifth House symbolizes his creativity in the field of writing. The Geminian duality is expressed in the fact that Fleming, known as the creator of James Bond, also wrote children's books, among them *Chitty Chitty Bang Bang*, which is about bicycles. And what could be more Germinian than a bicycle?

Their love of variety and novelty can be seen in a constant attraction to new acquaintances — youthful, lively, intelligent people, and those who remain perennially young at heart.

These people don't regard children with particular affection. In fact, they don't find them particularly interesting until they have learned to speak, when they start to become people in their own right. It's possible for people with this placing to have twins.

Gemini in the Fifth House bestows many and varied talents, especially in the fields of writing, movement and dance. Such people are fond of travel, reading and any games requiring mental effort. They have many hobbies, especially those demanding manual dexterity, from handicrafts to sleight of hand and conjuring. Some of them are attracted to hobbies related to the exchange of information and communication, such as ham-radio operating and Morse Code.

CANCER — THE CRAB

Water, Cardinal, The Moon

Love is something to be treasured, for people born with Cancer in their Fifth House. They are very sensitive, romantic and sentimental, and cherish every memento of their love lives, from letters and snapshots to dried flowers and even old bus tickets. The date on which they first met their loved one is inscribed forever on the calendars of their hearts. People with this placing cling to their loved ones like climbing plants, weaving their tendrils around them and smothering them with love. They also try their hardest to create an atmosphere of cosy domesticity. Like a bird bringing nourishment to its fledglings, these people express their emotions by feeding the object of their love. Small wonder, then, that when in love they spend most of their time in the kitchen!

But even when nothing is cooking in the romance department, they will spend many hours in the kitchen, because cooking is one of their favourite ways of expressing their creativity. Inspired by their Muse, they will conduct an orchestra of pots and pans in a symphony of exquisite tastes. Their culinary imagination ranges far and wide, and they can invent new recipes every day.

People with Cancer in their Fifth House will do their utmost for their children, who will regard their parent as a source of never-ending love and encouragement, and a tower of strength and security. Such parents tend, however, to be overprotective; as soon as their little chicks spread their wings, trying to leave the nest, they succumb to worries and black moods.

These people prefer to spend their free time at home, safe in the bosoms of their families. Their greatest hobby is collecting — mainly stamps, coins, manuscripts and china, but anything will do, so long as it can be collected. They also enjoy interior decorating, photography and sailing.

LEO — THE LION

Fire, Fixed, The Sun

A burning vitality and a warm, generous heart typify people with Leo roaring in their Fifth House. Their love lives are very active indeed, and brim over with romantic affairs, but when the spark of true love is kindled in the Lion's heart, it becomes the eternal flame.

The way to the hearts of these people isn't open to everyone. When Leo reigns in the House of love, these people want to take pride in their 'heart's choice' — a title they bestow only on someone worthy of their esteem and admiration. For the chosen one, they will roll out the red carpet, making them their life consort and not just king or queen for a day. The royal heart is nothing if not loyal.

Leo in the Fifth House indicates a great love of children, and people with this placing enjoy their company and will happily spend hours playing with them. But despite the fact that they may play as though children themselves, their authoritative image is not weakened in the slightest by their romping, and their children will never forget who the real ruler is.

These are pleasure-loving people, and can paint the town red in their

Pisces in Marc Chagall's Fifth House accurately indicates the mystical/hovering/floating motifs in the great painter's works.

Leo in Frank Sinatra's Fifth House reflects his stage personality and his extraordinary success as a singer and actor.

passion for amusement. In some cases, those with Leo in the Fifth House are really overgrown, playful kittens who, faced with the choice of work or play, will always choose the latter. The ancient Romans' love of games is associated with Leo the Lion, the symbol of the mighty Roman Empire.

The Leo brand of vitality and enthusiasm is also expressed in creativity, particularly in the dramatic arts. Those with this placing tend to express themselves dramatically, and love the spotlight, basking in it like a lion in the glare of the African sun. They certainly don't hide in the wings, and their theatrical presence makes it clear to everyone that they are born actors and actresses. With the royal sign in their Fifth House their motto is 'The bigger the better', and they are drawn to the grand and imposing. In other words, everything has to be king-size! If going in for the arts, for example, they will not only prefer to paint larger-than-life pictures, but will sign them with huge, flourishing signatures.

VIRGO — THE MAIDEN

Earth, Mutable, Mercury

People with Virgo in their Fifth House bring a refined expression of emotion and a rather puritanical approach to romance. A constant desire for moral purity and perfection colours their attitude to love. They approach the subject in a cerebral, fairly sober way, making them hardly likely to be blinded by the dazzling light of love — well, not for very long, anyway! Sometimes, it seems as though people with Virgo in the Fifth House view their loved one through a magnifying glass, as though to remind themselves at all times of their beloved's shortcomings. Although Virgo is the sign of health, these people's tendency to be overly critical and censorious does very little for the well-being of their romantic lives. When the heat of love begins to cool, the health of such people is likely to be affected and, although not the most romantic of people, they are liable to become, quite literally, love sick. Nevertheless, Virgo in the Fifth House also denotes a readiness to work at a relationship, to mend and improve it.

These people are often shrinking violets — introverted, shy and withdrawn in the company of the opposite sex, and who avoid loud parties and discotheques. Quieter forms of entertainment are more to their taste, especially those involving some form of activity, because these people don't like sitting idly, being busy doing nothing. They much prefer to be productive, investing all their efforts into a hobby or developing their creativity.

The Virgo form of creativity steers clear of anything abstract and aims for the utmost precision. When drawing, for example, their sketching will be painstakingly accurate, showing the most minute details. The signature, on the other hand, will be tiny, and barely discernible.

Embroidery is another favourite hobby, but the creativity of these people is best expressed in writing.

They have a very responsible attitude towards children, and pay great attention to their offsprings' health and nutrition, as well as their clothes, cleanliness and manners. In some cases, their attitude may be uncomfortably strict and over-critical.

LIBRA — THE SCALES

Air, Cardinal, Venus

When the Scales are swinging in the Fifth House, they denote a refined expression of emotions, and a sensitivity to beauty and to the charms of the opposite sex. These people are in love with love, and will try to maintain harmonious relations with their beloved at all times. Whenever a misunderstanding arises between the lovers, the Libra-affected one will be the first to try to heal the rift, kiss and make up. Somehow, they are always the ones who assume the role of dove of peace, ever ready to make compromises and concessions. So, it's hardly surprising that their love lives seem to be all sweetness and light. The Scales are, indeed, in a state of heavenly balance and equilibrium in the Fifth House. All the same, it could be argued that the reason this state of perfect balance isn't upset by romantic storms is that the emotional weight on these people's scales is light as a feather. They may be charming and refined, but they can hardly be accused of putting their lives in the balance.

People who have Libra in the Fifth House like togetherness — as far as they are concerned, no enjoyment is complete unless it is shared with their nearest and dearest. They get on admirably well with their children, and strive to instil in them moral values and the appreciation of aesthetics.

The highly developed sense of beauty, which is so characteristic of Libra in the Fifth House, is often expressed in creative endeavours as well. Whatever form this creativity may take, whether writing, music or painting, balance and symmetry are their hallmark, and the work will exude culture and refinement.

SCORPIO — THE SCORPION

Water, Fixed, Mars and Pluto

Deep, tempestuous emotions and stormy passions seethe under the surface when the Water sign of Scorpio is in the Fifth House. These people can feel love, all-powerful as death; jealousy, cruel as the grave; and bottomless hatred. Needless to say, the emotional lives of these people are tempestuous; tossed violently hither and thither, and at the mercy of emotional storms which threaten to pull them under. Is it to be wondered, then, that their romantic lives are such heady brews, so replete with dramatic events that, even if they were diluted with ample amounts of water, they would still be much too strong for most people's taste? Not surprisingly, even those people with Scorpio-affected emotions have difficulty at times in swallowing their own potions.

The creative endeavours of people with Scorpio in their Fifth House are bound to be infused with the passionate nature peculiar to this Sign. Their creativity will burn up their spiritual and mental faculties, seizing them in a demon-like grip and erupting violently like a volcano. The resulting work of art will not necessarily be beautiful in the conventional sense, and very often it will have a mixed reception, revealing as it does a disturbing inner truth. Their work is essentially expressionistic, often of deep psychological significance or erotic impact. The presence of Scorpio (which also indicates other people's money) in the Fifth House suggests that people with this placing might have to depend on the financial generosity of others in order to create. In fact, in many cases, those with Scorpio in their Fifth House are the beneficiaries of financial support or a study grant, which enables them to further their artistic pursuits.

These people love their children deeply. However, at times, they may display an overly possessive attitude towards them, and try to run their lives in the belief that only they know what is best for them.

Being influenced by a Water sign, these Scorpio-affected people love the sea, and many of them are excellent swimmers and divers. They are attracted to any activity which pits them against the forces of nature or the mysterious depths of the mind. These are the powers which they simultaneously long to submit to, and to subdue.

SAGITTARIUS — THE ARCHER

Fire, Mutable, Jupiter

There is a feeling of frankness, and an optimism in love when Sagittarius is found in the Fifth House. Although Sagittarius is a Fire sign, his flame does not burn, but merely warms. When placed in the Fifth House, the House of love, the Archer warms the heart, but often aims his arrows at too many hearts at once. The love lives of these people are as lively and varied as fireworks exploding in all the colours of the rainbow, but often, are just as quick to fade.

People with this placing are attracted to those who broaden their horizons and set fire to their imaginations. They are also attracted to foreigners, or those of a different culture or religion. Their love may be set alight not only by spiritual or intellectual people, but often by sporty, outdoor types too.

Sagittarius is the sign of freedom and open spaces, so these people will neither limit their children nor restrict them in any way. They will never keep them on a short leash, and will give them every possible leeway.

Sagittarius in Pablo Picasso's Fifth House represents the famous painter's abundant creative ability, and the extraordinary success he achieved – Sagittarius being a lucky sign.

Sagittarians are often good at sport and Sagittarius in Mark Spitz's Fifth House reflects the acclaimed swimming champion's athletic abilities.

The sign of the Archer bestows an abundance of talents, which find expression in an extraordinarily wide range of creative endeavours, especially those demanding intellectual ability, such as writing. Other possible creative outlets for the talents of these people are those requiring vitality and suppleness, such as dancing and gymnastics. Sagittarius symbolizes, among other things, a love of movement and sports, with particular emphasis on riding and other activities which allow one access to the wide, open spaces.

A favourite Sagittarian hobby is travel — which is understandable enough, considering that people with this sign in their Fifth House are especially 'turned on' by strangers . . .

CAPRICORN — THE MOUNTAIN GOAT

Earth, Cardinal, Saturn

The placing of Capricorn in the Fifth House denotes people who have a responsible, mature and serious attitude to love, and who are often attracted to those considerably older than themselves. Such people are far from being incorrigible, hopeless romantics. Instead, their emotions are well balanced, and usually under control. In most cases, love is not a goal in itself, but rather a means of achieving other more important practical aims, such as marriage. In some cases, the emotions are perfectly calculated, aiming at such worldly targets as the furthering of social status, career or income. These people are wont to pace their romantic progress to the tune of jingling coins and the rustling of bank notes . . .

Capricorn is perhaps the most ambitious of all the signs. Small wonder, then, that those with the Mountain Goat climbing in their Fifth House, the House of creativity, will strive for an appreciation of their artistic endeavours, and devote a great deal of time and effort to developing their talents. And though the road to the top is far from easy, these people are likely to get there. Mountain-tops and peaks are central motifs in their creative endeavours, and rocks and boulders also hold places of honour. In many cases, the creativity of people with this placing is expressed by sculpting in stone.

The Capricorn love of ascent is often seen in a love of mountain-climbing. In most cases, however, people with Capricorn in the Fifth

House prefer to spend their free time in fairly conservative ways, such as listening to classical music, reading serious books or playing chess. They are also drawn to hobbies which have a practical side, such as carpentry, and like to fashion things in stone, clay or ceramics, choosing to work with dark, sombre colours. Being drawn to the past, these people are enamoured of anything with an old-world atmosphere, such as houses, furniture, books or coins. Another typical Capricorn hobby is collecting, especially unusual rocks and pebbles. This is a sign that favours practicality and purposefulness, so a hobby can often become a profession or a source of income.

Those with Capricorn in their Fifth House tend to raise small families. Their attitude to their offspring is responsible, strict and conservative, often severe, with an exaggerated insistence on achievement.

AQUARIUS — THE WATER BEARER

Air, Fixed, Saturn and Uranus

The Air sign of Aquarius in the Fifth House imparts romantic feelings and the desire for a pure, spiritual, exalted and sublime expression of love. Such a love means, to people with this placing, more than physical love, and the greatest romance of their lives may well be platonic. These dreamy idealists hear the music of the spheres in their beloved's voice, and just holding hands can send them to seventh heaven. At times it seems as if the laws of gravity don't apply to them!

The refined atmosphere associated with this Air sign may not burn with the fires of carnal desire, but it is certainly charged with electricity. Cupid doesn't aim his arrows, but hurls bolts of electricity at these people instead. Yet, perhaps because of the electric shock, people with this placing may give the impression of being withdrawn and somewhat detached, even in the midst of a mad, thousand-watt love affair, and their apparent apathy may short-circuit the relationship. But even though the contact may be broken, these people will try to maintain friendly relations and to prove, at least to themselves, just how fair and objective they are.

Parents with Aquarius in the Fifth House get on well with their children, and give them a progressive upbringing and education, aimed at developing the uniqueness of each child. Their relationship will be based on trust and friendship. These people treat children as equals, always doing their utmost to understand, seeking for a common language — they may even learn computer language — in order to bridge the generation gap.

In the creative sphere, this placing gives an original, innovative approach to art. Aeronautics is a typical Aquarian hobby, but even those who can't fly aeroplanes will settle for flying kites instead.

PISCES — THE FISHES

Water, Mutable, Jupiter and Neptune

Tender, poetic feelings and an idealistic attitude to love are the hallmarks of people born with the Water sign of Pisces flowing through their Fifth House. They find it hard to navigate the stormy seas of emotion while listening to the enticing songs of the sirens, those legendary nymphs who lured seafarers to their deaths on the rocks of the deep. The Piscean 'love boat' may drift, caught by the tide of sentiment, unable, or perhaps unwilling, to drop anchor at a safe harbour. In most cases, the feelings of these people are their vulnerable spots and their hearts their 'Achilles' heel'. With Pisces in their Fifth House, they may become enslaved and engulfed by waves of emotion, sometimes even drowning in them. Then they may flap around like a fish caught in the net, and what was a 'love boat' will have turned into a 'ship of fools'.

The sign of Pisces is associated with seclusion. When in the Fifth House, it signifies romantic attachments connected with hospitals, convents and boarding schools, or romantic affairs that are conducted in secret.

These people have very emotional attitudes towards their children. Sometimes, however, there may be something that has to be kept secret in connection with a child. Often a great deal of self-sacrifice is demanded for the children's sakes.

Pisces in this House bestows inspiration, especially in music and poetry, and an impressionistic approach to painting. They usually love the sea. Strange as it seems, these people can be inspired by water in all its manifestations — sometimes, even when they are soaking in the bath! So, when the skies open, the heavens roar and the thunder crashes, their Muse does not remain silent, either!

THE SIXTH HOUSE

Work; Service; Subordinates; Health; Nutrition

ARIES — THE RAM

Fire, Cardinal, Mars

People who were born with the sign of Aries in the Sixth House give their all to their work. They much prefer to be their own bosses, because they find it difficult to take orders and obey commands. They also tend to rely solely on themselves, rather than delegate responsibility to others. Most people with this placing are attracted to occupations demanding a quick response, personal initiative, the ability to make and implement decisions, mental effort and physical stamina. Above all else, they are drawn to careers in which they can make their mark.

Those with the Fire sign of Aries burning brightly in their Sixth House are indeed afire with enthusiasm for their jobs. They work rapidly and intensively, burning off a great deal of excess energy, and not resting until they have achieved what they set out to do. However, they may finish themselves off before finishing the task in hand, as their feverish pace threatens to impair their health!

Inflammatory and high fevers can afflict people with this placing. There is also the danger of burns. Sometimes they may have an allergy to wool. The head is the most vulnerable part of the body for those born with Aries in the Sixth House.

TAURUS — THE BULL

Earth, Fixed, Venus

Those with Taurus the Bull grazing in their Sixth House may prefer, just like Ferdinand the Bull, to rest on a bed of flowers rather than on wreaths of laurels. Yet, despite their love of ease and comfort, these people are not necessarily lazy: once they consider a task worthy of their effort, especially if it is financially so, they will really put their shoulders to the wheel. But although the choice of occupation is dictated by financial considerations, these people will be happy in their jobs only if they give them the chance to express their creative and constructive drives. Once they have found suitable employment, these people will be content to get into their ruts and plough away. Among the professions that may attract people with this placing are those related to agriculture, gardening, construction, architecture, real estate, finance and economics.

Most people with Taurus in their House of health are as strong and healthy as the proverbial ox. They have healthy appetites, which can lead some of them to overeat. They are also susceptible to diseases and injuries of the throat and neck. Such peoples' financial situations may have profound effects on their health, and pastoral atmospheres and surroundings are most beneficial.

GEMINI — THE TWINS

Air, Mutable, Mercury

Professions demanding a persuasive manner, eloquence and which involve frequent changes, much variety and mobility, are admirably suited to those with Gemini in the Sixth House. They tend to change their places of employment frequently, and often do several jobs at once. They are also not averse to changing their careers, and willingly undergo professional retraining.

Intellectual lively occupations, such as journalism, radio and television — professions guaranteed to put one in the centre of things — all attract these people. Other suitable jobs are teaching, brokerage, clerking and in any field related to transportation and travelling. Sometimes, there is a tendency to get involved in bubble-schemes, which often burst. Quite a few of those with this placing work closely with members of their family or with their neighbours.

The health of these people depends to a great extent on the state of their nerves. Nervous tension is liable to express itself in breathing difficulties and allergies, particularly to feathers. The vulnerable parts of the body are the lungs, arms and hands.

CANCER — THE CRAB

Water, Cardinal, The Moon

Cancer in the Sixth House indicates an attraction to vocations in which these people can find an outlet for their need to nurse and take care of others, and their desire to serve society and protect its weaker members. It's not surprising, then, that those with the Crab in their Sixth House are drawn to medicine, nursing, baby-care, geriatrics and the social services. Other typical Cancerian professions are those related to hotels, restaurants and nutrition, as well as varied occupations and careers connected with the sea and housing. For example, architecture, real estate, and home repairs and maintenance can all appeal. As the sign of Cancer has a deep connection with the sea, water and liquids in general, many people with this placing are drawn to seafaring professions. Others are attracted to jobs related to swimming or public baths, spas or laundries, while others become barmen.

Since Cancer is the sign of the home, people with this placing tend to regard their place of work as their home-away-from-home, and their colleagues as members of one big happy family. In many cases, they

Leo, the sign of the stage, in Robert Redford's Sixth House symbolizes the acting profession.

The sign of Cancer in Benjamin Spock's Sixth House represents the caring profession as practised by the famous children's doctor and bestselling author of *Baby and Child Care*.

actually work from home, or in close professional co-operation with family members.

Cancer is a sign that craves security, so those with this sign in their Sixth House are very security minded. As a result, they may choose careers related to security, the secret services and defence.

The health of these people is strongly affected by their emotional states. In some cases, there is even a tendency to hysteria. The stomach, chest and womb are the most vulnerable parts of the body. Nutritional problems can sometimes occur, because these people are often allergic to many kinds of food.

LEO — THE LION

Fire, Fixed, The Sun

People with Leo, the Lion, roaring in their Sixth House long to hold centre-stage at their places of work, which they regard as their own private kingdoms. They throw themselves wholeheartedly into their work, thus earning the admiration of their superiors, who ease their way on the road to professional advancement and promotion.

A hobby may become a full-time job when people have this placing. They are also suited to occupations requiring creativity. Very often, their love of children draws them to careers related to youngsters.

Nearly all of these people will be attracted to jobs in which, sooner or later, they will be able to stand in the limelight. It should come as no surprise, therefore, that many people with this placing choose professions related to the worlds of entertainment and politics. Other careers symbolized by Leo are those demanding managerial and organizational skills, or those connected with jewellery and gold (which just happens to be Leo's favourite colour!). The presence of Leo, the sign of love, in the Sixth House signifies a love of work, and these people devote most of their time to their work— time spent pleasantly, especially since they often initiate and enjoy many an office romance along the way!

Their approach to work is truly wholehearted, and at times it seems that their hearts actually work overtime. In fact, many people with Leo in the Sixth House suffer from heart disorders. The parts of the body to be protected are the heart and the upper portion of the back.

VIRGO — THE MAIDEN

Earth, Mutable, Mercury

Virgo is the sign associated with work, and people who have the Maiden labouring in their Sixth House, which is the House of work, really enjoy rolling up their sleeves and working as hard — and as well — as they can. These people are quite happy to start at the bottom, teaching themselves systematically and thoroughly all there is to know about the job, stage by stage. By the time they are bosses, they'll know what their subordinates can and cannot do. In return, the employees will soon learn that they can't pull the wool over the eyes of their Virgo-affected bosses, but instead will always do their best — they know that only a perfect performance can avert that biting Virgoan criticism!

Jobs that require attention to detail, precision, a critical sense, a love of hygiene and cleanliness all appeal to people with this placing. Typical Virgoan professions include medicine, nursing, pharmacology, nutrition, physiotherapy, chemistry and biology, as well as anything related to the written and spoken word, such as journalism and teaching. Secretarial work and accountancy are also suitable careers, because they call for the methodical minds that these people have.

Keeping healthy is of paramount importance to these people, although sometimes they can border on becoming hypochondriacs, and are forever visiting their doctors, ready to discuss a new ache or pain. Fretfulness and nervous tension, however, can really make these people ill, and they can then suffer from digestive disorders and problems with their intestines.

LIBRA — THE SCALES

Air, Cardinal, Venus

'Easy does it' is the motto of these people when it comes to work. It's not that those with Libra in the Sixth House are frightened of hard work, but more that they try to keep it in perspective!

You won't find these people working themselves into the ground in an effort to get on in life — in fact, they find over-achievement vulgar. Instead, they work at a leisurely pace, as long as their place of employment has a cultured, aesthetic atmosphere. These people know how to work in co-operation with others and quite easily achieve harmonious relationships with their colleagues. They prefer not having to work alone and are ideally suited for teamwork, either working with their spouse or with a business partner. Being the sign of marriage, when Libra is found in the Sixth House it often means that a relationship begun at work will lead to the altar. Among the professions that attract people with this placing are those related to art and beauty, law, and any job that demands day-to-day contact with people, tact and diplomacy.

Libra also indicates balance where health is concerned. People with the Scales in their Sixth House succeed in treading the golden path between activity and rest, and ensure that they eat a balanced diet. On the whole, their health is satisfactory, but when their emotional balance becomes upset they can indulge themselves in orgies of over-eating and will gorge themselves on comforting sweets and cakes. As a result, they can develop some weighty problems, making their bathroom scales tip dramatically!

These people are lucky enough not to be particularly sensitive to either heat or cold. It's as if this Airy sign blessed them with internal air-conditioning systems! Although their health may be generally good, they should take care of their kidneys.

SCORPIO — THE SCORPION

Water, Fixed, Mars and Pluto

It may come as no surprise to learn that Scorpio makes people with this placing very intense in their attitudes to work. They are serious and thorough, and willing to invest a great deal of energy and mental resources in their jobs. Taking assignments upon themselves, these people won't rest until they have completed the task in hand. They drive themselves mercilessly, hardly ever resting and, as a result, often jeopardizing their health.

When Scorpio is placed in this House, it indicates people whose work involves an element of danger. In many cases, their jobs are cloaked in secrecy. Sometimes, rather complex relationships develop between themselves and their colleagues, involving jealousy, rivalry and intrigue. Typical Scorpio professions require a sharp insight into human psychology and the ability to penetrate beyond the obvious. Suitable careers include psychology, criminology, police work, intelligence work, scientific research, especially in medicine and biology, the discovery of natural resources, such as diving, mining or prospecting, and any other work that involves digging beneath the surface.

The sign of Scorpio is associated with other people's property and money. Therefore, its presence in the Sixth House, the House of work, may signify a professional training which is funded by grants. Sometimes it is the medical or scientific institution at which these people work that receives a grant. Alternatively, this placing may indicate a profession which directly involves the property and money of others, such as insurance.

Overwork can definitely harm the health of these people. Sometimes, they may suffer from recurring inflammatory diseases, especially in the secretory and sexual organs. There is also a possibility of food or water poisoning, as well as a danger of being bitten by scorpions or snakes.

SAGITTARIUS — THE ARCHER

Fire, Mutable, Jupiter

Like an arrow shot from a bow, people with the Archer in the Sixth House aim to get as far as possible in life. They loathe restrictions of any form, and can't stand being chained to set working hours and confined within four walls. Instead, they are drawn to jobs in which they can feel 'born free', such as the liberal professions or any field which gives them a free hand and the opportunity to travel. Sometimes they aim their arrows at too many careers — after all, the Archer has many strings to his bow — from those requiring a talent for sports and a love of open spaces to those demanding intellectual ability, higher education and an open mind. Typical Sagittarian professions are sports, working with animals (mainly horses and dogs), publishing, anything connected with tourism, law, teaching, philosophy and theology. Even when lacking an academic degree, they may be connected professionally with universities, law courts and religious institutions.

This is the sign of plenty, and these people are endowed with an abundant vitality and excellent health. But many of those with the Archer in their Sixth House have a tendency to overeat, which often results in obesity. Too much rich food and heavy wine can also lead to liver trouble. The vulnerable parts of these peoples' bodies are the pelvis and the vertebrae of the lower back.

CAPRICORN — THE MOUNTAIN GOAT

Earth, Cardinal, Saturn

'Ambition' is the keyword for people born with Capricorn, the Mountain Goat, clambering through their Sixth House. They are lured on by the prospect of attaining the peak of success, and so can be enticed into making supreme efforts in order to reach the summits of their particular mountains.

These people appreciate formality, ceremony and status symbols at work. The more established the hierarchy, the more their Capricorn sense of competitiveness grows, spurring them on to climb higher and higher up the ladder of success. But, at times, the atmosphere at work can be so conservative and uninspiring that it becomes stultifying.

Capricorn is a sign associated with government and politics, and many people with this placing work in these fields. Other suitable Capricorn professions are agriculture, real estate, finance, economics, exact sciences, history and geology.

Too much ambition and hard work can impair the health of people with this placing, and they should take particular care of their bones, joints, knees and teeth. They are also prone to rheumatism, which can sometimes become so severe that they find it difficult to move. There is also a possibility for these people of suffering from hardening of the arteries.

AQUARIUS — THE WATER BEARER

Air, Fixed, Saturn and Uranus

An idealistic and original approach to work are the chief characteristics of people born with this placing. To them, work isn't merely a means of earning a living, but can also be a way of helping a worthy cause. Whatever their job, these people feel that it is their duty to serve society and humanity as much as possible. They approach the task with the sense of having a real mission in life, truly wanting to enrich humanity with the life-giving waters that flow in unending streams from the Water Carrier's jug, watering the seeds of progress and making them sprout and blossom.

Conservative ways of working are anathema to these people, who will try to find more efficient (and interesting!) methods of getting the job done. Unfortunately, their brainwaves don't always work, which tempts them into trying out one new idea after another. It's almost as though they were fated to work in a tense atmosphere — the air being almost charged with electricity, and threatening to short-circuit at any moment.

As you might expect, people with Aquarius in the Sixth House are attracted to jobs linked with humanitarian organizations, or closely associated with large groups. Professions that are particularly Aquarian include those connected with electricity, electronics, computers, aeronautics, television, astronomy and astrology.

Nervous tension and circulatory problems are the main health worries for these people. They can also become health freaks, and will experiment with every food fad (good and bad) which comes their way.

PISCES — THE FISHES

Water, Mutable, Jupiter and Neptune

Just as there are two Fish depicted in the glyph of Pisces, so there are two sides to the Piscean attitude to work. The first, and positive one, is idealistic. These people believe in maintaining a high standard of service. They are very altruistic, always ready to do their utmost for anyone in need, and to answer any call for help. More often than not, their work involves an isolation of some sort, is associated with closed institutions such as prisons or hospitals, and is frequently shrouded in secrecy.

But not everyone with the Fishes swimming in their Sixth House is a do-gooder, or a self-appointed martyr. The other Piscean attitude to work is quite a different story. These people feel out of their depth at work, and will often try their hardest to avoid it in a fishy, slippery fashion. Occasionally, the only occupation of people with this placing is fishing for suckers to trick.

Acting and music attract many of those with Pisces in the Sixth House. However, the majority of these people can be found working in the caring professions, such as medicine, nursing and the social services. Other Piscean careers are those associated with the sea, oil and its by-products, textiles and anything connected with the feet, such as chiropodists, shoe manufacturers and salesmen, and shoemakers.

Many people with this placing fool themselves into thinking that their job offers better prospects than is really the case. As if that weren't bad enough, they often work in atmospheres that are vague and confused, even with an element of hostility — some of their colleagues may try to gain the upper hand in an underhand way. The conditions under which they work are also liable to change frequently.

Strangely enough, the feet of people born with this placing are truly their Achilles' heels. They are also susceptible to illnesses that are difficult to diagnose. Sometimes, these people fall victim to imaginary illnesses, which serve as refuges from the rigours of work and the demands of life.

THE SEVENTH HOUSE

Marriage; Close relationships; Partnerships

ARIES — THE RAM

Fire, Cardinal, Mars

Fiery Aries in the Seventh House symbolizes a strong urge to form ties with members of the opposite sex, often leading to early marriages or hasty romantic attachments. People who have the Ram cavorting in their Seventh House are constantly aware of the need to find their 'other halves', since only in the loved one's presence can they find fulfilment. These people are drawn to forceful, dominant and firm personalities — all qualities they admire in others, yet feel, rightly or wrongly, that they themselves are lacking. As a result, they may develop an exaggerated dependence on their life-partners, often to the extent of feeling lost and helpless in the absence of a close personal attachment.

Aries, whose symbol is the Ram, leader of the flock, indicates that the partners of these people will be energetic, active, dynamic and full of initiative — in other words, they will play the leading part in the marital drama. Not infrequently, those with this placing become attached to aggressively domineering partners. Any sign of weakness on the part of those who have Aries in their Seventh House will not only fail to appease the spouse, but may actually goad them into renewed aggression. Aries is ruled by Mars, the planet of war, and married life under this Martial influence may sometimes seem like a pitched battle.

People with Aries in the Seventh House must learn to rely on themselves, and to look for strength from within, not from their partners — only then will they succeed in grabbing the Ram by the horns and taming him.

TAURUS — THE BULL

Earth, Fixed, Venus

A desire for peace and prosperity within the framework of marriage is the main motivation of people born with Taurus in the Seventh House. Small wonder, then, that people with this placing are drawn to strong, reliable life-partners who appear to be very basic and solid. With such partners they feel they can safely build a lasting relationship. In many cases the partners have country backgrounds, or are connected with building or real estate in some way.

These people hope to find in marriage the secure foundation and solid base which are frequently lacking in other departments of their lives. That is why it is of the utmost importance for them to preserve and nurture the stability and permanence of their married lives. They are afraid that breaking the marriage bond may rock the ground under their feet, thereby undermining their existence. Although in many cases the marriage may be one of convenience, perhaps for financial reasons, the couple may well celebrate not only their silver, but their golden wedding anniversary too.

The spouse of people with this placing may be rather dull and conservative. But it is precisely these qualities that win the hearts of these people, who will have learned from experience that all that glitters is not gold. The trouble is that they may discover that all that does not glitter is not necessarily gold, either . . .

GEMINI — THE TWINS

Air, Mutable, Mercury

Relationships have to be based on an intellectual affinity for people born with this placing. This Air sign signifies an attraction to a life-partner who is intelligent, even brilliant, and imaginative — but who is also apt to get carried away by flights of fancy. Sometimes, though, it may be the people with Gemini in this House who have too flighty an attitude towards marriage. Those who are influenced by the dual sign of Gemini in their close relationships may have a tendency to serve two masters (or mistresses). Thus they are likely to conduct affairs with two people at the same time, and usually get married more than once. A few of them may even go so far as to commit bigamy! But no matter how many times they marry, they are often attracted to people who are very young. After all, the Twins are the sign of youth!

Although Mutable Gemini in the Seventh House indicates people who need change and variety in their close relationships, they may nevertheless become attached to one life-partner, providing that the loved one has a multi-faceted personality, is as intriguing as a riddle, and as sparkling as a diamond. Yet at times these people may be taken in and dazzled by mere polished glass . . .

CANCER — THE CRAB

Water, Cardinal, The Moon

Much-needed emotional security is to be found in close relationships for people born with Cancer in the Seventh House. They see marriage as a safe harbour, a refuge from the storms of life. In fact, their urge to marry stems mostly from a need for domesticity, and not necessarily from any romantic yearnings. They prefer the familiar to the unknown because, for them, familiarity breeds love. When it comes to choosing a partner for life, they prefer people whose origins and backgrounds are similar to their own — someone with whom they can feel at home. Involvements with people they don't understand, and have nothing in common with, leave them cold; nor will people surrounded by an aura of stardust lead them to the altar.

Taurus, the sign of property, in Jacqueline Kennedy Onassis' Seventh House symbolizes her marriages to the super-rich.

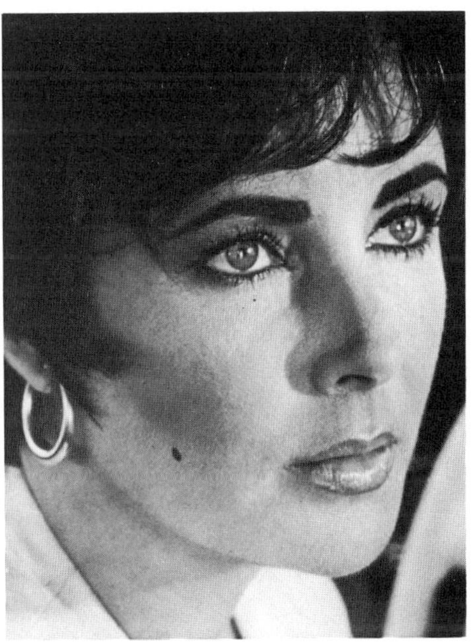

Aries in Elizabeth Taylor's Seventh House reflects her strong urge to form close ties, expressed in her many marriages.

Far more enticing are the charms of a kitchen wizard, because food is the love potion of people born with this placing. Romantic, moonlit, star-studded nights don't appeal to them. Instead, the way to their hearts is through their stomachs! When it comes to choosing a partner for life, these people definitely prefer gastronomy to astronomy.

The life-partner is usually an affectionate homebody, who wraps up their beloved in a cosy cocoon of warmth and security, and takes great delight in spoiling them. It goes without saying that such a partner will also excel in the culinary arts! When a man has Cancer in his Seventh House, it indicates that he will marry a woman who is motherly, or who reminds him of his mother.

LEO — THE LION

Fire, Fixed, The Sun

People who are born with Leo in their Seventh House long for an admirable spouse, in whom they can take real pride. And very often, they get their wish, because they choose partners who are attractive, imposing, and who radiate warmth, vitality and vigour — qualities which are all characteristic of the sign of Leo. As far as the people with this placing are concerned, their life-partners are not just superstars, but the suns of their lives, while they, planet-like, revolve happily around this radiant centre, basking in its reflected glory.

Although people with Leo in the Seventh House are ready — of their own accord — to play second fiddle to their beloved, they will strongly resent being dominated, and perhaps even patronized, by their spouse. Although Leo in this House denotes a love match, friction can arise due to the life-partner's bossiness. Conflicts over matters of pride and principle can also create a feeling of tension.

Despite all that, majestic Leo, being a Fixed sign, means stability in marriage, and the people who win the hearts of those with Leo in the Seventh House may rest assured that they will not just be Kings or Queens — for a day. If the people with this placing can learn the secret of taming the royal beast, while giving it due respect, then they are likely to live happily ever after with their loved one.

VIRGO — THE MAIDEN

Earth, Mutable, Mercury

'Holy Virgin' or 'Worldly Virgin'? People born with the sign of Virgo in the Seventh House will adopt the attitude of one or the other of these two categories as far as marriage is concerned.

The Holy Virgin is a symbol of purity, and when applied to this House, she signifies the yearning for perfection in all close relationships. People with this attitude towards marriage are very particular in their choice of life-partner, because they expect them to be paragons of every possible — and impossible — virtue.

The other Virgoan attitude, as its name implies, is more worldly and shows the need to find an ordered, secure existence through marriage. People who think in this way won't be captivated by the saintly type. It's pragmatic, down-to-earth people who win their hearts — people who have practical ideas in their heads rather than saintly haloes shimmering over them. Hard-working, realistic people whose feet are firmly planted on the ground are the ideal life-partners for those with the Worldly Virgin attitude to committed relationships. It is only people like this who can bring a semblance of order into the usually vague, chaotic existence of those with Virgo in their Seventh House.

Gemini, the sign of youth, in Roman Polanski's Seventh House indicates the famous film director's attraction to girls much younger than himself.

Leo, the royal sign, in movie actress Grace Kelly's Seventh House reflects her marriage to the Prince of Monaco.

Being disorganized and lazy by nature, people with this placing expect to be waited upon hand and foot by their spouse. Therefore, they subconsciously form ties with those from a lower social class, or who are real workaholics. In most cases indeed, the partners of those with Virgo in the Seventh House keep as busy as bees. However, if they suspect that their nearest and dearest are shirking their duties and not doing enough for the common cause, they will try to goad them into action with incessant nagging and stinging remarks. The lazy partner, in their turn, may accuse their spouse of pettiness, spite and lack of understanding. Is it surprising, then, that those with Virgo in their House of marriage often marry more than once?

LIBRA — THE SCALES

Air, Cardinal, Venus

The sign of Libra, the Scales, delicately balanced in the Seventh House symbolizes a yearning for an ideal, harmonious marriage between two love birds. Therefore, people with this placing are likely to choose good-looking, gentle partners with pleasing manners, who are well liked by one and all, and who are considerate and thoughtful, ever-ready to compromise for the sake of marital harmony.

People born with this placing, although often somewhat uncouth, may well lose their rough edges with time, under the cultured and refining influence of their spouse. The way to achieve a successful, happy relationship is through give-and-take, and the ideal partner is the one who extends the olive branch, while still holding it firmly in their hand, expecting their spouses to do their share of compromising and meet them half-way. However, people who subdue their own personalities in order to please those born with this placing are missing the point, and upsetting the delicate balance of their relationship. Even though people with the Scales in their Seventh House wish for partners as peaceful and gentle as doves, nevertheless they expect them to be more than featherweights when putting their feet down on the marital scales.

SCORPIO — THE SCORPION

Water, Fixed, Mars and Pluto

Strong, even tempestuous, emotions and relationships that cut deep into the soul are typical of people born with Scorpio in the Seventh House. They may well experience tumultuous personal involvements, which can give new meaning and flavour to their lives. These people are attracted to partners who are strong, magnetic and complex in character.

In some cases, this attraction may lead to entanglements with rather complicated characters, or with people who are already married or involved with someone else. Just as Scorpio is associated with other people's possessions, those with Scorpio in the Seventh House may be tempted to taste forbidden fruit. However, these people will soon learn that such adventures lead nowhere. Since Scorpio symbolizes deep waters, people with this sign in their Seventh House may find they are out of their emotional depth and, unless they learn to swim, the powerful currents might sweep them off their feet, and eat away at the firm foundations of their personalities.

Scorpio inspires these people with fidelity, devotion and a willingness to follow their partners through thick and thin. Because the sign of Scorpio is a Fixed one, it implies a need for permanence in relationships and a tendency to take 'till death do us part' literally. However, very occasionally, the Scorpion-like nature of the relationships may become so poisonous that a break-up seems the only course of survival. The ensuing rows over money and property could well be typical of the entire relationship.

SAGITTARIUS — THE ARCHER

Fire, Mutable, Jupiter

Optimism and trust in close personal relationships are the main traits of people born with the sign of Sagittarius in the Seventh House. They need a fair amount of freedom and independence, if they are to be happy, avoid close ties if they threaten commitment, and are willing to give their partners as long a rein as they require themselves. People with this placing also want to experience the entire gamut of human relationships. As you may imagine, they have to aim far and wide if they are to achieve this goal, will zero in on more than one target, and may well marry more than once. On the other hand, those with the Archer in their Seventh House can make do with pointing their bow and arrow at one target only, providing that person is as fascinating and as multicoloured as a rainbow. Only people in whose personalities intelligence and spiritual interests intermingle with a love of adventure and a true *joie de vivre* will be able to keep those with this placing spellbound. They will then quit the happy hunting grounds and abandon the notion that the furthest pasture is also the greenest.

People with this placing are often attracted to foreigners or travellers — people whose free spirits roam the wide open spaces and soar to the higher spheres of knowledge. The chosen partners are often connected with law, religion, the humanities or sports.

CAPRICORN — THE MOUNTAIN GOAT

Earth, Cardinal, Saturn

The need for steadiness and security are the main motivations for marriage when Capricorn is in the Seventh House. These people regard others in a way that is serious and mature, responsible, yet judicious and cautious. They usually marry relatively late in life, or choose partners considerably older than themselves, since they are attracted to sedate, authoritative people of serious intentions, who will be towers of strength and provide shelter whenever it is needed. However, this shelter may prove to be too confining, making these people feel walled in, as though they were struggling for air — especially if the over-protective spouse is also of a strict, pedantic and unbending nature. In spite of that, people with Capricorn in the Seventh House will do their utmost to preserve their marriages, fearing that a break-up would undermine their security.

Sometimes, because Capricorn is an Earth sign, this placing may indicate a rather worldly approach to marriage, resulting in a cool and calculated choice of partner, based on ambition. These people may choose life-partners of higher social standing, or large bank balances. In other words, the spouse will have been chosen to contribute, in some way or other, to the material comfort of these people. In a woman's horoscope, Capricorn in this House often suggests marriage to a man who is a father figure.

AQUARIUS — THE WATER BEARER

Air, Fixed, Saturn and Uranus

There is an original approach to marriage, and a yearning for a unique and unusual partner, when Aquarius is found in the Seventh House. These people, characterized by airy Aquarius, have an elusive, ethereal quality, which makes those attracted to them all the more determined to captivate and capture these 'space walkers' — and not necessarily by remote-control! These manoeuvres are disagreeable to the people with this placing, who expect rather more freedom. Indeed, such respect and understanding wouldn't be misplaced, because Aquarius in the Seventh House signifies a trustworthy and faithful partner. Though they may roam in spirit and get carried away to distant galaxies, these people will inevitably be drawn back to their one-and-only sun, the centre of their universe.

Never expect to receive continuous love signals over the air from your space traveller, since these people prefer extrasensory communication to mere words. But their silence speaks volumes!

PISCES — THE FISHES

Water, Mutable, Jupiter and Neptune

Marriage is viewed rather idealistically when Pisces is in the Seventh House. In fact, it often leads to sentimental involvements with partners in need of help or care. People with this placing are therefore often attracted to unworldly, vague or artistic types whose feet hardly ever touch the ground. The disorder which, more often than not, reigns supreme in the lives of these disorganized people makes those with this placing long to tidy up after them.

Sometimes the partner's artistic qualities amount to no more than their ability to play havoc with the emotions. People with the Fishes swimming in their Seventh House should therefore beware of being hooked by drug addicts, alcoholics and other fishy folk. Because they are sensitive and affectionate, they're easy prey for professional spongers and leeches. But unfortunately, people with Pisces in their Seventh House may often have unrealistic views of their relationships, which are based on delusions. They may also feel that they are contributing more than their fair share to the marriage, or committed relationship, by giving up too much or giving in too often — both situations that will make them feel trapped. The Water sign of Pisces often symbolizes a rather fluid and murky state of affairs when it comes to marriage.

THE EIGHTH HOUSE

Sex; Death; Other people's money

ARIES — THE RAM

Fire, Cardinal, Mars

Expect inflamed passions and a tendency to play with fire in sexual matters, when Aries is found in the Eighth House. The Ram is no innocent little lamb, and his presence in this House induces the strong sexual urges that he symbolizes. This placing not only suggests an active sex life, but often sexual initiative and adventurism too. Inspired by Aries' ruler, Mars, the planet of war, people with this placing may set out on a campaign of sexual conquests, laying siege to everyone who takes their fancy. This sign, especially in a man's birthchart, represents a very strong sense of identification with the sexual act, in the sense of 'Sex is me'. These men are convinced that the proof of their masculinity lies in their sexual abilities, and will try to use them to head off potential rivals. The Ram in this House often indicates a Don Juan who wants to cuckold as many husbands as possible.

People with Aries in the Eighth House have a very personal attitude towards other people's finances, and often choose careers that involve handling other people's property. Sometimes, they may even take control of their spouse's or partner's money, basing their actions along the lines of 'What's yours is mine'.

The question of death frequently occupies the minds of those with this placing. The Fire sign of Aries burning in this House can mean that danger may fire the imaginations of people with this placing, and excite them. They tend to play with fire and flirt with danger and, in extreme cases, may even imperil their own lives. Head injuries are especially dangerous and can sometimes prove fatal.

TAURUS — THE BULL

Earth, Fixed, Venus

Taurus the Bull really lives up to his name here by giving people with this placing a very strong sexual urge! Being an Earth sign, the Bull induces basic, earthy and fundamental desires which, although strongly sensual, are nevertheless stable and controlled. Those with Taurus in the Eighth House don't believe that the grass in their neighbour's yard is always greener. On the contrary, they are perfectly satisfied with enjoying themselves in their own pasture. After all a bull can hardly flutter like a butterfly from flower to flower!

Taurus is the sign of property, and the Bull in the Eighth House usually indicates that the financial situation of the life-partner is firm and stable with money often being invested in land or real estate. Although the finances of those with this placing are very often provided by their partners, they are not usually passive recipients of their beloveds' bounty, but will willingly contribute their share through hard work. As well as being lucky enough to establish themselves on the solid footing of their partners' property, they also have the talent to make it bear fruit — and their incessant ploughing of this ground often produces a very rich crop indeed.

A peaceful departure from this world, and a painless death, are the prospects for most people with this placing. However, in some cases, there may be a danger of death by suffocation or through an injury to the throat or neck. A tendency to overeat, and the resultant weight problems, may also shorten the lifespan of these people.

GEMINI — THE TWINS

Air, Mutable, Mercury

Change and variety in sex are the spice of life for those born with flighty Gemini in the Eighth House. They have a rational attitude to the passionate and dark side of their natures, and try to develop an intellectual awareness of it. People who have the mercurial, communicative Twins in their Eighth House feel a need to express their most intimate experiences in words, and often commit them to paper (which can make fascinating reading!) They devote a great deal of thought to everything connected with sex, psychology, and the mysteries of life and death. Some of them even write books or give lectures on these subjects.

Other people's property and money is another subject to which these people may devote much time and thought. They often take care of the property of their business or life-partners, which entails a great deal of paperwork. As most of their partners' property is invested in stocks, their financial condition is obviously not a very stable one. People with this placing may receive an inheritance from a relative or someone living nearby, but this usually involves a lot of correspondence and many short trips.

Traffic accidents are a danger for those with Gemini in the Eighth House. They can also suffer from injuries to the respiratory system, or to their hands.

CANCER — THE CRAB

Water, Cardinal, The Moon

There is an emotional attitude to sex when the Crab is found in the Eighth House. These people associate sexuality with being taken care of, or taking care of someone else. Women who are born with this placing tend to express their maternal feelings sexually, while men with Cancer in the Eighth House may have an Oedipus complex, and link sex with the mother figure.

The sign of Gemini in the Eighth House of Sigmund Freud, the famous investigator of the soul of man, reflects his theory of psychoanalysis, based on sex.

Mercurial Gemini in the Eighth House of Casanova, reflects the diverse sexual life of this legendary Don Juan, who immortalized his conquests in print – the sign of Gemini is associated with literary composition.

They are quite careful in money matters, striving not only to preserve their own property, but also taking good care of that of others. In many cases, they are called upon to handle these affairs, and can even be chosen to act as a guardian. Their life-partners tend to save, and are good at taking care of their homes and joint family finances. People with this placing often inherit silver heirlooms, houses and land from their parents.

People with this placing should beware of accidents in the home, and also not take any risks with water. In rare cases, Cancer in the Eighth House can indicate family problems which are not conducive to lengthening the lifespans of these people.

LEO — THE LION

Fire, Fixed, The Sun

A hot temper and tempestuous passions rule those who have the king of the jungle roaring in their Eighth House. These big cats usually turn out to be real sex kittens, who love sex and enjoy it both as entertainment and as a diversion. In some people, however, the sexual instinct may be sublimated, and the drive directed into areas of artistic creativity instead.

These people's life-partners may profit handsomely from their artistic abilities and their financial situation will be solid. People with this placing tend to organize and control the financial affairs of their partners, whose money is usually invested in gold or jewellery.

An urge to live it up, to get out and enjoy life, if taken to extremes can actually harm people with the Lion in the Eighth House. Many of them suffer from weak hearts and, therefore, when they behave riotously or are too active sexually, they may really be tempting Fate.

VIRGO — THE MAIDEN

Earth, Mutable, Mercury

Sex is regarded in one of two ways by people born with Virgo, the Maiden, in their Eighth House. The first is characterized by a pure and chaste attitude, and a healthy expression of sexual emotions. The second is hypocritical, often sick and warped, and sometimes leading to sexual aberrations. A lack of sexual self-confidence may make these people seek the company of lovers whom they feel are inferior in some way.

There is an honest and business-like approach to other people's financial affairs when Virgo is found in this House. These people are good at handling their partners' money, and often manage it more efficiently than their own property or funds! They are, therefore, often successful in professions connected with managing other people's finances.

People with this placing should be aware of possible dangers arising from intestinal diseases, dehydration, or from the strain of overwork.

LIBRA — THE SCALES

Air, Cardinal, Venus

Libra in the Eighth House indicates people who have a well-balanced and harmonious attitude towards sex. They abhor any expression of sexual coarseness or vulgarity, and associate sex with beauty and aesthetics.

These people have a balanced and considered approach to joint finances. They never attempt to tip the scales in their own favour in money matters, but always maintain a fair and objective point of view. They can see the other side of the coin and understand the economic point of view of the other person, therefore they are always willing to give in or strike a happy medium. In fact, this talent for compromise, which is brought out by the Scales balancing in the Eighth House, may find best expression in jobs dealing with monetary law. They may also receive an inheritance from their spouse.

This placing indicates a relaxed, serene and painless death, under tranquil and harmonious circumstances, and in the presence of the spouse. Libra, the sign of marriage, may also symbolize the shared passing away of a couple whom even death does not part. In extreme cases, people with this placing may be in danger from their life-partners. Injuries to the lower back may also cause problems.

SCORPIO — THE SCORPION

Water, Fixed, Mars and Pluto

Deep, powerful and tempestuous instincts abound in people with the Water sign of Scorpio in their Eighth House. When their sexual drives aren't given free expression, they may be driven into the 'underground' of their subconscious — in extreme cases the foundations of these people's personalities may even be undermined. They may also experience ingrained and complex sexual problems, even violent outbursts. There is a tendency towards clandestine sexual behaviour, and many of them love tasting forbidden fruit, in the form of lovers who are already spoken for elsewhere.

Scorpio points to a strong attraction to everything connected with mysticism and psychology, and people with this placing like to delve into the mysteries of life and death. In fact death fascinates them, so that they are tempted to flirt with danger. And danger is something that lies in wait for them wherever secret activities are involved, or in everything relating to the underworld, literally as well as figuratively. Subterranean and underwater places can be especially dangerous for these people, as are venomous reptiles, contagious diseases and injuries to the genital areas.

There is a strong element of secrecy when it comes to these people's dealings with the finances of their business or life-partners. Sometimes, they betray an underhanded attitude to other people's money!

SAGITTARIUS — THE ARCHER

Fire, Mutable, Jupiter

Fiery Sagittarius in the Eighth House gives those with this placing free expression of their instincts and a frank and open approach to sex. Their sexual emotions abound, and may even overflow at times, because these people believe that variety is the spice of sexual life. Those with the Archer hunting in this House may aim their arrows at many sexual targets, but won't forget to direct at least one of them to the heavens — for the religious and philosophical aspect of the eternal questions of life and death intrigue and fascinate them.

There is a chance of legal difficulties arising from joint money matters. These people may win a sum of money through litigation, or could benefit from a large inheritance. A grant for studies is another possibility, as is some form of financial support from abroad. People with Sagittarius in the Eighth House choose partners who are particularly generous, but very often their approach to money is characterized by overconfidence or a tendency to gamble.

Complacency and over-optimism can spell danger for people with the Archer in the Eighth House, and they may also suffer from injuries to the pelvis, and the effects of overeating. Sagittarius in this House can also signify death on a voyage, or while staying in a foreign country.

CAPRICORN — THE MOUNTAIN GOAT

Earth, Cardinal, Saturn

The presence of Capricorn in the Eighth House tends to cool, limit, harness, and even repress the passions, and indicates self-control in everything connected with sex. Sometimes, people with this placing may regard sex as a means of proving themselves, and may therefore indulge in exaggerated sexual activity in order to feel good. They may also use their sexuality to gain standing, or to control someone else. In certain cases, they can even gain dominance over a large group of people by appealing to their most primitive drives or to their herd instincts.

When it comes to the financial affairs of others, these people are very responsible, and may even choose a career bound up with other people's money. Also, Capricorn in this House points to a tendency to rely on financial support from others, in order to further ambitions and gain status. However, difficulties sometimes arise where shared property or an inheritance are concerned.

The Mountain Goat in this House denotes possible danger as a result of falling, injuries to the bones, or from a serious cold. This placing could also signify death in the line of duty, and posthumous decorations.

AQUARIUS — THE WATER BEARER

Air, Fixed, Saturn and Uranus

Aquarius is not a sign that abides by convention, and people with the Water Bearer in the Eighth House are no exception to this rule. They don't rest on their laurels where sex is concerned, but will try different, and even unusual, sexual experiences. Their approach to sex is both innovative and experimental, and some of them may even be prone to sexual aberrations.

The Water Bearer in the Eighth House bestows strong intuition, and sometimes even mediumistic powers. It often seems that these gifted people have ethereal antennae that receive transmissions from other worlds! They will develop original views concerning life and death, and not only are they interested in the enigmas of existence, but in the very secrets of the universe as well, and they can devote a great deal of thought to inexplicable phenomena.

The property of their life-partners is tied to large corporations, especially those dealing with electronics, computers, aeronautics or electricity. However, they should be warned that unexpected developments may arise with respect to these holdings. Some people with this placing may also receive an inheritance from a friend.

Electricity and flying can both endanger the lives of these people. But, for many of them, death will be unexpected, and will take place in the presence of friends or during a social gathering. Very occasionally, a friend will constitute a real danger to the life of a person with this placing.

PISCES — THE FISHES

Water, Mutable, Jupiter and Neptune

There is an idealistic approach to sex, and a subtle, poetic expression of even the strongest of passions, for people born with the Fishes in their Eighth House. Sometimes they sublimate their sexual desires and channel them into creative activity instead. Their approach to sex is very secretive, and some of them see it as taboo. They may even attempt to shackle their instincts, and to bind and imprison them. For others with this placing, the reverse is true. Anything goes for these people, yet they themselves are held prisoner, hostage to their passions and enslaved by them. People who have the Fishes in their Eighth House may drink like fish, get hooked on drugs, or indulge in inordinate sexual activity. Nevertheless, the more they attempt to flee from reality and from themselves, the more they will find themselves entangled, trapped like fish in a net.

Pisces in Marilyn Monroe's Eighth House reflects the mysterious circumstances of her death.

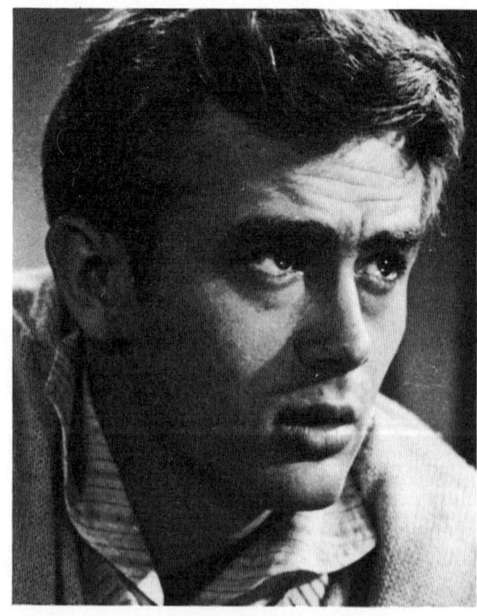

Gemini, the sign of mobility, in the Eighth House of movie idol James Dean points to his death in an automobile accident.

Pisces in this House denotes secrecy and a lack of clarity when people with this placing deal with mutual property. They should therefore refrain from managing other people's belongings, in order to avoid potentially unclear and embarrassing situations. In many cases, these finances are connected with closed institutions such as prisons, orphanages and hospitals, or with philanthropic activities. Sometimes, they can receive an inheritance or financial support from a secret source. This placing may also hint at a tendency to fish for other people's money and to sponge on them.

Drugs, drink and drowning all hold dangers for these people. They can also suffer at the hands of secret enemies. The mysterious sign of Pisces in the House of death can indicate an end of life that is shrouded in mystery. In extreme cases, these people have a tendency to be self-destructive, and they may threaten their own lives.

THE NINTH HOUSE

Abstract thought; Inspiration; Moral values; Philosophy; Religion; Law; Higher education; Spiritual journeys; Travel; Far-away places

ARIES — THE RAM

Fire, Cardinal, Mars

A burning zeal in spiritual matters, and a strong identification with religious, philosophical and moral values, are to be found in the personalities of people with fiery Aries in the Ninth House. They could even be described as warriors in the service of justice, always ready to fight for a cause, and never hesitating to gore their ideological adversaries. This Fire sign, symbolized by the Ram, is found in the Ninth House of those spiritual leaders who go like pillars of fire before their flocks, to light their way.

In most cases, the pioneering spirit of Aries can be seen in a search for the Self. These people want to discover themselves by treading a spiritual path, and will set out on an odyssey of self-discovery to do so. In other cases, they will search for themselves through more mundane activities — trips, tours and journeys to far-away places will reveal not only new worlds, but also a new self. Travel to foreign shores will depend to a large extent on personal initiative, and these people show a marked preference for journeys that require a strong sense of adventure.

Higher education is something else that attracts these people — they see it as a journey of the mind. They prefer to study subjects in which the emphasis is on 'know thyself', such as philosophy and psychology. Many of those with this Martial sign in their Ninth House are drawn to military studies, or to subjects connected with mechanics, metals and engineering.

TAURUS — THE BULL

Earth, Fixed, Venus

When the sign of Taurus is found in the Ninth House, it indicates people who have a basic, down-to-earth attitude to life, which is well-anchored in reality. They avoid abstract ideas — those arrayed in mundane garb are more to their liking. Even when these people are drawn to lofty ideas, although their heads may be in the clouds, their feet will be always firmly planted on solid ground. Their ideas, far from floating in the air, are rooted in sense, so that they will blossom and bear fruit. These people have the knack of putting their ideas to good use.

The Earth sign of Taurus represents firm, solid, stable values, cornerstones that can be trusted and built upon. Fairness and honesty are the inalienable assets of people with this placing. They are loyal to their beliefs and tend to be conservative. For some of them though, the symbolism of the Bull is seen in a tendency to follow the herd, to hold fast to materialistic values and to worship the golden calf.

People born with the Bull grazing in their Ninth House believe that the

Aries in the Ninth House denotes a fighting spirit in the spiritual and religious realms. It burns fiercely in the Ninth House of many spiritual leaders, among them Martin Luther, the German pastor, who bravely opposed the Catholic Church and was the founder of Protestantism.

Daring Aries in the Ninth House of the astronomer Galileo Galilei, reflects his courageous battle against the Catholic Church who threatened him with the Inquisition because he championed the revolutionary concept of Copernicus, which said that the earth revolves around the sun.

further away the grass, the greener it is. Small wonder, then, that these people often graze in foreign pastures. And, indeed, they will find many opportunities for financial profit in foreign lands, and their travels are usually connected with business or financial matters.

Earthy Taurus in this House indicates that even journeys along spiritual paths may have a practical aspect to them. In many cases, the choice of studies is dictated by material considerations, and these people tend to acquire knowledge in the fields of agriculture, economics, mathematics and architecture.

GEMINI — THE TWINS

Air, Mutable, Mercury

Spiritual subjects such as philosophy and religion appeal to people born with Gemini in the Ninth House. They need to express their views, ideas and beliefs, and often set them down on paper. Although airy Gemini in this House inspires people with high-minded ideas, most of these soon dissolve into thin air . . . They are interested in everything under the sun, but tend to change their field of interest frequently, flitting from one subject to another as the mood takes them.

People born with the dual sign of the Twins in their Ninth House are blessed with the ability to see both sides of every coin, even when it is a spiritual one. They are gifted with intellectual flexibility and with the ability to understand other people's viewpoints. Being so open to new ideas, they may well change their ideology or religion as they learn more. Gemini bestows quick adaptability, not only to ideas and beliefs, but to new surroundings as well. Changes and journeys are what make life interesting for these people. They travel abroad extensively, and may study in a foreign country. Studies requiring a flair for communication and a talent for languages draw these people like magnets.

CANCER — THE CRAB

Water, Cardinal, The Moon

People born with this placing have an emotional attitude to life and believe that only through the emotions can true understanding be attained. The families of those with this placing will have a very strong influence in the development of these people's moral values, their ideology being influenced to a great extent by their mothers. They gain great confidence and reassurance from their spiritual values and feel protected by their beliefs. Cancer in the Ninth House also denotes a longing to shelter under the wings of a faith in which the mother-figure is the central image.

There is a very emotional, even sentimental, approach to spiritual and ethical values. These people may be moved to tears by high-minded ideas or noble behaviour. Their ideal is to protect, defend and take care of those in need, and to feed the hungry. As the sign of the Crab is associated with food, its placing in the Ninth House indicates spiritual nourishment — these people can digest the most abstract spiritual ideas easily, and feel quite at home in the higher spheres. Their minds simmer with ideas, and it seems to be in the kitchen, of all places, that they see light. Small wonder, then, that their shopping lists and recipe books are adorned with scribbled snatches of their thoughts!

When it comes to choosing subjects to study, they are often influenced by their families, and will generally opt for something that one of their parents studied, especially if it is connected with one of the caring professions. These people long for far-away places, and may live abroad for extended periods of time. They also enjoy sea travel in the company of their families. When born with the domestic sign of Cancer in their Ninth House, people look for security and the comforts of home even while travelling, because they need to feel that wherever they drop anchor is their home port.

LEO — THE LION

Fire, Fixed, The Sun

When the Fire sign of Leo blazes in the Ninth House, it denotes spiritual fervour. People with this placing are often blessed with creative ability in intellectual and spiritual spheres, shining sunlike in the higher realms of thought, and are drawn to faiths that are rich in ritual, pomp and circumstance.

The presence of the king of the jungle in the Ninth House symbolizes status achieved in anything connected with the humanities, religion or philosophy. But the prestige of these people is not only raised by intellectual travel; very often, they may achieve honour and be lionized through real journeys — many explorers and discoverers have the Lion in their Ninth House. Even in everyday life, people with this placing love to travel in the grand manner, and will always go first class. Journeys are associated with pleasure, amusement and romance, and they may develop emotional ties in another country, or fall in love with a foreigner. Their intellectual journeys have a romantic side to them too, and they may fall in love with someone whom they will regard as a spiritual teacher. Their children will also have close ties to foreign countries, whether being born abroad or living there for a long time.

Higher education appeals not only to the minds of these people, but to their hearts as well, since they have an innate love of study and enjoy extending their mental boundaries. They are attracted to studies in creative fields, particularly those associated with the arts and drama. Subjects connected with management and organization are also of interest.

People with Leo in the Ninth House may be convinced of their intellectual and moral superiority over others. They may even be unwilling to admit that they ever make mistakes. Some of these people display an intellectual haughtiness and supremacy, and expect everyone to bow to their mental prowess and authority.

VIRGO — THE MAIDEN

Earth, Mutable, Mercury

The Maidenly Virgo symbolizes the puritanical virtues of modesty and work, and a longing for integrity and perfection in the spiritual sphere. This aspiration for perfection may be expressed by an overly critical attitude towards faith, religion and spiritual matters in general. Yet, people born with Virgo in their Ninth House are at the same time very

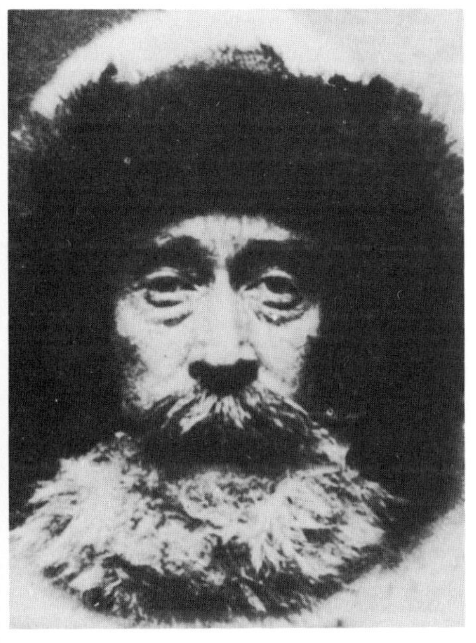

Daring, pioneering Aries is in the Ninth House of Robert Perry, the first man to reach the North Pole.

Leo, the sign of fame, is in the Ninth House of Charles Lindbergh, the first man to fly across the Atlantic.

practical and pragmatic, and may cover up ideas which do not further their interest. This is especially true when their work is connected with matters that they do not necessarily agree with.

This placing also indicates spiritual work. This may either be in the service of religion, or in any sphere that carries a spiritual or educational message, such as teaching, or jobs connected with law and justice.

The Virgo approach to spiritual matters is realistically down-to-earth, and people with this earthy sign in the Ninth House may have profound reservations about very mystical or abstract schools of thought. They demand facts and proof before accepting anything, and can be sceptical in the extreme. Generally, they tend to look at everything as though through a microscope, and will only focus on small matters. Sometimes, they may even display intellectual short-sightedness. Whenever they are in contact with the tree of knowledge, these people may notice the most microscopic details of the nearest leaf, but will fail to see the whole tree for its leaves. In many cases, the modest and buttoned-up Maiden in this House symbolizes a difficulty in grasping the naked truth, preferring it to be clad in more acceptable attire.

When these people choose higher education, it is usually in subjects requiring great accuracy, love of detail, and a highly-developed critical sense. Any trips abroad are connected, as a rule, with work or health.

LIBRA — THE SCALES

Air, Cardinal, Venus

Libra, the second of the three Air signs, gives a harmonious, balanced outlook on life, a striving for justice and high moral values, and an extremely liberal approach to faith and religion in general. People born with this sign in the Ninth House can see both sides to every story, even when it has a spiritual message. They respect the beliefs of the other people, and view them fairly and objectively, without trying to tip the Scales in favour of their own viewpoints. Nor do they sneer at creeds or concepts different from their own; their balanced attitudes enable them to see the all-prevailing unity which lies beneath the surface of all the world's religions and ideologies. They usually hold liberal and pacifist opinions, and believe firmly in the dove of peace.

This placing represents higher studies which require an objective judgement and an ability to weigh matters and compare them, as well as a sense of proportion and harmony. These people lean towards studies in the fields of comparative religions and cultures, international relations, law and art. They prefer to study in a group and may develop strong personal ties in the course of their higher education. While some of them may meet their one true love while engaged on journeys of the mind, others will do so when making less cerebral journeys of the body. Cupid also lies in wait for them in houses of worship and courts of law. These people are drawn to educated and cultured life-partners, who have very high moral values. They tend to be influenced by the opinions of their spouse, even to the extent of embracing another faith. In many cases, the life-partner belongs to a different nationality and/or religion.

SCORPIO — THE SCORPION

Water, Fixed, Mars and Pluto

Stormy emotional experiences (especially those connected with death) for people with Scorpio in the Ninth House will heighten their awareness of the eternal values and the meaning of existence. Many of them have a strong belief in an afterlife, and a deep interest in extrasensory phenomena. There may also be a profound interest in ideas pertaining to the spiritual realms, religion and philosophy. Sometimes people with this placing have a tendency towards religious and ideological extremism, which can border on fanaticism. Scorpio is an extremely secretive sign and its placing in the Ninth House, which is the House of faith, denotes people who are very secretive in everything connected with their belief. They are often drawn to secret ceremonies, and may even be attracted to black magic.

If people with this placing become involved in higher education, they will choose subjects dealing with the subconscious, or matters that are concealed from the naked eye, such as psychology, criminology, biology, medicine, scientific research, archaeology and oceanography. They may also study subjects that deal with other people's finances, such as business administration, accountancy and insurance. In other cases, they may apply for grants in order to continue their higher education. When they travel, their fares are often paid for by other people, or their journeys are connected with the finances of other people. Very often, their travels are linked to a secret mission.

SAGITTARIUS — THE ARCHER

Fire, Mutable, Jupiter

The fiery Archer aflame in the Ninth House gives those with this placing fervour, an optimistic attitude to life, a developed sense of justice, broad horizons and an open and liberal approach to everything connected with beliefs, religion and philosophy. These higher spheres are of great attraction to the people with this placing, who aspire to higher education and high moral values. Their intellectual abilities open up a wide range of possibilities in the field of advanced learning. Nevertheless, these people will do best if they concentrate on a few topics, rather than try to learn everything at once! The subjects in which they are most likely to succeed are law, philosophy and theology.

Being adventurers, these people don't only want to soar high into the spiritual spheres, but they long to roam the wide open spaces as well. They travel far and wide, often finding their luck in far-flung corners of the globe. Journeys are usually connected with the broadening of the mind, and sometimes with religious matters, such as missionary activities.

CAPRICORN — THE MOUNTAIN GOAT

Earth, Cardinal, Saturn

Those with Capricorn in their Ninth House have constructive, sound values and a pragmatic, realistic attitude to life. They try to prove that they are people of principle, and win respect in appreciation of their moral strength. Very often, these people have a conservative view of religion, preferring its form to its teaching, and therefore attributing undue importance to its ceremonious aspects. Most people with this placing need an authoritarian framework in moral matters, and rely on a rather rigid set of values in order to be guided down the straight and narrow path.

Because Capricorn is an Earth sign, these people sometimes have a materialistic, even cynical, view of life, and believe that the end justifies the means — especially when the goal is self-advancement. Some people with this placing have a tendency to self-righteousness, and will use religious and moral arguments to further their interests.

The Mountain Goat climbing in this House also indicates great ambition in the search for knowledge, especially in practical subjects, simply in order to improve their status or social standing. Just as these people's journeys of the mind have a rather earthy aspect, so do their travels, which are mainly devoted to furthering their careers and ambitions. They often see travel as a status symbol, so will use it as a means of one-up-manship.

AQUARIUS — THE WATER BEARER

Air, Fixed, Saturn and Uranus

Airy Aquarius blowing through this House bestows abstract thought and the ability to delve into the content, significance and true meaning of spiritual values. It also gives an idealistic, original, progressive attitude, and an independent spirit. People with this placing regard all ceremony, pomp and circumstance as nothing more than empty rituals. Overlooking the external, they look for the eternal values in life. Those who have the Water Bearer overflowing in their Ninth House believe in humanitarian values, friendship, and the brotherhood of man, and try to live accordingly. Occasionally, people with Aquarius in this House may also have weird, eccentric views, and iconoclastic — even anarchistic — leanings.

Many of those with Aquarius in their Ninth House are drawn to studies in the fields of electronics, aeronautics, cybernetics, computers, astronomy, electricity and astrology. Many of them are also avid readers of science fiction. Being fascinated by the shape of things to come, they

The winds of the future blow through the Air sign Aquarius, which is in the Ninth House of the writer Jules Verne. As early as the 19th century he foresaw the conquest of space and described the launching of the first spaceship to the moon with incredible accuracy.

The spirit of tomorrow is present not only in the spiritual voyages of those with Aquarius in their Ninth House, it inspires daring explorers such as astronaut Neil Armstrong, the first man to step onto the surface of the moon on 20 July 1969.

often feel that they have been born before their time. They also feel, spiritually at least, that the winds of tomorrow already waft around them. Small wonder, then, that Aquarius in the Ninth House can be found in the birthcharts of many astronauts, while in the charts of 'mere mortals', Aquarius in this House signifies unusual journeys, and surprising, unexpected developments which occur during these voyages.

PISCES — THE FISHES

Water, Mutable, Jupiter and Neptune

The placing of watery Pisces in the Ninth House gives people great sensitivity and spirituality. They are very aware of the suffering of others, often to the extent of identifying themselves with the sufferers. In addition, they are inspired by ideas that extol sublime spiritual and moral values. However, the Fishes floating in the Ninth House can sometimes give a tendency to vagueness, Utopian ideas and to drifting along in a nebulous, ideological fog. There is also a danger for these people of falling under the spell of a so-called spiritual charlatan who is out to ensnare them.

The mystical, arcane and occult sides of life are often of great interest to those with this placing. They tend to be very secretive about their beliefs, often regarding them as sacred and, therefore, unwilling to share them with the uninitiated. They may even go so far as to decide to retreat from the world of the senses to a monastery or convent, in order to live in the atmosphere of spirituality that their souls crave. Pisces in this House often gives people inspiration in the mystical and spiritual realms and, not infrequently, extrasensory perception. These people hear the music of the spheres, and swim in the realms of the abstract just like fish in water.

If their mental voyages have a mystical aspect, then their earthly travels are often shrouded in mystery, or have something secret about them. These people may, for example, travel on highly confidential, secret missions. In other cases, they may have to travel incognito or as stowaways. Given the chance, these people will always choose to travel — whether in secret or openly — on board ship. They feel an affinity with water.

Most people with Pisces in their Ninth House are drawn to spiritual or hermetic studies. They may choose to study in a closed institution, such as a religious retreat, or will choose a subject that is veiled in secrecy. Sad to say, these people may encounter hostility in academic circles.

THE TENTH HOUSE

Career; Status; Prestige; Aspirations; Ambitions; Achievements

ARIES — THE RAM

Fire, Cardinal, Mars

A powerful drive to achieve prominence is indicated by the presence of Aries in the Tenth House. People with this placing have such strong aspirations to be leaders of their own particular orchestra that, in many cases, they won't even consider playing first violin, insisting on being a soloist instead. Those with the Ram in their Tenth House, the House of status and career, won't easily be shoved aside, and are always willing to blow their own trumpets. They can be very assertive in everything pertaining to their honour and status, ready to butt anyone who doubts their authority.

Very often, Aries symbolizes the achievement of high position, thanks to one's own efforts, initiative, energy and drive. These people identify themselves with their own status, regarding it as an integral part of themselves. Paraphrasing Louis XIV's claim that 'The State — is I', these people believe 'My career — is I'.

People who have the combative sign of Aries in their Tenth House are attracted to careers which require much initiative and a fighting spirit, giving them ample opportunities to express their personalities.

TAURUS — THE BULL

Earth, Fixed, Venus

The self-respect of those with Taurus in the Tenth House is influenced to a considerable extent by the number and nature of their achievements. But in spite of that, these people may at times feel that their careers are stuck in ruts. However, if they can grab the Bull by the horns and harness it to the plough of their ambition, some perseverance and hard work will make their fields bear a rich harvest. Their careers will not only blossom and flourish, but will become firmly rooted and will thrive for many years.

The status of these people greatly depends on their ability to gain the trust and appreciation of others. They take care to build their livelihoods on solid foundations — fidelity and reliability being the cornerstones — and it is no coincidence that their work is often connected with construction: they may well be architects or building contractors. Other suitable careers are economics, finance, agriculture and real estate.

The worthy Bull plodding through this House suggests that people with this placing tend to identify their status with the concept of value and, indeed, Taurean achievements are often of lasting value, and gain wide appreciation. Sometimes, Taurean aspirations are literally monumental, and they long to see their social standing reflected in something tangible and substantial — and concrete, like a building! They often realize this ambition by living in an imposing-looking house, or by contributing to the construction of a building that commemorates their name. The Taurean connection with money could hint, in some cases, at people who give generous donations to charities and societies as a means of becoming pillars of society.

GEMINI — THE TWINS

Air, Mutable, Mercury

As far as those with Gemini in the Tenth House are concerned, they seek approbation through their intellectual abilities and find recognition in professions requiring an ability to communicate, such as writing, teaching or the media. These people devote considerable thought to their social standing and, thanks to their high intelligence and talents, achieve impressive positions at relatively early ages.

The Twins, being a dual sign, suggest that these people are pulled in two directions by their status, and are not always at one with their public personas. Outwardly, they may display images completely different from their true personalities, which in most cases may be quite shy and retiring. As a result, the more prominent they become in public life, the more this feeling of ambivalence increases, and the greater becomes their desire to preserve their privacy. They sometimes try to keep their private and public selves in separate compartments by assuming a different working name, like an author using a pseudonym.

However, these people usually express the duality of the Twins by running two careers at once, or by frequently changing their jobs. A typical Geminian career is one that is rich in variety and mobility, requiring a gift of improvisation, quick adaptability, flexibility, agility and alertness. Many people with this placing choose careers that depend to a considerable degree on their ability to express themselves articulately, such as journalism, writing, teaching and anything to do with the media. Other Geminian professions are those connected with transportation, trade, agencies, office work and communications, such as postal and telephone services.

CANCER — THE CRAB

Water, Cardinal, The Moon

Their families are the main influence in the status and careers of people born with Cancer, the sign of the home and family, in their Tenth House. Very often, they come from well-connected, influential families who can help them in their climb to the top. Sometimes, the Crab in this House indicates that the concept of 'family' extends beyond the boundaries of these people's homes and families, and gains a broader, more universal, world-embracing significance. They want to take care of the whole world, and to keep everybody safe. As a result of this feeling, they often choose careers in medicine, child-care, social work of all descriptions, or anything to do with defence and security.

Other professions that can attract them include those connected with hotels, restaurants and catering in general, or those associated with housing or real estate. In most cases, their careers are bound up in one way or another with their families. It's hardly surprising, then, that they feel at home in their work. Quite often, though, the care these people lavish on their jobs is at the expense of their homes and families. When Cancer is found in this House, it often signifies people whose sense of security depends to a large extent on their status, and that they are liable to be over-sensitive in this respect.

LEO — THE LION

Fire, Fixed, The Sun

Only the best is good enough for Leo, so only being the best at work will do for people born with the sign of the Lion in their Tenth House. Already blessed with an inborn talent for putting themselves in the spotlight, these people usually manage to achieve imposing positions in their careers. Creative professions attract them, whether in art or drama, or in any other field in which they will be able to express themselves. The Sun is the ruler of Leo, and so the Sun signs of these people often suggest the type of work that will attract them. The Sun in Aquarius, for example, gives an air of originality and individuality to the working life, and indicates an attraction to Aquarian careers. If the Sun is in Virgo, on the other hand, then people with Leo in the Tenth House will be drawn to jobs that require the meticulous attention to detail, and communicative abilities, so typical of this sign. This rule also applies, of course, to the rest of the Sun signs. But, whatever job they choose, one thing is certain: people who have the royal sign of Leo ruling over their Tenth House will aspire to wear the crowns of their chosen careers.

Leo roars in the Tenth House of Margaret Thatcher – the first woman to be elected to the exalted position of Prime Minister of Great Britain.

Leo in Charlie Chaplin's Tenth House reflects the fame he achieved in the dramatic arts as actor, director and script-writer of his films.

VIRGO — THE MAIDEN

Earth, Mutable, Mercury

Hard work holds no terrors for people with this placing! On the contrary, those with Virgo in the Tenth House, the House of career, long to achieve perfection in their working lives, and will put in a great deal of effort in order to achieve it. These people have a deep respect for everything that the term 'work' implies, and are the living embodiments of those who take pride in their careers. Yet the people whose ambitions are symbolized by Virgo, the Modest Maiden, don't want to stand out from the crowd, and may even shy away from the limelight.

Virgo is a mercurial sign, so people with this sign in their Tenth House often change professions, or have two different careers at once. They are ideally suited to jobs that demand accuracy, meticulous attention to detail, highly developed critical faculties and excellent verbal abilities. Any occupations in the fields of communications, education, health, hygiene, nutrition, chemistry, biology, pharmacology, office work and accounting will attract them.

LIBRA — THE SCALES

Air, Cardinal, Venus

People with the sign of Libra, the Scales, gracefully poised in their Tenth House conduct themselves honourably, have harmonious, tactful and diplomatic dispositions, and will always observe the professional ethics. The positive image they project helps them considerably as they scale the ladder of success. And thanks to their balancing skills, enabling them to perform like high-wire acrobats, they succeed in advancing in even the most precarious situations, while others only trip and fall.

For many of those with this placing, the Scales of Justice draw them to careers in law, and often lead them to specialize in the drawing up of marriage contracts, or other agreements between parties. A Libran career entails contact with the public, and these people's career prospects not only depend greatly on their popularity, but also on the support of others, and their life-partners in particular.

Libra, the sign of marriage, in the House of career can sometimes hint at a close link between the chosen profession and marriage: in most cases, marriage helps further the careers of these people, and their loved ones encourage them in their ambitions. For women with this placing, their husbands may not only encourage them to pursue an independent career, but also will be ready to do their share of the housework, too. But, whichever sex, people with this placing are wedded to their work.

Other occupations that attract these people include those connected with weddings: marriage counsellors, wedding photographers, and running dating agencies, wedding halls and bridal boutiques. Other typical Libran professions are those involving diplomacy, or related to the arts and beauty.

SCORPIO — THE SCORPION

Water, Fixed, Mars and Pluto

Sometimes, people with this placing are so jealous of their honour and status that they can react with venomous spite when they feel that these qualities are being encroached upon. To other perhaps more enlightened people with Scorpio in the Tenth House, the concept of honour not only applies to the individual, but also to the more universal theme of human rights — an ideal for which they are ready to fight with zeal.

Many of these people are given a helping hand financially along the road to success, but they can find it almost impossible to admit that they owe anything to anybody, and will sometimes even resent the very people

Libra – the sign associated with beauty – in Helena Rubinstein's Tenth House represents her glittering career in the world of cosmetics.

The sign of Cancer in John F. Kennedy's Tenth House indicates his distinguished family which propelled him towards achievement, as well as representing his aspiration to benefit the American people by diverting many resources to social welfare.

who helped and supported them! In the long run, this flaw in their characters makes it difficult for them to get along with their superiors, whose authority they tend to contest. The waters of Scorpio don't always denote calm sailing where the career is concerned. Stormy weather can alternate with halcyon days, and disruptions and fresh starts are likely.

Jobs that call for secrecy and an enquiring mind are perfect for these people — criminology, police work, intelligence, psychology and scientific research (especially in the fields of biology and medicine) all fit the bill perfectly. Since Scorpio is a Water sign, other possible professions are related to the sea, such as diving, underwater research and anything to do with submarines. They are also drawn to mining, plumbing, taxation, insurance and jobs in which they manage other people's money.

SAGITTARIUS — THE ARCHER

Fire, Mutable, Jupiter

The sky's the limit when optimistic Sagittarius is in the Tenth House. People with this placing look for jobs that will give them the widest scope and opportunity when it comes to realizing their ambitions. Sometimes, they feel like big fish in little ponds, and may decide it's time to aim their Archers' arrows at more ambitious targets, such as achieving international fame!

Sagittarius is the sign of plenty, and brings many opportunities — sometimes, perhaps, too many. It should come as no surprise then, that some people with the Archer in their Tenth House do too many things at once, and often miss the main chance. They tend to have too many irons in the fire, and may be kindling more than one career at a time, jumping from one to another. Perhaps one lesson they should learn is the art of being selective!

The career possibilities open to these people are almost unlimited, as you might imagine, because Sagittarius in this House symbolizes the widest range of professions, from those in the spiritual sphere, such as philosophy and theology, to those involved in the spreading of knowledge and higher education — for example, teaching and lecturing. Other suitable occupations include law, diplomacy and foreign relations, not to mention anything connected with tourism, animal husbandry and sports.

CAPRICORN — THE MOUNTAIN GOAT

Earth, Cardinal, Saturn

Never underestimate the ambitions of people with Capricorn, the Mountain Goat, in the Tenth House, because they can be very strong indeed. Honour, position, authority and power all beckon to them. These people long to prove themselves through their achievements, and to have a mission in life.

Those born with the sign of the Goat clambering through this House will spare no effort in attaining the summit of their ambitions. Progress is not always easy or swift, and the road to the top is often strewn with boulders, but those who plod on with patience and determination will eventually succeed in turning the stumbling blocks on their serpentine path into stepping stones.

These people want to be part of a hierarchy, and to climb the ladder of success rung by rung, in order to reach the top. As well as commanding respect, they want to command other people, too, and are often attracted by the civil service, whether on a local or national level. Other people with this placing may choose to work in mathematics, physics, astronomy, history, geology, agriculture, mining, stonemasonry, carpentry or real estate.

Capricorn in this House often represents people who are over-ambitious, crave power, and have rigid and competitive minds. In extreme cases, they will push out of the way anyone who obstructs their path to the top. All too often, these people will reach the summit only to tumble down again, neatly illustrating the saying 'Pride comes before a fall'.

AQUARIUS — THE WATER BEARER

Air, Fixed, Saturn and Uranus

The clear waters of Aquarius flowing in the Tenth House imply that honesty and flawless conduct on the part of those with this placing will win them the esteem of their fellow men. Sometimes, these people are driven by a humanitarian spirit that makes them want to be of help to mankind, or they will choose to work in a subject dedicated to the study of man, such as anthropology or sociology. Other possible careers are those of electronics, aeronautics, computers, radio and television, astronomy and astrology. An interest in antiques may provide further possibilities for people with this placing. The presence of Aquarius, the sign of originality, in the House of career, points to unusual professions. In most cases, these people's occupations are bound up with large groups of people, and they may work for organizations, corporations or political parties.

Achieving social standing and popularity are two of the ambitions of people with this placing. Very often, their dreams come true through the help of excellent business connections and friends in high places.

PISCES — THE FISHES

Water, Mutable, Jupiter and Neptune

When people are born with Pisces in the Tenth House, they want to realize a dream or an ideal through their choice of career. They may choose professions that demand self-sacrifice, renunciation and secrecy, and which are often associated with self-contained institutions, such as hospitals, boarding schools, monasteries or convents, army bases or prisons. Being a Water sign, Pisces in this House signifies fluid conditions, frequent changes and frequently a fog of uncertainty surrounding career matters. These people can easily fall into the Piscean mire of self-delusion, which can swamp them in their careers. This sign in the Tenth House hints, as well, at a wish to play a part in public, and to adopt an image that fulfils some kind of ideal or dream. Since the flexibility and fluidity of this Water sign, and the duality of its nature, are frequently seen in the talent of portraying different characters, quite a few of those with Pisces in this House choose a career in acting. However, these people may play a part not only on the stage, but behind the scenes as well, pulling many strings and spinning yarns which, while elusive and intangible, may prove quite entangling . . .

Suitable jobs include those connected with textiles, and other industries which weave and spin dreams and sell illusions, such as cosmetics, perfumes, alcohol, costume and set design. As the sign of Pisces is associated with the feet, some of those with this placing become chiropodists, or work in the shoe trade. Still others may choose jobs associated with oil, plastics, the sea and music.

THE ELEVENTH HOUSE

Friends and acquaintances; Attitude to social problems

ARIES — THE RAM

Fire, Cardinal, Mars

Being one of the flock doesn't appeal to these people in the slightest — they want to be leaders, not followers! Some of those with Aries in the Eleventh House want to be at the head of organizations and groups, while others want to blaze a trail in social areas.

When it comes to their relationships with other people, those with this placing are no meek lambs, hiding in corners at social gatherings. Instead, they are dynamic and open, and will easily start up conversations. They enjoy very warm friendships and like making new social contacts. Because Aries is ruled by Mars, the planet of war, these people often have many friends in the army.

In true Aries style, these people tend to be fairly impetuous and not discriminating enough in their choice of friends, and although their attitude to others is very straightforward, they are not always tactful or tolerant. Being quick to anger, even the slightest provocation can fuel the bonfire of their wrath. So, people with the butting Ram in their Eleventh House can clash head-on with others — even goring them at times.

TAURUS — THE BULL

Earth, Fixed, Venus

People with the sign of Taurus, the Bull, in their Eleventh House have a very practical approach to social matters, and are always willing to give donations to charities and organizations formed for the advancement of humanity.

Friendship is not something that these people take lightly. Although they don't form relationships at the drop of a hat, once they have found someone they like they will nurture that friendship as though it were a plant, encouraging it to bud, blossom and bear fruit over the years. Usually, they are attracted to worthy, down-to-earth people who come from good backgrounds, and who can be trusted and relied upon. People with this placing will be only too glad to lend a helping hand whenever their friends need it, and they know that they will get the same support should they ever be in difficulties. They tend to make friends with those connected with economics, banking, architecture and agriculture, and with the landed gentry.

GEMINI — THE TWINS

Air, Mutable, Mercury

There is a lively interest in social matters for people with this placing. They also enjoy expressing their views on social and humanitarian subjects, and often put these ideas down on paper.

Those with the Twins cavorting in this House find it easy to communicate with others, and choose friends who are their intellectual equals. They are attracted to those who are young in spirit, alert, intelligent and light-hearted. Most of their friends are connected with the communications and transport industries, journalism and education. Although they make friends easily, those friendships are not very deeply-rooted and, like castles in the air, can be here one minute and gone with the wind the next. After all, Gemini is an Air sign . . .

CANCER — THE CRAB

Water, Cardinal, The Moon

People with this placing are sensitive to social issues, so much so that they very often decide to take active roles in dealing with social problems, and extending warm and tender care to the needy.

Cancer, the sign of home and family, in the House of friends signifies people for whom familiarity breeds — in this case — friendship. Not only do those with this placing foster strong and affectionate ties with their relatives, but they also keep in close touch with childhood friends and delight in reminiscing with them about the past. People feel comfortable with those who have the homely Crab lodging in their Eleventh House. They love cooking and baking for their friends, and dish up everything with their own soothing brand of tea and sympathy. No wonder that friends who come to supper may well end up spending the night! More often than not, these people will share a house or flat with a friend for a considerable period. As you might expect, their friends are usually nice, simple, unpretentious people.

LEO — THE LION

Fire, Fixed, The Sun

Impressive social status is what those with this placing long for, and they hanker to be at the top of social groups or organizations. People born with the king of the jungle roaring in this House aspire to be among the social lions, and to bask in their reflected glory. Usually, they would rather be a tail to a lion than a head to a fox.

These people love to enjoy themselves in truly regal fashion, to socialize with celebrities, to move in affluent circles and to rub shoulders with VIPs. Those with the Lion in this House want, with all their hearts, to belong to the 'top cats' of society. Their circle of friends will sparkle with members of the upper classes and glamorous, creative people — especially those from the world of the theatre.

The sign of Cancer in Florence Nightingale's Eleventh House represents her desire to give patients warm and caring treatment.

Leo in Elizabeth Taylor's Eleventh House reflects the glittering social and theatrical circles in which she moves.

VIRGO — THE MAIDEN

Earth, Mutable, Mercury

A willingness to serve and to further humanitarian goals, even in the most modest and routine way, is the keynote to those with this placing. They strive for integrity, perfection and order in day-to-day communications, and these high expectations can make them very critical of the social order.

The Virgoan attitude to people is, in most cases, rather reserved. These people tend to be introverted and shy in large groups, and usually prefer to mix in a small circle of friends. They expect perfection in their relationships with their friends, but usually manage to find fault with them! They also tend to befriend those whose social standing is lower than their own. Many of those with this placing form friendships with their colleagues, and also relationships based on a common interest in health, nutrition and hygiene.

LIBRA — THE SCALES

Air, Cardinal, Venus

When the Scales balance in the Eleventh House they indicate people who have a balanced approach to social issues and who strive for social justice and equality.

People with this placing are extremely popular. In most cases they are social butterflies, flitting from party to party and adorning each social gathering with their delightful presence. It seems as if they feel obliged to spread their charms around! Because they have a strong desire for harmony in human relationships, they will gladly give in or compromise in order to avoid friction and fights. The Libra connection with marriage hints that friendships of these people may often lead to the altar, or to business partnerships. Sometimes, they feel married to their friends, and rumours may abound that they will never even contemplate marriage, fearing that it may interfere with their social lives. Whether they are close friends or simply acquaintances, high intellect and cultural refinement will be the common characteristics of those who know people with Libra in the Eleventh House.

SCORPIO — THE SCORPION

Water, Fixed, Mars and Pluto

Those with Scorpio in their Eleventh House have a radical, often extreme, attitude to social issues that may, at times, take a conspiratorial turn. Scorpio in this House occasionally denotes an extraordinary dedication to a humanitarian goal, with these people even sometimes being ready to sacrifice their lives for their ideals.

Secretive Scorpio in this House may suggest that not everything is always quite open and above-board between friends. In more extreme cases, the Scorpion lurking in the House of friendship means that relationships between friends may turn rather poisonous, with envy, intrigue, plotting and scheming thrown in for bad measure. Unfortunately, Scorpio in the Eleventh House often points to snakes in the grass. Sometimes, these people's friends may have ties with secret or underground matters, and can even be linked with the underworld. As in some cases there could be a tendency to become involved socially with rather shady characters, these people should do their utmost to be very discriminating in their choice of acquaintances, since with friends like these, who needs enemies?

SAGITTARIUS — THE ARCHER

Fire, Mutable, Jupiter

Arrows are aimed at many social goals by people born with Sagittarius, the sign of the Archer, in their Eleventh House. They are blessed with an idealism that extols the values of universal freedom and higher education, and sometimes they may even be social visionaries.

These people show excellent intuition in their choice of friends, and have an open, optimistic and sympathetic attitude towards others. They try to widen their horizons through friendship, and have a large circle of acquaintances and a veritable network of social connections that spans the globe. They will make friends on their travels, and are drawn to foreigners. Among their numerous friends may be found sportsmen and characters full of adventure, as well as people connected with law, philosophy and religion.

CAPRICORN — THE MOUNTAIN GOAT

Earth, Cardinal, Saturn

The cautious sign of Capricorn in the House of friendship gives people with this placing a sober, conservative attitude to social issues, and endows them with a sense of etiquette.

These people are inordinately ambitious when it comes to climbing the social ladder, and will seek out the company of the influential and important, even trying hard to gatecrash their way into the ruling classes. They are cool and calculating in their relationships, their motto being 'Respect and suspect'. Small wonder, then, that their circles of acquaintances are rather limited, as are their social lives. They may also encounter difficulties and disappointments in their friendships. Among their friends will be people much older than themselves, or those who may be of help in furthering their careers.

AQUARIUS — THE WATER BEARER

Air, Fixed, Saturn and Uranus

When people are born with the sign of Aquarius, the Water Bearer, in their Eleventh House, they long to bestow upon humanity a never-ending abundance of spiritual waters, helping mankind bloom with the help of their advanced, innovative and sometimes revolutionary ideas. However, because Aquarius is an Air sign, these people's ideas are not always rooted in solid earth, dissolving sometimes into thin air . . .

Progressive, liberal people, usually with an original turn of mind and who are often rather eccentric, attract people with this placing. In most cases, they will meet under the most unexpected and unusual circumstances. The friends of these Aquarian-influenced people include those who work in aeronautics, computers, electronics, radio and television.

PISCES — THE FISHES

Water, Mutable, Jupiter and Neptune

Social ideals, which can sometimes border on the Utopian, abound in those born with the Fishes floating dreamily in their Eleventh House. They have sympathetic, understanding attitudes to others, and will help them whenever possible. They may develop friendly ties with someone who is confined in some way, such as hospitalized, institutionalized or imprisoned. In many cases, these people will try to save some poor fish who is hooked on alcohol or drugs.

The symbol of the two Fishes suggests that some of these people's relationships are not altogether free of duplicity. In extreme cases, hidden enemies may scheme against them under the cover of amity — planning to catch them with compliments. Their friends can include drifters and people surrounded by an aura of vagueness. They often feel drawn to secret societies.

THE TWELFTH HOUSE

The subconscious; Hidden weaknesses;
Self-undoing; Escapism; Behind the scenes activities;
Secret enemies; Chronic sickness; Seclusion; Confinement;
Inner sources of strength; Sacrifice; Charity

ARIES — THE RAM

Fire, Cardinal, Mars

The sign of Aries, when appearing in the Twelfth House, indicates strong impulses and drives, which batter at the unconscious of people with this placing. They may appear to be innocent lambs, but their lambskins mask hidden aggression. Deep down these people are wilful children, convinced that the entire world revolves around them and exists for the sole purpose of fulfilling their whims and desires. They are often slaves to their impulses and, being driven by their instincts, will act without too many inhibitions.

Fiery Aries ablaze in this House shows people smouldering with an inner fervour. They have difficulty restraining their burning passions, and may be scorched by the fire they play with. Their urges, straining to break loose of their bonds, batter at the walls of the unconscious, and their pounding will block out the voice of reason. These people rush ahead, oblivious to the possible consequences, quite often getting hit on the head in the process, sometimes even literally. Hospitalization as a result of a head injury is possible, as well as headaches whose causes are often rooted in the subconscious.

Sometimes, these people are their own worst enemies, and their overly impulsive and aggressive behaviour in personal matters may lead them to the precipice of self-destruction or detention. Small wonder, then, those who have the Ram in this House are often considered to be black sheep.

Many with this placing may want to develop an awareness of their most hidden and secret subconscious motivations, working along the lines of

'Know thyself'. If they remain unaware of their impulses and instincts, these may trample them like a stampeding herd. But if they succeed in grabbing the Ram, which is butting in their subconscious, by the horns, they may become the leader of their wild herd of drives, and masters or mistresses of themselves.

TAURUS — THE BULL

Earth, Fixed, Venus

The natural, healthy feelings of love and sensuality are often suppressed by those with Taurus in the Twelfth House, who will replace them with an exaggerated materialistic attitude and acquisitiveness. These people believe that money will buy them the security that love has failed to provide, and are aware of their worth only when they feel that they are worth their weight in gold. They believe that only a secure economic base can buy them peace of mind and security, and that only by virtue of their land and property will they acquire their own 'God's little acre'.

At times, their belief in the golden calf is liable not only to sway their minds, but their faith as well, and they will be ready to sell their souls to Mammon. Believing that the grass on the other side of the fence is greener, they are eager to graze in their neighbour's pasture — and crop it down until only stubble remains. But instead of minting security from their silver coffers, these people might discover that, as their wealth grows, so do their worries. They become slaves to their property, and its prisoner — chained to a golden cage by silver fetters. For these people, the Bull is brought to his knees by the golden ring in his nose, which only serves to lead him into captivity.

People born with the weighty Bull crouching in their Twelfth House may at times feel burdened by their consciences, especially if they are very materialistic and prefer to balance their books rather than their own souls. They may find some kind of relief in donating a sum of money to charity (as a subconscious atonement), or will be driven by an illogical compulsion to spend their money wildly. They may also punish themselves unconsciously by a foolish move that results in bankruptcy, brings ruin upon their heads, or even leads to imprisonment.

Taurus in this House represents covert financial transactions, secrecy with regard to property, and secret sources of money. Despite a longing for security and serenity, people with this placing are unlikely to feel at ease in pastoral surroundings, because the peaceful atmosphere makes them feel confined.

Because the sign of Taurus is linked with money, its placing in the House of secret enemies suggests that any hostility these people arouse may be well earned, and is often linked with financial matters. The adversaries they acquire are stubborn, determined, inflexible characters connected with economics, banking and agriculture, and those involved in real estate may really plot against them.

The Bull's strength lies in his earthiness and deep-rooted bond with the land, and his spiritual strength depends on his proximity to nature. Only then will these people discover that Taurus in the Twelfth House is not a big bully in the slightest, but is an amiable and peaceful beast.

Who says there are only sacred cows? It appears that there are heavenly bulls as well. They are attuned only to the rustling of the wind over green pastures, and never to the rustle of banknotes. They listen to cowbells and not to the clink of coins. The only desire of this heavenly bull is to dwell forever amidst the serene green pastures of the eternal grazing grounds . . .

Aries, the sign of the Ram, in the Twelfth House of Vivien Leigh, symbolizes the beautiful actress's attacks of violent rage which eventually led to her hospitalization.

Leo, the sign of love, hiding in Oscar Wilde's Twelfth House hints at the secrecy that enveloped the writer's love life, his involvement in a 'forbidden' romantic attachment and his subsequent imprisonment.

GEMINI — THE TWINS

Air, Mutable, Mercury

Any unpleasant thoughts of people with the sign of Gemini, the Twins, in the Twelfth House are usually suppressed, and hidden away in their subconscious minds. This habit may result in duplicity and insincerity, a subjective view of life, and may make them lapse from reasonable judicious behaviour.

The dual sign of Gemini in this House symbolizes a certain split within the subconscious, where conflicting forces jostle and pull these people in opposing directions. This doesn't necessarily mean that their personalities mirror those of Dr Jekyll and Mr Hyde, but even if they seem like those mischievous imps, Tweedledum and Tweedledee, it can be enough to drive them round the bend.

These people often feel that talking to someone is the best way for them to relieve tension. In fact, psychologists who use astrology in their work have noticed that most of their patients have this sign in their Twelfth House. But don't think that this placing, more than any other, indicates a tendency to mental imbalance. Instead, it means that these people are more aware of the workings of their subconscious than others, and have a greater need to express themselves, uncover the unknown and bring it to light. Airy Gemini signifies a need to air things verbally, to talk over intimate problems, bring them into the open, and give vent to one's feelings. Since the chambers of these people's minds are kept well-ventilated, problems don't have a chance to fester.

Thoughts can buzz around these people's brains, giving them sleepless nights. In fact, it is at night that their minds do their most productive work. Often these people will go to sleep worrying about a problem, and will wake up the next morning with a bright solution. They are also blessed with the innate ability to absorb knowledge and scraps of information subconsciously, without being aware of doing so. They then find that they know things without recollecting how they acquired that knowledge. They also have a knack for correctly guessing other people's secret thoughts, and understanding their hidden motives. They want to understand their subconscious minds and are interested in psychology. Another trait is being able to put into words complex ideas and thoughts, which others find difficult to express and explain clearly.

These people's inclinations to discuss their thoughts and feelings are, for the most part, a good thing. But since Gemini is a dual sign, there is another, less desirable aspect to it. Sometimes, these people talk too much and may give themselves away, or they may be indiscreet in writing or speaking, which can lead to their undoing. It's quite likely that some people in their close environment are secretly hostile and will spill the beans, making their secrets common knowledge. Respiratory ailments can be another problem.

CANCER — THE CRAB

Water, Cardinal, The Moon

The sensitivity of some people with this placing can be their downfall. They may try to conceal their tenderness under a defensive shield of tough armour, as though sheltering their crablike softness in a shell. Sometimes this shell can become a self-imposed cell, isolating them emotionally. These people can suffer from a subconscious fear of abandonment and injury to their feelings, and they may try to mask their vulnerability behind a façade of exaggerated confidence.

Their over-sensitivity and lack of self-confidence usually stem from their early childhoods, and often their ties with their mothers appear restricting. As a result they may feel that the umbilical cord, binding them to their mothers, has not been severed. In some cases, the mothers themselves might be involved in a difficult situation. Sometimes, they may even have been detained temporarily in a closed institution, a time which might prove crucial to the development of those with this placing.

People with Cancer in the Twelfth House may feel confined in their own homes, as though the very walls were closing in on them, and may have a sense of being enslaved by their families. Very often, they will react by

Cancer, the sign of the family, in Marilyn Monroe's Twelfth House reflects the secrecy surrounding her family background, and the fact that her mother was institutionalized.

Virgo, the sign of service and medicine, is present in the Twelfth House of Albert Schweitzer who founded a leper colony in Equatorial Africa.

attempting to break loose from their family bonds — sometimes at a very early age. In other cases, people with Cancer in the Twelfth House may react in the opposite way by becoming excessively dependent on their families, and housebound. In extreme cases, they may even become recluses in their own homes.

There is a deep empathy within these people for the suffering of others, and they will open themselves emotionally towards those in need. Caring for the weak strengthens their sensitivity — the very trait they want to suppress! They find fulfilment in caring for the needy and destitute in closed institutions, developing warm, familial relationships with their inmates and feeling at home there. In some cases, however, these people seek the company of those who are down and out just to patronize them and feel one-up.

The Crab hiding in this House hints, at times, that there might be something secret, obscure or not really above-board in the family's background and, occasionally, there may even be a skeleton hiding in the cupboard . . . A feeling of hidden hostility may lurk among members of the family. These people may also experience enmity from women or from ordinary people.

The strong point of these people is their soft point — their sensitivity to the suffering of others, which may help them to develop a more tolerant approach to their own weaknesses. By identifying with the sorrows of others, they tune into their own vulnerabilities, whose existence they tried to deny. Becoming aware of their inner weaknesses is the first step on the road to overcoming them.

LEO — THE LION

Fire, Fixed, The Sun

The position of Leo in the Twelfth House can symbolize the suppression of animal vitality, enthusiasm and *joie de vivre*. People born with the Lion in this House inhibit the eternal child dwelling within them, imprisoning him or her in the innermost chambers of their Twelfth House, under lock and key. Suppressing the vital, impulsive side of their characters, these people put their heads between the lion's jaws — and may risk being torn to pieces by the animal confined in their subconscious. Their bottled-up desires give them no peace, making them as restless as a lion pacing nervously in its cage. In some cases, there may be a distortion of romantic feelings, a yearning for forbidden love, and secrecy in matters of the heart.

The Lion locked up in the Twelfth House does not roar. Therefore, these people may be very unassuming on the surface, often swallowing their pride, but in their heart of hearts they are aware of their inherent value. They have an inner majesty and a serene dignity, and if others are unaware of their worth — well, that's their problem. Sometimes these people even glory in their humility. They are superstars behind the scenes, the hero or heroine of their own private drama. However, they aren't always content to settle for behind the scenes fame, and may want to prove to themselves that the Lion in their Twelfth House, although behind bars, is still the king of the jungle. In extreme cases, there may even be a tendency to megalomania, with these people being convinced that they are 'the greatest', social lions at the very least — or even Napoleons. (Napoleon, by the way, was a Leo.) It is said that pride goes before a fall, and in this case, these people march straight into the lion's den.

Leo in the Twelfth House sometimes denotes undoing through pride. The hostility of their adversaries stems, in most cases, from points of honour — but very often matters of the heart could be at the heart of the matter . . . They may get entangled in their romantic ties and become prisoners of love, this captivity leading sometimes to downfall or retreat. The hearts of these people are their Achilles' heels — literally, in many cases. They may even be hospitalized because of a heart condition.

VIRGO — THE MAIDEN

Earth, Mutable, Mercury

A tendency towards psychosomatic illnesses and hypochondria often occur in people born with Virgo, the sign of health, in the Twelfth House. Their mental conditions and subconscious fears affect their health, and some of them can be tempted to become ill in order to escape from work.

Many people with this placing suffer from feelings of guilt, and may be subconsciously displeased with themselves. On the positive side, the Maiden here symbolizes an inner need for perfection, and to overcome shortcomings. Virgo being the sign of work, working overtime will not deter these people who, in an attempt to compensate for their faults, will often choose a demanding profession which entails a degree of self-sacrifice, such as a job dealing with institutionalized patients or with a secret service.

The Maiden hiding in the Twelfth House indicates people who are shy, even insecure. This insecurity can lead to excessive criticism, directed at themselves as well as others. They are very aware of their weaknesses, and can find fault with themselves wherever they look. To try to make up for any real or imaginary blemishes on their characters, these people may be given to obsessively washing their hands, like Lady Macbeth, or can be overly concerned with cleanliness. Virgo here symbolizes an irrational fear of anything unclean, of germs and disease. Sometimes even everyday, trivial matters may drive these people to their wit's end, making them see specks of dust, or the common cold, as their mortal enemies. An untidy room or a picture hanging crookedly gives them gooseflesh, and drives them up the wall. However, they will usually stay within the confines of their homes. They like their privacy, work best in calm, quiet atmospheres, and prefer jobs carried out behind the scenes.

LIBRA — THE SCALES

Air, Cardinal, Venus

The placing of Libra, the Scales, in the Twelfth House represents people who display a subconscious dependence on others and a need for someone to lean on. However, if they lean too heavily on someone else, they will tip the scales and lose their emotional balance. If they expect to be rescued by Prince Charming, their dreams might lead to disaster, especially when the prince turns out to be a frog . . .

On the other hand, if these people choose to make judicious use of the Scales in their Twelfth House, seeking truth and justice, they will eventually find harmony and peace within themselves. Only then will they be able to overcome their reliance on others: they will no longer be subconsciously dependent and incomplete, but become people in their own right.

Those with the Scales of Justice weighing heavily in their Twelfth House are sensitive to the slightest alteration in balance, and will not ignore any weights on their consciences. These people won't wait for the Day of Judgement to set the record straight: for them, every day is a good day for soul-searching and spiritual book-keeping.

The pangs of conscience symbolized by the sign of Libra may strike at these people's kidneys, and even lead to hospital treatment. Their spouse or partner may also be secretly hostile towards them.

SCORPIO — THE SCORPION

Water, Fixed, Mars and Pluto

This placing is a very powerful one, since it symbolizes the repression of intense emotions and heated passions, which writhe like poisonous snakes in the recesses of the subconscious. People with Scorpio entrenched in their Twelfth House are apt to hide, even from themselves, so-called ugly emotions such as jealousy, and push them into remote corners of their minds — they believe that the further away, the better! In extreme cases, these people are liable to be touchy and suspicious, vengeful and spiteful, and may choke on their own bile. However, they will more than likely deny these feelings and attribute them to the people surrounding them, imagining that the venomous vipers are part of others rather than themselves. They dread the moment of truth when the curtain will rise and the spotlight will illuminate the darkest regions of their souls, because they fear that, once their Pandora's box is opened, all sorts of reptiles will emerge. These people guard the skeletons in their closets like Cerberus, Pluto's dog, keeping watch over the secrets of hell. They have to keep the scorpions of their souls locked up, fearing that, once they have wriggled free, they themselves will become the captives of these beasts.

In order to overcome their inner scorpions, these people must be fully aware of their existence and be prepared to face them. If they can muster the courage to delve deep into the gloomy, labyrinthian netherworld of their Twelfth House and confront the dragons that plague them, they will come up the winners — even saints.

Sometimes people with Scorpio in their Twelfth House are convinced that they are being shortchanged, and that the world as a whole is in their debt. This attitude may lead to their sponging on and using people. In extreme cases, these people may take the law into their own hands and find a surreptitious way of reclaiming something of what they believe to be their own, but they should be warned that this can lead to imprisonment!

People with this placing may show their anger in veiled, vile ways. They can acquire many enemies due to their malevolent wrath, never missing an opportunity to sting with their poisonous tails or strike below the belt — which is the part of the body associated with the sign of Scorpio.

SAGITTARIUS — THE ARCHER

Fire, Mutable, Jupiter

People with Sagittarius in their Twelfth House are likely to suppress their yearnings for freedom, and subdue their optimism. Sometimes these stifled desires may break all bounds, and burst out in an unchecked urge for expansion — often at the expense of others. When these people let their pent-up emotions loose and their desires run wild, they blow up and take over, like a genie let out of the bottle. Should this hankering after boundless liberty take a dare-devilish turn, it may end in disaster and confinement of some sort or another. However, should people with the Archer in their Twelfth House establish high moral targets for themselves, they will discover that the freedom they have been seeking lies within them after all.

Sometimes, these people may be forced to conceal their religions, beliefs and views. In extreme cases, they may become the victims of persecution for religious or ideological reasons. Sagittarius in the Twelfth House denotes that those hostile to these people are usually very learned, or connected with foreign countries. Their secret enemies may hurl their slings and arrows at those with this placing for moral, legal, religious or academic reasons.

CAPRICORN — THE MOUNTAIN GOAT

Earth, Cardinal, Saturn

The repression of unpleasant experiences connected with the father, or a lack of confidence due to the absence of a father figure, are symbolized by the placing of Capricorn in the Twelfth House. These people can sometimes even have a subconscious fear of the outside world. They may repress their worldly aspirations, which their subconscious sees as a challenge to their fathers. As a result, they may develop a fear of success, dreading that behind the summit something is lurking in ambush, waiting to overthrow them. Because of this fear of heights, the mere suspicion that they are nearing the top will make them — unbeknownst to themselves, of course — slip down and destroy all that they have achieved (in order to appease their fathers' jealousy towards them).

If they lean towards self-discipline, responsibility and self-reliance — developing in themselves that positive father figure they miss so much — they will have taken the goat by its horns at last! When the challenges they set for themselves are in the spiritual-intellectual sphere, they will manage

Scorpio lurking in Feodor Dostoyevsky's Twelfth House indicates the Russian writer's inner turmoil which is reflected in his works.

Capricorn in the artist Auguste Renoir's Twelfth House represents the arthritis which disabled him and forced him to paint with the brush tied to his hand.

to rise to the summit of their superegos and climb the slopes of perfection to the heights of their personal Himalayas.

Capricorn in this House symbolizes not only inner aspirations turned towards spiritual and intellectual worlds, but also the realizations of secret ambitions, as well. It also represents achieving an aim in life in a somewhat hidden fashion, such as being the power behind the throne, or having a career in a closed institution. In extreme cases, people with this placing have unbounded ambition and exaggerated rigidity, which may lead to self-destruction or isolation. Elderly people, or those of high standing, may be secretly hostile towards those with Capricorn in this House. Injuries to the bones and joints may call for a stay in hospital.

AQUARIUS — THE WATER BEARER

Air, Fixed, Saturn and Uranus

There is a repression of ideals, dreams and hopes, and a subconscious fear of people and society, when Aquarius is in the Twelfth House. As a result, people with this placing may develop misanthropic feelings and withdraw from society. In other cases, the reverse may be true, and these people will feel compelled to join large groups, sometimes to the point of wishing to lose their identities. They long to drown their individuality in the Aquarian waters, to dissolve their distinctiveness in group consciousness and to be absorbed by it, hoping to turn into just another drop in the ocean. Dreading the feeling of separateness, they subdue their anxieties by melting into a group.

However, when the water in Aquarius' jug is the water of life, it awakens a thirst for sublime social ideals. Thanks to this water of life flowing in their Twelfth House, these people are endowed with an inner purity, which they project on humanity. Because they have positive expectations of mankind, they are reconciled not only with themselves, but with society too. They want to contribute to society from the waters in their jugs and, hoping to help and improve the lot of the underprivileged, are active in humanitarian projects, especially those associated with hospitals or prisons, or which take place behind the scenes.

Sometimes, people with this placing have some revolutionary hopes and wishes, or unusual tendencies, which may lead to voluntary retreat. In other cases, these people feel the need to conceal their personal truths in the innermost chambers of their Twelfth House. They must be extremely cautious in their social connections, since wrong ties may entangle, bind, chain and enslave them, and occasionally may even lead to detention or self-destruction. Circulatory problems or injuries to the lower limbs can lead to spells in hospital for these people.

PISCES — THE FISHES

Water, Mutable, Jupiter and Neptune

A subconscious fear of losing one's identity is characterized by the Fishes in the Twelfth House. As a compensation, these people may try to reinforce their egos by emphasizing the barriers between themselves and others, resulting possibly in extreme egotism and aggressiveness which hide a subconscious feeling of weakness and helplessness — a gnawing feeling which they try to hide at any price, even from themselves.

The Fishes swimming in the Twelfth House suggest that people with this placing are captive to vague fears, which glide through their subconscious like mysterious sea-creatures in the ocean's depths. These people are beset by hidden fears of uncertainty, and by a dread of drowning in the depths of the unknown. These ambiguous fears close in on them from all sides, until they may feel that they are being held prisoner by hidden, unknown jailers — those same mysterious forces lurking beyond the threshold of their consciousness. To counteract this, they may develop a clear-eyed, realistic, know-all attitude, which denies all mystery, spirituality and vision — imprisoning the intangible behind locked doors in the furthest recesses of the Twelfth House.

In some cases, however, these people may try to flee from reality and to escape the confines of their emotional prisons with the help of drugs or alcohol, hoping that they will provide a short cut to spirituality. Thus they may drift on the waters of the unknown without bothering to learn to swim in them. If they try to achieve instant nirvana, as if it were a cup of coffee, they may discover that the drug route doesn't lead to their long-awaited freedom after all, but turns instead into a one-way street ending in enslavement, addiction and imprisonment of some sort. The drug path becomes their personal Via Dolorosa. They may become slaves to a desire for unlimited freedom and to their urge to rid themselves of all responsibility. But when they shake themselves free of all ties, they find that they are more fettered, bound and chained than ever before. Their dreams of boundless freedom are nothing but illusions and false visions.

But when they yearn for liberty while admitting to the limitations and responsibilities of their earthly existences, they may find freedom even in bondage. Only after accepting the fact that they cannot be as free as birds will they be able to call their souls their own and set their spirits free. In order to release themselves from the fetters of their egos, they will have to knock down the barriers separating them from their fellow men. The watery sign of the Fishes denotes that only by letting their feelings flow freely will they at long last feel like a fish in water.

Pisces in the Twelfth House denotes fishy, shifty, slimy and slippery hidden enemies lurking in the murk. They lie in wait for people with this placing, using all sorts of lures and inducements to make them rise to the bait. Some people with this placing may be admitted to hospital for some undetermined illness, over-use of drugs or an injury to the feet. In some cases, they may also be in danger from water, and especially the sea.